# MUG PUNTING
## Short Tales About Long Odds

**David Atkinson**

*Dedicated to every cheapskate thrill seeker
who ever backed a long shot in blind faith*

*and to Quixall Crossett*

*Quixall Crossett achieved a cult following after 'beating' the British record for the number of consecutive defeats. When his trainer Ted Caine retired him in 2002, the horse had run 103 times without once getting his head in front. Jonny Beardsall, regular jockey to Quixall, said, "He may be as slow as a hearse, but he's a very safe ride!" In deference to his unparalleled record, Ted Caine once remarked, "We don't push him too hard….". Quixall has made the frame on two occasions. The Racing Post in assessing one of these performances commented that the serial loser "ran a cracker by his standards when he was second of two finishers."*

**CONTENTS**

1. Let's Get Connected
2. Exit Stage Left
3. Declarations
4. First Festival Fever
5. Basic Instinct
6. The Value Betting Emporium
7. What's the craic in Ireland?
8. Arcane Agricultural Anxiety
9. Never Bet at Brighton
10. Grim, Dull and Fruitless
11. Unfantasy Cricket
12. Brandy Chasers
13. The Cheltenham Posse
14. Acne in Hackney
15. Boundary Boys
16. Three blokes at the Oaks
17. Blue Eiderdown
18. Bountiful Tales
19. Lay Hedging
20. Cheltenham the Third: Roosted
21. Cheltenham the Third: At the Double
22. Cheltenham the Third: Bookie Massacre
23. Vodkatini
24. Sunrise at Sandown
25. Toaster
26. Up and Down the City Road, In and Out The Eagle
27. Sunset at Sandown
28. Cheltenham 2004: Hardy Perennials
29. Cheltenham 2004: Paddy's Day
30. Cheltenham 2004: The Rollercoaster
31. The Charming Dash
32. Rival Attraction

## 1. LET'S GET CONNECTED

*"Take me there, anywhere,
Just so long as there's an atmosphere
We'll be round, round around"*
The Wildhearts, *I Wanna Go Where the People Go*, 1992

'De-de-de der de-der' The pony express jingle trumpets the arrival of a small envelope icon on my computer screen. E-mail has just arrived. In the wider sense, rather than just on my desk-top. It's a brand new shiny novelty for those of us who earn our crust in the public sector. There is no end to the fatuous junk, jokes and witty observations that we suddenly feel obliged to share with colleagues and acquaintances that otherwise would, and probably should, remain buried in dark crevices of addled brains.

I'm working in an open plan office. Some days I see natural light, but I wouldn't guarantee it as a regular occurrence. I bob along in a sea of desks arranged in clusters and stars as far as the eye can see. Chest high partitions, festooned with jolly slogans such as "You don't have to work here to be mad.....", designed to break the ebb and flow of sight and sound have recently been removed "to improve communication". So now shrill electronic symphonies bounce around the floor announcing the arrival of more e-garbage. Everyone has a different tune to distinguish their own mail delivery from a neighbour's. I can have Bohemian Rhapsody on speed to accompany the swelling of my in-box. Roll on the technological revolution.

Now that's off my chest, this is infact an e-mail I'm delighted to see. It's from Steve. And he's waxing lyrical. He does from time to time.

> "Ah. The Cheltenham festival. A celebration of the very best that steeple chasing has to offer. The pinnacle of national hunt racing. The unchallenged zenith of the season. A chance for pretenders to become champions, for owners, trainers and jockeys to carve their name deep into the walls in the pantheon of greatness; where, however fleetingly, they come to rub shoulders with the current luminaries of the jumps game and drink a toast to the legends of the past. Let us conjure with the names. See More Business, Istabraq, Limestone Lad and Flagship Uberalles of this year's vintage, bidding for comparison with the Jodami, Desert Orchid, One Man, Viking Flagship, Beech Road. And further back, Mill House, Sea Pigeon, and let us dare utter it...Arkle himself. Yes, Dave, count me in. I'm available for a day at the races. Gold Cup Day. An unfulfilled ambition. Bring it on."

OK, so I'm embellishing his enthusiasm a little. But only a little. My electronic enquiry has unleashed a monster. Until this e-mail, Steve's passion for horse racing has lain dormant, or at the very least hidden from the rest of us. This is a revelation. Nay, an awakening. I've always fancied the nags a bit. Indeed I have pursued many a lost dream, driven by undiagnosed mug punting up and down this fair country's racecourses and betting shops. But I thought I was alone amongst us. Steve's passion has taken me by welcome surprise.

Bryn is next to declare his hand. He strikes a less effusive tone, but picks up the mood of Steve's e-mail. "Dave, haven't got a clue about the horses, but this sounds like a right laugh. Count me in and I'll start my research". Never has a truer word been spoken. No-one takes their sport more seriously than Brynaldo. If he says he's doing some research, I know that by March, he will have selections lined up for every race and a solid, logical basis to his punting strategy. No worries.

Vaughany's a confirmed runner too. "I think I'm available. A quick look at the diary suggests that Tuesday and Wednesday look difficult, but Thursday is free and I'm happy to pencil this event in. Look forward to hearing more details." No flies on Vaughany. The only man I know who would have a couple of social engagements booked in for 5 months hence. The enigmatic, detached Mr Vaughan is another who will be fully briefed from a standing start come the big day. Top stuff.

Stendo can't make it. "Happy to do the fantasy football and the cricket, Dave, but the horses are probably stretching my gambling instincts too far. Think I'll decline your generous offer and leave you to indulge." That's Stendo. Straight bat. Checks his guard. Always knows where is off stump is and plays to his strengths. No show Stendo then.

Nick's not so sure. "Horse racing? It's all luck isn't it? Not so sure about this. Go on then. Count me in I suppose." This is an antidote to Steve's exuberance. Deliberately so, no doubt. Reading between the lines, I'd say he was quite close to being a non runner. Without the guarantee of a good laugh and a few beers, Nick would be seriously reluctant to chuck good money after bad on losing horses and have to pay entrance money for the privilege. Nick is carrying mental scar tissue from an afternoon he and I spent watching Royal Ascot in a boozer outside Lord's during a rained-off test match. Not just watching, though. Sipping ale and slipping next door to the bookies too. He lost a bob or two and I broke even. I was insufferable because I backed a winner. Mostly by chance though naturally I claimed it was form-inspired. Nick wasn't having any of it and became convinced that picking winners was a lottery. He sticks unerringly to this view. Nevertheless, he's up for the Cheltenham trip. His true spirit is shining through.

That's five of us in. That's enough for a serious day out.

## 2. EXIT STAGE LEFT

*"Come on come on*
*Hurry up Harry, come on*
*Come on, come on*
*Hurry up Harry, come on*
*We're going down the pub*
*We're going down the pub"*
Sham 69, "Hurry Up Harry", 1978

In some ways, racing is a bit of a departure for us lot. All mates have some shared experience; a common bond twisting its way through circumstance. For us, working in the same organisation is the circumstance part. The common bond is sport. And at the heart of this common bond, pumping eagerly and consistently is a dark fascination with fantasy cricket. So maybe a day losing money at the nags is a logical step.

Our anorakesque fascination with fantasy cricket needs further explanation. A good few of us in the office belong to a highly competitive league where the honour of victory and pride of ownership of a small, battered plastic trophy are worth far more than the prize money that accompanies it. The league tends to bring out the best and worst in us - a diversionary competitive zeal where no quarter is neither asked nor given. We assiduously follow every twist and turn of the English domestic season. Every half-century racked up by Graeme Hick is mentally converted into points and offset against the five wicket hauls plundered by spin-King Saqlain Mushtaq. Everyone's transfers are keenly debated over a couple of swifties after work, each nuance of rule interpretation is analysed and argued over.

Escapism, of course is a very powerful thing. Making the day pass a bit more swiftly. We've all been in the Service far too long. We all moan about the job from time to time and we all struggle to raise enthusiasm for the business. As my mate Mike wearily but accurately observes, "We are just mental prostitutes for the Government....". The pub is a place of refuge though. Griping about work takes up only a small part of the banter down the boozer. Without wishing to pursue more amateur psychology than is strictly necessary, there is clearly an element of therapy about all this escapism. I'm sure there is some kind of cleansing quality about walking out of the office and picking over the bones with your work colleagues about something totally unrelated to the mundane processes of the day. As Ron Atkinson once said, "It's a bloke thing. For me, if you can't escape the days' grind by losing yourself in a big football debate then what's it for, if you like?" Less helpfully, he also said "there goes the striker down the channel at the back stick, giving it the little eyebrows" but even more unforgivably, "Marcel Desailly, he's a f****** lazy n*****..." for which offensive and inappropriate remark he paid the ultimate price. Big Ron's display of ignorance has cost us forever the unique thrill of listening to a graceful language put through a merciless simile wringer.

The best feature of our league, without a shadow of a doubt, is the highly sought after Manager of the Month award. The manager accumulating the most points each month wins a trough of beer purchased by his competitors to be consumed over a lunchtime. Alcohol, of course, is the language of success. This glorious event on too many occasions stretches across the whole afternoon. We become lost in a blizzard of guest ales, player stats and hard luck stories. Fantastic stuff.

The Stage Door is the chosen hostelry for the Manager of the Month events. The pub is also the venue for a number of increasingly regular 'unexpected' sessions after work. It is a venue of accidental choice. Proximity to the new office is clearly the crucial criterion. That said, the landlord puts on a few barrels of decent guest ale every week. This is a very important feature. Nick and I seem to end up in here at least once a week for at least a couple. Sometimes it's not *at least*. Sadly, irretrievably, it can be *at most*. The Belgian beer experiment continues to haunt me. Why we decided that bottles of Leffe Brun were a natural progression from a few reasonable pints of Adnams Broadside escapes reason. But there we are. A nasty intestinal incident in the doorway of the Silverlink County service to Bletchley bears testament to faulty judgement of my alcohol resistance.

Nick and I not only work in the same organisation, but the same office, too. This has some inevitable consequences. We are our own worst enemies and as the clock ticks round to 5pm it only takes a little look or a leading question and we are making for the door.

We are in the Stage Door early tonight. There are a couple of familiar faces. At the end of the bar sits a Leeds fan, holding court with a couple of other customers. I don't know his name, but he always has a lot off. He's a carpenter and he fancies one of the barmaids badly. He has one of the most unsubtle, lecherous, building-site ogles I've ever seen. We have a quick word with him as we order our pints, but he's one of these guys who talks to you as if he's talking to the rest of the pub. He doesn't want a conversation, but he's happy to use you as convenient opportunity to share his largely uninformed views with a largely uninterested clientèle. He finishes his beer, orders a couple of carry-outs and takes his thin, hirsute and tattooed body off to somewhere in Camden.

Another regular face, Dave the Lecky, is wedged in at the bar sipping a Fosters and pretending to read the Evening Standard. We last met Dave on that infamous Leffe evening during the course of an expensive fruit machine escapade. He had ingratiated himself with some uninvited banter about how he'd cleaned out that particular machine twice the previous evening so there was no point sticking in any more of our lolly. He sounded like a bullshitter, but it was true that we didn't get the machine to drop any spends.

Bryn joins us later on this gorgeous Summer evening for a couple. By then the SD (as it is rather unimaginatively known) is rammed. A new season of

'Buddy' has been unleashed at the Victoria Apollo and the pre-theatre G'n'Ters are sipping their fill. The three of us are squeezed tight against the bar. No point wrestling for a seat amongst this transient mob. We are well in tonight, though. Mike, the camp, cheeky, Scottish barman recognises us and takes my order. He's full of offensive bullshit, but it's all welcome as he proclaims to waiting customers,

"Sorry girls, these lovely gents were here alreeeeady".

Nick reckons he fancies me.

"OK, short-arse, better be quick. What are ye having?"

Top stuff!

"Three pints of wife beater and have one y'self ye dodgy old bastard".

Ha ha. It feels like a local!

The theatre crowd move on before we have emptied our glasses. An element of normality is restored. It's not long before we are pounding the jukebox. This is a third reason for our residency at the SD. A mere £1 affords a partnership in rhyme with a host of 70's and 80's rock 'n' roll heroes. And we are so, so predictable. At some point during the evening, without fail, I will request Motorhead 'Ace of Spades', Led Zep 'Kashmir' or The Scorpions 'Rock You Like A Hurricane'; and Nick will call up The Clash 'Should I Stay Or Should I Go', ZZ Top 'Legs' or Black Sabbath 'Paranoid'. Only when Bryn is around do we get a bit of cultural enlightenment, or a dose of 90's chic. So tonight we are soaking up some Massive Attack. Dave the Lecky is still around and casually drops in on the conversation on his way back from the bogs.

"I emptied that fucka ova there the night after yooze two bastads threw your money away."

There's a hint of a grin around his thin lips as he nods over at the fruit machine. We go with the flow.

"Oh aye? Yeah, good going".

"Yeah. Piece o piss", he continues, "you know how to tell when the bugga's ready to drop divn't ya?" He's tantalising us.

"Go on then ...?"

He glances from side to side, like he's checking for eaves-droppers. Not easy because he has the heaviest eyelids I've ever seen, drooping over his semi-obscured eyeballs. Moving them must be a real effort. He pauses for further dramatic effect and speaks slowly.

"The reels slow down. Reet down, like there in slur murtion. That's how you knur when to keep pumpin' it. That's how I cleaned up on Tuesda neet."

Sounds like more bullshit to me. Nick - to whose wisdom I always bow on any matter
of fruit machine technique is similarly unimpressed. His forehead furrows.

"I've never seen that. You sure the machines are programmed to do that?", Nick probes.

"Ah, well. You have to know what you're looking for. Trained eye, it takes."

Bryn moves us on.

"D'you work round here Dave? We always see you in here early." Turns out he's been working on our office. The Department had recently moved into a new building just off Victoria Street. The whole move was rushed and we were decanted from our old office before the new glass sided eco-friendly, smart building was ready. We have joiners, builders, software consultants and, as it now transpires, electricians crawling all over the site. The move - surprise, surprise - was a logistical nightmare of over packed tea-crates, underfloor wiring carnage and missing desks. The situation had become farcical with fire exits blocked by slabs of concrete, sprinkler systems going off at random and a flood of water cascading down the main hard wiring ducts. The last incident resulted in two-thirds of the building's power was knocked out. Dave is wise to all this of course. That's partly why he's on the site.

"I could a told 'em it was all gannin' pear-shaped. They was cutting corners all urver the place to get the job finished on teem. Not me like. I wouldn't cut corners. But we was making some serious dough, wurking round the clock, like."

I feel as though I'm on the set for 'Auf Wiedersehn, Pet'

He gives us a classic story about how he was doing some "urvateem" and stumbled on one of our Directors doing a bit of his own overtime with the secretary across the desk. It sounds like a Carry-On moment and we have a rambling and incoherent discussion trying to work out who the Director is. We never do and maybe we don't entirely buy the story.

Manager of the Month booze-ups in the Stage Door continue unabated. Next time we see Dave he's lodged at the end of the bar as usual, scanning the racing pages of the Evening Standard. Now we are getting to the real point of this ramble. Amongst his many and varied talents - fruit machine king, master electrician, piss artist - he also claims to be making a killing on the nags. Of course, we've got Cheltenham just around the corner, so we reckon we know a thing or two about the racing game by now. Dave unfurls his secret over the ordering of a few beers. Our ordering, his beers. It emerges that Dave's cousin is an apprentice jockey riding out of Willy Haggas's yard called Jo Hunnam. We must sound reasonably interested, so Dave continues in his hushed tones, eyes doing that flitting thing, lips working faster than needed .

"...so, I just waits for the call, y'know - the wurd - and then, y'know...."

It's all unspoken and Dave's twitching, clucking and raising his eyebrows. A nod's as good as a wink to a blind man and all that. It's like talking to a secret agent, all bleedin' dodgy handshakes and secret codes. I frankly do not believe a word of it and I want to take the piss mercilessy, but Dave is deadly calm and resists our provocations with a serious approach.

"I nur when she's on a dead surt, nur two ways aboot it. Ah, ya divn't have t'believe me. Nur skin of my nurz."

A couple of days later, I bump into Nick in the street. I happen to be carrying the Evening Standard. I show him the results of yesterday's

Windsor evening meeting and in particular a winner trained by Willy Haggis and ridden by Jo Hunnam. A coincidence, surely? Or did Dave get a tip off?

It's a good while before we hook up with Dave again. We are often in the SD at the same time, but not always pissed enough to talk to him. And more than that, he keeps an understandable aloofness a lot of the time. Why would he want to be seen devaluing his hard won tradesman credentials by talking to a bunch of unskilled bureaucrats?

There is a good crack going in the SD. In addition to Mick, the offensive Scottish manager, there is an ever changing cast of wise-cracking Aussie bar maids whom Mick fails to keep under control with his tart little comments and bitchy one-liners. A couple of the Aussies in particular are a real laugh. It's the best local I've ever had. I often get 'Ace of Spades' turned down on the jukebox and Nick regularly gets 'Eye of the Tiger' interrupted by some smoochy number of 'Music to Watch Girls By' or some such. Surely a sign of acceptance! Only Bryn brings a modicum of respectability in the eyes of the bar staff with his modern ditties, interspersed with a surprisingly wide range of classic rock that his years belie. The Boy is not yet 30!

I know Bryn from a previous job. He's just about the most dedicated sportsman I've ever met. Not only does he compete and win at international level across a range of sports - he holds honours at football, cricket and athletics - but he has an encyclopaedic knowledge of televised sport. He will be the bloke buying the pay-per-view boxing matches to be shown at 3am. But he will also be the one staying awake to watch it whilst others collapse into an alcoholic stupor. He baffles me with stats about American Football and baseball. Sports that are simply not on my radar. Bryn is partially sighted and has introduced me to a few of his mates who also compete at a high level under the umbrella of the British Blind Sports Association. They are a driven and competitive bunch.

But Bryn hates losing. Whether it's the 200m relay at the Barcelona Paralympics or a game of video golf in the pub. I don't know whether some of the drive comes from trying to compensate for a disability or whether he and his team-mates are just made that way. Maybe a bit of both.

The Civil Service is supportive of his sporting endeavours and he is often able to take special leave to participate in representative events. I used to work with a guy called Sean O'Brien who was blind and had a similar sort of arrangement to compete in blind chess tournaments. Sean was an old rogue. Once he disappeared off to the pub at lunchtime there was virtually no chance of getting an ounce of work out of him in the afternoon. Christ knows how he got away with it for so long. "Did anyone die because I missed this deadline?" he once hollored back at his Boss.

He told us a cracking story about the British Blind Chess Association's trip to Brussels a year or two back. After one of the competition sessions the group had headed off on a session of a different nature with Sean leading a tour of fine Belgian ale hostelries. After a few hours of krieks, Trappists and wheats they made for their hotel. Inevitably the group, to a man, was taken short on the way back. They decided to sneak down an alley to urinate against the wall. This was literally the blind leading the pissed blind and it was only as some shouts and screams disturbed their flow that they realised something was wrong. Turns out that these eight or nine middle aged, drunk, blind chess players were stood in a line, todgers in hand, relieving themselves against the glass-sided wall of one Brussels finest Michelin-rated restaurants. The diners who had paid a pretty penny for their window seats were apparently rather upset to have their lunch disturbed by this revealing sight! The maitre d' sent the group packing. Quite how he explained what was going on is lost in translation. A remorseless Sean found the episode side-splittingly hilarious.

Vaughany is down in the Stage Door most nights too. He's my boss back at the office. Always gives the proceedings a respectable air does Vaughany. Oxbridge education, Austin Reed attire and cheekbones you could hang your coat on.

As the Summer gives way to Autumn fantasy cricket awards and finally to Winter tours, we have established our little Cheltenham expeditionary party. Steve is around a bit more these days and his awakened zeal for the upcoming festival ensures that racing talk is creeping into the post-office cricket banter.

Today we make a scandalous early departure from the office on the basis of another Manager of the Month drink up at lunch-time. It's not long before we are well oiled and giving Dave some earache about a shite Newcastle Utd defence and even worse wiring that still causes our building to short out every so often. His latest patter is more outrageous than that of a month or so ago. Now he's working as the foreman of a gang of leckies wiring up the fiddly bits of the Jubilee Line Extension. He comes out with some astonishing four-figure weekly wages he claims to be pocketing that a minor Football League fullback wouldn't turn his nose up at. I still don't buy it.

    "So why are you drinking round here then?", I probe.

    "Ah, I've got connections round here, business to take care of". He even taps his nose and settles his heavily lidded eyes on us, the mysterious bastard.

    "Anyway, we're ganning on streek tomorra. We're tekkin' Management on over wurking conditions and 'ealth 'n' safety and arl that, like. Them lads'll do 'owt on ma say su-o."

I can't take anything he says seriously, but sure enough in the next day's Standard I read about an electrician's strike and further delays to the already late tube extension.

A couple of weeks later, we are bending his ear again. Nick is screaming for mercy from another onslaught of 'Kashmir'. Bryn and me are giving it some serious emotional moments about the track's unique dark and brooding power. Nick, on the other hand, just thinks it's dull. He seeks out Dave on one of his forays to the bog.

"How are you doing on the gee gees?"

Nick must be in pain if he's kicked off this conversation under his own steam. It succeeds in diverting our attention.

"Oh, y'know." His face is illuminated with the most disarming of smiles, "not bad."

We press. Nick goes for the jugular.

"Had any big winners?"

Dave looks casual as usual: denim jacket, blue jeans, open shirt, loafers. And out comes the casual gambling patter.

"Aye. A few of us have got together, y'know, pooling the money like. We've had a few winnas at £200 a time."

I'm still not satisfied.

"So who's studying the form? Who decides the bet of the day?"

Dave's ready with the answer.

"Ah, see, we get a phone call once a day with the infurmyation that mattas. Then we lump on. £200 a month buys you in."

I'm staggered.

"So it's a tipping service then. That's it?"

Dave's cool.

"Well, you might want to call it that if you want." His eyes do that heavy-lidded shuffle again. "But it's just a club for us what likes a punt on the nags like. I'm not complaining about the money I'm stickin' in me back pockut."

Yeah. Neither would I, I guess.

He slopes off to the bog and then out of the pub without another word. On reflection, I think he's closer to the set of The Likely Lads than Auf Wiedersehn Pet.

## 3. DECLARATIONS

*"Barry's looking through the Racing Post,
orders coffee, another round of toast"*
Saint Etienne, *Mario's Cafe*, 1993

Racing might not quite have displaced the national Summer game in the collective psyche of our little group, but whilst Steve is around, it runs us close. Every pub conversation is now laced with thoughts of next March and the onset of Cheltenham. We congregate in the Willow Walk these days, a hot, sticky and noisy pub round the corner from Argos. We've moved on from the Stage Door. Dave the Lecky is long gone. Dunno where he went, he just stopped coming in. Then Mick the barman disappeared. I heard from someone else who used to drink in the SD that he got a bit too familiar with one of his customers. The filthy bastard. The brewery moved him to a smaller, less conspicuous pub. Relegation. Then the Aussie bar maids all moved on within a few weeks of each other. Then - calamity - the guest ales went too. It was the final straw. So did we.

The WW (naturally) is OK, serving at least one decent guest ale a week, which usually runs out by Wednesday. So today must be Monday. Steve is a man of routine. He gets out for a couple of swifties to shoot the breeze about the shape of the Cheltenham ante-post markets and then he's off somewhere between 6pm and 6.30pm. Tonight we are discussing final declarations and prospects for horses over the weekend. I pinch myself. It's hard to believe this revolution in our midst. Steve is a whirlwind of stats, I'm trying desperately to keep up. He sits at the table looking for all the world like Matty Hoggard with his new crew cut. Except for the glasses. When Steve gets excited about a subject his foot starts tapping on the floor, pumping out a military tattoo of nervous energy, shaking the table with pent up anticipation. He's doing it now and he's rubbing his hands up and down his dancing thighs as he describes the runners for tomorrow's show-piece chase at Haydock or somewhere.

"Moral Support is the one to be on, lads. Laid out for the race and he'll get the ground he wants." Nick is shaking his head in bewilderment. "Don't give me that 'it's all luck' nonsense Jenkins."
Steve is screwing up his eyes in mock disgust, barely suppressing a grin that suggests he doesn't quite believe it all himself yet. Vaughany is nodding sagely but the suspicion of a patronising smile hangs on his face. Bryn's creased brow betrays the look of a man trying to get to grips with all this. Racing is one of the few blind spots in his sports make-up.

Steve and Vaughany depart early. One for the Parent/Teacher meeting, the other for the opera. Steve's monologue has left its mark on Bryn and Nick, though. They have waited for his departure and now frame a revealing question.
"So, the Gold Cup, Dave".
"Mmmm?" I nudge.

"Well," Bryn has a furtive look in Nick's direction, he's seeking support. "Is it run over fences, y'know, the Grand National bastards, or the little hurdle things?"
I roar with laughter. No wonder they waited until Steve had gone. He will be so disappointed. I say that if they are referred to as obstacles in all future conversations then they won't go wrong.

Steve's emergence as a guru on all things National Hunt is as quick as it is complete. I have to remind myself that it was me that suggested the trip. I thought I would need to convince the others and maybe impart a bit of my own wisdom about the jumping game. After all, I've got all this useful grounding in horse-racing through the family and there is that priceless moment in a St John's Wood boozer with Nick. So when Steve begins to throw off the dusty layers of betting inactivity to reveal his extensive racing knowledge, I find I am barely in his slip-stream, stretching my threadbare knowledge across an expanding subject matter. I soon give up. A few e-mail exchanges about the chances of Limestone Lad versus Istabraq quickly expose my shallow understanding of some pretty basic concepts, such as handicapping, the grading of races, relevance of ground conditions….. And the rest.

But what staggers me is not just that Steve has a welter of experience and knowledge that we previously knew nothing about, but also that he has rediscovered his voracious appetite for the subject. Within days of our planned Cheltenham outing, he is quoting ante-post markets, past performances of the leading contenders, and extracts from recently devoured books on betting and gambling. He has exploded all over the subject. I've been left behind. I reckon he has been waiting for something like Cheltenham to rekindle his smouldering ambition. He has as much reason as any of us to seek escapism. Steve has been in the same job for years. He's bored rigid by tree preservation orders, even if he has become the world's leading expert. I met Steve when we worked in the same division. Such is the nature of the civil service that his job was later moved overnight, lock, stock and tree-trunk from Rural Policy Division to the Urban Directorate without touching suburbia on the way. Fantastic. A geographic u-turn of EU referendum proportions! But of course Steve doesn't physically move. His team stays in exactly the same place amongst his erstwhile rural colleagues. It's just that the hierarchy above him shuffles around a bit. Infact long after me, Nick and Vaughany have all done our own shuffling, chasing jobs up and down Victoria Street, Steve is still in the same post, same seat, same desk, same boss. Whilst all around is transient squawking, Steve remains as constant as the ravens at the tower of London. He reminds me of a (local authority protected) Magic Faraway Tree in the Enchanted Forest. Unmoved and unswayed despite the regular passage of dream-like lands swirling around his head. Bet-as-much-as-you- like Land is his favourite.

The other boys are as gobsmacked as me. Down the pub, Bryn's going,
"What's happened, mate? Where's all this come from?" He shakes Steve's arm "Who are you? What have you done with Steve?"

We chuckle. But it's an adventure for the rest of us too and as Cheltenham approaches, we are all getting carried along with the enthusiasm. Steve's gone home early-ish as usual, but me, Nick, Bryn and Vaughany are on a roll. It turns into a sad and desperate night. Three of the Cheltenham party - me, Steve and Nick - are married. There's something about this fact that makes squeezing in a stolen pint in the pub feel like an act of rebellion. Turning an unfinished conversation into a session when you should really be heading for home. This night becomes a spontaneous Cheltenham-inspired session.

I struggle in to work the next morning feeling crap. My tongue feels like stale bread, my mouth like an ashtray, my head like the sound check for a Metallica gig and my guts like a spin dryer. In support of my condition, there's already been a bit of an e-mail exchange early this bright day. Steve's clearly perplexed about the events of last night:

> "Before leaving the pub last night, Nick insisted he'd be in the Willow Walk betting ring for no more than a couple of pints and a sugar lump. Eight pints later he thought he'd better phone Denise before getting home on the Dawn Run.
>
> I've heard some things in my time, but citing Vaughany as a bad influence takes the dog's chocolates. What was your excuse David?
>
> Wayward Lads, the lot of yer."

Could it really have been the mild mannered Andrew Vaughan that led us astray? I respond:

> "No, no, I fully support Nick's position. We were well and truly on the reigns last night until Vaughany, doing his Whisky Lad impersonation entered the parade ring at about 6 o'clock and led us a good gallop around the shorts optics.
>
> Nick - Vodkatini shall we call him - was in trouble at the third when he phoned the stable and the head lass knew he was on my phone in the boozer. The going instantly turned heavy and the price on a damn good dog-housing shortened considerably.
>
> As for me, well despite sending signals to the Hertfordshire Gallops, the tactics didn't pay off and it was a frosty canter to the childminders this morning."

But Steve's apparently far from convinced:

> " A wonderfully entertaining, but ultimately unconvincing account of last night's reckless workout. Vaughany - the Tardy Boy - a front runner? That's a stark reversal of form is that. In my experience it's Nick, he of the Blowing Wind, who makes the early

pace with yourself the Yorkshire Edition sometimes disputing the lead. Tardy Boy likes to tuck himself up close behind and no knowledgeable punter would have him down as an out-and-out stayer.

What should have been a two-mile chase ended up a four mile point-to-point. As for me, I was tucked up in me box nice and early after a spot of grooming from the head lass."

Hilarious stuff. See what I mean about Steve? He's even got the impenetrable language of the racing world off to a tee! Bryn sets up a new e-mail account for these exchanges known simply as 'classics'. At this point I should confess another entry in this section. Whilst recognising that the following entry probably paints me in a less than favourable light, it does, if nothing else, underline that the balance between those stolen pints and domestic bliss can get out of kilter:

"Boys

I think I was well pissed by the time I left the Wetherspoons.

Helen was OK about me getting home late, but not too delighted about what she found this morning.

I think I must have thrown up on the way to the bog after going to bed. I made a reasonable attempt to clean the vom off the stairs, but I see this morning that I missed a fair bit on the floor and walls.

I did have the presence of mind to put my puke-encrusted dressing gown in the washing machine. Only to find this morning that it was already full of newly washed clothes, the machine having completed its cycle.

Oh dear."

Bring on the Festival. We are ready now.

## 4. FIRST FESTIVAL FEVER

*"Out there is a fortune waiting to be had
If you think I'll let it go you're mad"*
Judas Priest, *"You Got Another Thing Coming"*, 1981

Steve has come up with a cracking idea to encourage our interest in the full three days of the festival rather than just for the day we are there. Fantasy Festival, building expertly on the proud history of our football and cricket competitions, is born. The rules are devastatingly simple. A fantasy £100 pot is to be spent by each competitor across ten top class Festival races, in mixtures of singles, doubles and each-ways. £10 minimum bet. Winner takes all. There's even a tacky trophy! And tantalisingly, we are offered the 'bust the bookie' option. If, collectively, we end up with more cash than we started with, then Steve is forking out for a bottle of finest malt whisky. There is no better incentive!

The big day arrives. Damn, it's exciting! I think I'm all set, but I'm not sure. Do I need all the Racing Post or just the bits about today's racing? I fancy having the binoculars for the totty, but do I need them slapping round my neck all day (the bins not the birds...ho ho). The hip flask is a must have, but it leaks. Inevitably, I take them all. But the indecision is costing me and I'm now late. I'm running down the road, RP sticking out of one trouser cargo pocket, hip flask sloshing around in the other, binoculars gouging my ribs from the inside of my coat.

Still, I'm on the train - my usual work train as it happens – with seconds to spare. We rumble into Euston and as I begin to tuck the paper away, a slow spreading damp patch reveals itself across my thigh. It's accompanied by the sharp smell of single malt whisky, though mixed with perspiration and clothes conditioner. One would be hard pressed to name the distillery.

The exits off the train quickly become clogged in the commuter crush and I find myself staring at a former work colleague. We are on reasonably friendly terms, but at this very moment he has me at a disadvantage. I stink like a brewery, I'm soaking wet down one leg and it's only 08.58!
    "Morning Stephen", I nod in quick acknowledgement before hastily losing myself in the barrier surge. I'll explain another day.

The boys are at the station before me. Nick and Bryn are also hip-flasked to the hilt, but otherwise travel light. A Daily Mail racing page pull-out between them. Vaughany, typically, looks the part. The very essence of a country gent. All he needs is a shooting stick and he would fit the bill for a day at Gatcombe Park. Shame we've only got tickets for the cheap seats in the Courage Enclosure. On the train, Steve is cornered by some 'been-there-done-that' geezer who boasts an almost unbelievably robust Cheltenham record. He landed See More Business in last year's Gold Cup at outrageous ante post odds of 40/1. Apparently.

"Lump on Castle Sweep in the Cathcart. Got a great chance. Can't lose"
Steve takes note, but I think he's a bit sceptical.

There is a right old grapple at Cheltenham Station. Knees and elbows come into play as we struggle off the platform and out into the car park. I thought Cheltenham Station would be laden with Cotswold charm and quiet sophistication. I was expecting a spruce, tidy hall with bright décor and maybe an understated flower arrangement, discreet yet confident wrought iron swirls and maybe a couple of grand limestone porticoes. But if the place ever knew any glory, it is long since crumbled and faded. There are only two narrow platforms, uneven and rutted; dilapidated wooden and stone walls, peeling paint and a roof with too many panes missing. This is no cathedral of steam, more a chapel of rest.

We squeeze on to the shuttle bus up to the track for a bargain £3. The double-decker lurches through the back streets on a riotous crusade. This is the crack that was missing on the train. It's all human life up here on the top deck. A group of scousers up front are already bladdered and are swapping tips for the day, offering advice to anyone who will listen. "Ere, mayte. I reckon tha' Irish nag's gowinna clean up t'dayee. Limestone thing-gee. Lad. Yeah. That's it. Fuccck'n gerronit" A bit more advice then. Nick's grinning. Behind me there are a couple straight out of the Royal Ascot members enclosure with two debs in tow who think it's Ladies Day. Big hats, skimpy dresses and silly giggles. So it's wide brims and wide boys. There you go. All human life.

This is it then. My first view of the battlefield. There is a spot before the main entrance where you stand at the end of the track, beyond the finishing post. We all pause. It means more to some than others, maybe. But we all feel a tingle. A spiritual shiver. Like the first time you go to Wembley after growing up on the 1966 stories and all that; or to Lords after seeing Viv Richards destroy England in the first test match you ever saw on telly; or that first proper gig at the Royal Albert Hall after seeing the Remembrance Day service over countless years.

We savour the view. The hallowed turf is just a few feet in front of us, rising up to meet the path. The Corinthian spirit of horse and man straining for the line up that punishing incline is palpable. The empty grandstands present a coliseum-like aspect, sweeping away to the left. Down the hill, we can see the Guinness enclosure and almost away into the distance, rows of hospitality boxes lined up near the last fence and disappearing past the final furlong marker. Room for 50,000 inside. So we go inside.

We're early. That bit was inevitable. I was three hours early for my first ever gig, content to wait on the steps of Hammersmith Odeon for the doors to open. Nick has brought a disposable camera. Excellent stuff. There are a few hastily arranged group shots down by the winning post. Mementos of our debut at the big one. We are leaping around the enclosure with childish glee. Grasping the first beers of the day grinning at each other like we've landed corporate hospitality at the Cup Final. The place is filling up. We check out what the place has to offer. Plenty of bars, loads of bookies and a massive tented village out the back which is rammed with day-trippers already full-on into a serious rave.

Time seems to slip away. A couple of beers later and its time to mull over the runners and riders for the first. The Triumph Hurdle, a helter-skelter headlong 2 mile charge for 24 frisky four-year-olds.

Already the fantasy festival banter is cranking up. Nick has stolen into an early lead courtesy of a massive priced winner, Sausalito Bay, in the Supreme Novice Hurdle on day one. We stole a few hours on Tuesday to catch the key races of the comp on the telly in a local boozer. His face lit up like bonfire night when the Irish novice landed the race by the slenderest of margins. The horse had hardly pulled up before Nick whipped out from the depths of his pocket a brick of paper, which he unfurled until the name Sausalito Bay appeared on the list of naps from some website I'd never heard of. The Steeplechase Studio or something. This was to be his mentor for the next three days. So, it's Nick, the most reluctant gambler, the sceptic and the doubter who has put in the research and taken a skinny advantage into the final day. Andrew has done some shrewd punting, too and is hard on Nick's heels. But of course it is all up for grabs.

It's not all fantasy though. I'm here to take on the bookies. At least I think I am. I have the cash to flash and I reckon I'm reasonably up on the form. But I am quickly disabused. The Triumph is truly a spectacle. I back Bring Sweets who turns sour. But Steve is off to a flyer after backing Regal Exit each way at a very healthy 20/1. He flies up the hill to take 2$^{nd}$. French raider and favourite Snow Drop hoses home after drifting to a respectable 7/1. She ran a blinder at Kempton last time out. We were all talking about this horse on the train. Why on earth didn't we back it?

No-one eats into Nick's fantasy lead either. Next up, the Stayers Hurdle. I've got some serious dosh to lodge on this race. The Mother-in-Law, bless her, wants £2 each way on Limestone Lad. She's been listening to some drunken scousers down the Village Hall Bingo, I reckon. Anyway, I'm on Bacchanal with real money. So is Steve. In the Fantasy Festival Novices Cup, Nick is outrageously playing the percentage game. He's on favourite Lady Rebecca at a very skinny 5/2. It's an absolute screamer of a race. After two circuits of Prestbury Park Bacchanal has a clear advantage, but the Irish legend Limestone Lad hasn't given up. He prefers softer ground, but he's coming again at Bacchy. He goes best at 2 and a half miles, but he's coming again. Breathtaking stuff. Bacchy is an out and out stayer and he prevails by a length and a half. But what a game performance from the Bowes beast. What a race. I've done OK here, but Steve is ecstatic. He's on a roll. Two out of two.

Then pinnacle of the day is hard upon us. Here we are for the Gold Cup. I can't pretend I've put lots of work into researching the race. Steve and I have had a bit of e-mail chat about some of the line-up, but I haven't got my head round the form. It's all cursory stuff. I'm backing Gloria Victis from the Pipe yard. He's the brightest star in the pack. He's the novice in the field. He's the chaser that ripped up a decent Racing Post Chase field at Kempton only 5 weeks ago. That was a scintillating performance and I can't see past him. Bryn and Andrew go for him too. Steve's got double trouble with Looks Like Trouble rolling into Castle Sweep in the Cathcart Chase. He's only gone and lumped on the advice of the joker on the train this morning!

The Fantasy comp is set up for the glorious Gold Cup too. We are all in with a shout and it is getting very tense. Seriously tense. Nick is desperate for this one. I realise that whilst he might have a few quid to blow at the bookies, he has really set his stall out for the fantasy prize. Nick is a classic study of anxiety. He's pacing around the beer tent paddock like a cat on heat. He's chuffing away at his Marlboros like a chimney and he's all over his beer like a bad suit. His coat is open and flapping around in the breeze, revealing his cerise t-shirt-covered belly escaping from incarceration in his faded denims. But is there a slight twinkle in his eye?
"I just don't know what to do", he splutters between draws on his tab and gulps from his John Smith's smoothflow.
He leads by a few quid from Andrew and now Steve is right back in the mix following Bacchanal's win. Bryn's not had a winner, yet but he's looking at the big priced stuff and still has a shout in this. So Nick's next decision is crucial. And here it is. Oh, it's shamefully skinny. An each way bet on hot favourite See More Business. Scandalous. But then without drawing breath, I've only gone and done the same thing!

The race does not let us down. Vaughany and me step back from the crowds on the rail and watch the race from in front of the bar. We can see them all the way round from here and I'm glued to my binoculars.

Gloria, as game as they come, sets a scorching pace, stringing out the field.
"Gloria's setting a scorching pace", I say to Andy.
He jumps like a stag, but jumps out right.
"He's jumping right", I say to Andy.
The PA blares out:
"Gloria is jumping right at that one".
We are agreed then.

The chasing pack is closing and as Gloria tires, his jumping defect becomes more exaggerated. Twelve of the nation's finest chasers scream down the hill. I'm getting animated. Vaughany remains cool. Of course. Gloria holds a slim but diminishing lead and tries to put in a big leap at the penultimate fence, but he doesn't make it and comes crashing down. He was probably a beaten horse by then, but so game, who can say for sure. Looks Like Trouble has been going the best of the stalkers and now emerges to bolt up the hill. It's a foot-perfect Gold Cup win. Florida Pearl stays on for a very creditable 2nd. See More Business went off favourite and was never at the races and finished out of the frame. He didn't like the firmish ground. Jockey Mick FitzGerald was quoted later likening the horse to "a hen on hot griddles". Hmmm.

Steve is on fire. He's landed a hat trick. Three on the bounce. What a performance. The bookies are heading for the hills. Me, Bryn and Vaughany have all bought into the Gloria Victis hype. We've seen his sensational jumps round Kempton. But we haven't really seen anything else. Swept along by the story and the expectation. But Steve has been looking at the form, seeing the results in the proper context, judging the suitability of the ground. There is no place for sentiment and he's backed the best animal in the field. "It's so difficult for a novice to win the Gold Cup. It's such a tough race". He remarked. And so it proved.

What's more, he's now in line to bag the Fantasy wedge as well. Vaughany is still hanging on. There was never a doubt that he would be on the premises. Bryn is potless, absolutely stony broke. And I'm not far behind. Cathcart time. It's all cloak and dagger now, with the principles shooting each other knowing looks. Nick has to declare first. Rules of the game. The leader declares his hand first. He has victory in his sights and, bugger me – shit or bust – he's upped the stakes to a tenner and gone for Young Spartacus. Vaughany goes each way on Young Spartacus and weighs in with a saver on Tresor De Mai. Steve has his Castle Lane double ready to roll and also has a saver on Fadalko who has already turned out at the Festival in Tuesday's Arkle. Bryn goes for Majadon, but plays it canny. He's not risking his full stake. If Majedon crashes out Bryn crawls out of the wreckage with 25p still in the bank. Look after the pennies and the pounds look after themselves.

There is a classic moment when Nick's pick Young Spartacus falls. He instantaneously assesses the situation. Concluding with lightning logic that his best chance of making off with the lolly is for anything to get home before Tresor de Mai and Fadalko, he immediately starts screaming for race leader Stormyfairweather. "C'mon Stormy. You can do it!" The speed Nick's loyalty transfer is nothing short of mercenary. Bryn is crying with laughter.

By the time the field rounds the top bend, there are only two with a realistic chance of winning. Stormyfairweather and…..Fadalko! Nick and Steve! They are still together at the last. Nick is screaming now. Steve's heart is in his mouth. The jockeys are close enough to whisper in each other's lug holes. Desperately tight. The final flight is the decider though. Stormy puts in a top jump and gains a little daylight. From then he on has Fadalko's measure, to Nick's obvious and vocal relief. He's had one winner secured in the 1st race of the festival and managed to steal away with the wedge at the climax of the festival. Fantastic. The win, in the heat of tactical battle and against the fiercest of adversaries is very sweet for Nick. We are all grudging losers in the true spirit of the competition.

It's all too much for us by now. It's been a heady cocktail of emotion and alcohol. We run for home on a packed Paddington flyer and round off with a couple of beers in a dodgy boozer round the back of Paddington station, recommended by Brynaldo after one of his footballing adventures. Then it's the slow crawl round the district line back to Euston. Steve is heading off to Liverpool Street and we depart on a note of expectation, savouring the prospect of Gloria competing at the highest level next season. His enriching experience in today's thrilling Gold Cup can only stand him in good stead.

Following the drama of the Gold Cup, I take the day off work. Chance to collect my thoughts. I'm lounging about on the sofa, scanning the sports pages. I have to blink several times and swallow hard to take in what I'm reading. The Gold Cup gets the deserved back page headlines, but not in the way I'd imagined. There is deserved celebration of the victory by Noel Meade's star, but I'm stopped in my tracks by Andrew Longmore's headline in The Independent, "Gloria Victis a victim of his own brilliance – young steeplechaser is put down after crashing fall at Cheltenham." A sickening realisation sweeps over me. In a filthy twist of fate, the incandescent talent of this exciting chaser, not yet six, has been extinguished. In a bitter after thought, I am appalled that we were singing his praises and anticipating future glories long after the green screens had come and gone in front of 50,000 on-lookers. How were we the only ones in Prestbury Park not to know?

I read on and it seems that Gloria was taken back to the stable block in an ambulance before an assessment of the terrible injury to his leg was made and the decision to put him down. Tony McCoy, hard as iron, was inconsolable. Having earlier described him as one of the most exciting horses he had ever sat on, he said of the race that Gloria had more to give. Right there at the second last, there was still a bit more to come. Tragic.

Back at work and I pick up a commentary Steve has written about Fantasy Festival competition. Nick is rightly lauded for his spawny, brass-neck victory, but the mood is accurately reflected in Steve's obituary for Gloria:

> "We all know racing's terrible truth. Occasionally we are forced to confront it, try to make sense of it or come away from it with an unaltered mind. Day three of the festival was the starkest reminder of that terrible truth. In the first place, of course, we were there. And in the second place, we are talking about the greatest young chasing prospect in the greatest race at the greatest meeting there is. As Alastair Down said in the Racing Post, we hardly knew him."

## 5. BASIC INSTINCT

*"In the beginning*
*When we were winning*
*When our smiles were genuine"*
Manic Street Preachers *"Everlasting"* 1998?

I suppose I was always going to succumb to the subtle delights of horse racing at some time or another. The mental conditioning kicked in from very early days. My Dad loves the game. Thinking back, all those trips to the races and the drip, drip racing talk must have become embedded in dark recesses of my psyche. Stored like the fruity bits in a bottle of orangina: 'Shake the bottle, wake the instinct' or something. Dad still continues to talk a good race these days, even if he rarely makes it across the threshold of the bookies. Speaking of which, the local bookmaker, Alec Peacock was one of his mates and I used to knock about with his son at one stage. They lived in the biggest house on my street and Alec sold up to William Hill and retired to a pile in the country before middle age. There is a lesson here, surely.

Anyway, my early racing indoctrination was not confined to Dad and family days out at York, Ripon and Charm Park point-to-point on the road to Scarborough. My Uncle Terry also contributed. He is a loud, brash, enthusiastic racing man if ever there was one. My Mum's brother. The family used to get the horse talk in full-effect over the Christmas period. Boxing Day round at Terry's served as the traditional festive gathering of the Harper clan. My Mum is one of six - three sisters and three brothers. So plenty of family to go round.

I had two cousins, both boys and we were all about the same age. We used to tear around the place, torturing the younger kids - particularly my younger brother, Paul and destroying newly acquired Christmas gifts. Action men were always the first to go in a hail of matches and handkerchief parachutes. Downstairs, my Mam would be letting rip with her uproarious siblings.

There was always a fantastic spread of food and a sea of booze. Terry and Eileen never skimped. And they gave the heartiest of welcomes. But as I hit my truculent teens, the promise of enough grub to last a week and beer to sink a battleship became an increasingly unattractive proposition. Bloody hell, how times have changed! Such a prospect now would have me clawing at the door begging to be let in. By then it was a case of watching a new generation of kids tearing round the place, trashing action men.

Mostly I remember listening to Terry and my Dad talking about racing. Terry loves his racing. Looking back now, I wish I had listened a bit more closely. He knew his stuff and was passionate about it. The fact that Boxing Day was King George VI Chase day at Kempton Park was certainly of mild interest to me. Probably no more than that. But my Dad and Terry would chew the fat over the day's events for ages.

This was in the early 80's pomp of trainers like Jenny Pitman and Michael Dickinson. Jonjo O'Neill and John Francome ruled to roost on the track, but the local hero was Graham Bradley, mainly because of his Northern connection, riding for Dickinson's Dunkeswick stables near Harewood, which he had inherited from his Mother, Monica, who trained from many years. Terry and my Dad were big fans of the stable. Dickinson sent out a record 12 winners on Boxing Day in 1982 which strikes me as an awesome achievement. The trainer was still in his 30's! He had some cracking horses like Silver Buck and Bregawn.

But the chaser that really stood out was Wayward Lad. He made the King George his own, becoming the first horse to win it on three separate occasions. The third win was towards the end of his glittering career and after an indifferent season he was allowed to go off at 12-1. He stormed to a win and I can still remember Terry waxing lyrical about the performance.

"Did you see that bugger stroll up today at Kempton? Couldn't believe it at that price."

That was the same season he was narrowly beaten in an emotional Cheltenham Gold Cup by Dawn Run. It was an incredibly popular win by the game mare, but I was cheering on Wayward Lad that day. I don't think I even had a bet. Without the 5lb mares allowance that Jonjo O'Neill's charge received, the Lad would have surely claimed the Gold Cup victory he so deserved. Wayward Lad was also placed in Michael Dickinson's crowning glory when he saddled the first five home in the 1983 Gold Cup. Amazing stuff. I can still remember Dad and Terry's shock when Dickinson changed codes and took over the famous Manton yard for owner Robert Sangster. The switch didn't work and the trainer soon after emigrated to America to continue training on the flat. He continues to have considerable success there.

Terry had been around horses most of his life. He had owned a good few greyhounds and also dabbled with horse ownership. One horse in particular had some success shortly after I found excuses not to join the Boxing Day jamboree. Travel Home (initials TH after my Uncle, Terry Harper) was trained by local license holder Mick Ellerby, but by all accounts in was Terry that did much of the graft. Mick and Terry had bought the horse at Doncaster sales for a bargain. He certainly paid his way. Travel Home won a maiden and a couple of other pretty low-grade races at minor meetings around the North and Terry had some fun with the horse. I remember Dad telling me about Terry painting the town red (only a small pot required, Pickering's a little town after all) with prize money and his bookies wedge. One of Travel Home's wins coincided with his daughter's wedding, my cousin Theresa. Shocking planning! The story was that Terry sneaked out of the Methodist Chapel on Potter Hill to catch the race in Alec Peacock's bookies up the Market Place. I was at the wedding, but can't vouch for the accuracy of the story!

I think he enjoyed the crack around the courses too. Although it appears that Ginger McCain gave Terry short shrift the first time he took Travel Home racing. Terry was soaking up the vibes of the parade ring and went across to introduce himself to Ginger whom he had seen attending to his charge.

"Who are you? Piss off!"

I don't think the four-time Grand National winning trainer had much time for the game's minnows.

Terry did well to enjoy his success whilst he could. It didn't last long. In Travel Home's next race the horse broke down and never recovered. The story I've heard from Dad is that the jockey did not ride to instructions and ran it too hard. The horse was never the same. Nothing came close to touching the success of his first horse and for me captures the essence of the sport. It stirs up all those romantic notions about small time owners and trainers taking on the big boys and wiping the floor with the bookies for good measure.

I've had this ambition awakened in me quite recently. I'm seriously attracted to the idea of horse ownership. Something to do with reflected glory, maybe, but I would revel in my big day out at the races. I can see it all in my mind's eye. I'm not showy, I've placed the horse at a nice little characterful low key track. Somewhere like the Cartmel August bank holiday meeting, or a nice little Autumn meeting at Towcester. I'm poncing around the paddock, casting a knowing glance over my charge, passing the time of day with the trainer. Then the jockey comes up to me and tells me how he's going to run the race. I'm nodding and saying that it sounds like a good plan. "All the best, Ruby. Just bring him back in one piece". I'd slap him on the back and slope of to the Holy Grail - the bar with the sign outside that says "Owners and Trainers only", where I'd have a couple of single malts and quietly pinch myself in disbelief. And the race wouldn't have even started yet.

One day that will be me. It's a seductive idea. Every time I've been anywhere near the paddock, I marvel at the professionalism of the trainers and jockeys in the way they regard the owners. I'm content in my slightly naive, idealistic view that the small timers and the syndicates bask in a similar respect to that afforded to the big hitters who marshal strings of horses and who bring in the winners cheques. But the little guys, and increasingly the syndicates, are the lifeblood of the sport and they all pay the wages.

I read Stan Hey's book 'An Arm and Four Legs' about warts 'n' all horse ownership. It's a cracking read with frank account of the costs involved. Clearly, only a select few - the very wealthy residing at the classic and championship end of the market - enter into horse ownership to make money. For the majority, the game is about extracting reward from the thrill. It's an expensive hobby. There's a revealing piece in the book recording in painful detail his 'expenses' incurred on a grim and fruitless trip to a bleak Worcester where his horse under the care of Martin Pipe was running. But there's the promise of a nice pay-day occasionally. Very occasionally, according to Stan's advice. Even this solidly downbeat advice doesn't shake me from my dream. I noticed about a year after reading the book that Deadly Doris, Stan's quirky hurdler whom he lovingly kept in training with Nigel Smith as part of the Stan Hey and Partners team scored her maiden victory in a 2m novice hurdle at Towcester, coming home at a very tasty 14-1. I was genuinely delighted for him. He must have been thrilled. Nigel Smith said with great optimism that "there will be plenty more to come from her". She hasn't made the frame since.

Sometime after, I'm running my eye over the form in the Racing Post of a thin meeting at Uttoxeter. It's a pretty poor card in the week before Newbury's Hennessey Cognac Gold Cup meeting, when I get a vision of how this small-time, big thrill horse ownership caper can really be maximised. I'm not paying a great deal of attention to the fare on offer, but I do notice the silks of one particular owner appearing in nearly every race. It's an owner I have never heard of, John Pointon and Sons, sporting distinctive in red, blue and white silks. All the horses are trained by a certain Miss SJ Wilton - Sue Wilton out of a yard in Staffordshire. This intrigues me because it is quite common to see the big owners - JP McManus, Sir Robert Ogden, David Johnson, Jim Lewis, Trevor Hemmings, etc blanket covering meetings. Rarely do the small time owners use the same tactics and equally rarely do they have their horses with little known trainers. I was quite fascinated by the idea of the Pointons having a real day out at the races with their entire string, trained by a family friend. There I go you see, attracted to these romantic notions. Anyway, I checked the results in the RP next day: no winners; one second place; one non-runner; and one horse the subject of a steward's enquiry after finishing distressed. So not such a top day out after all.

## 6. THE VALUE BETTING EMPORIUM

*"I wanna be as big as a mountain*
*I wanna fly as high as the sun*
*I wanna know what the rent's like in heaven*
*I wanna know where the river goes."*
The Stone Temple Pilots, *"Where The River Goes"*1992

What on earth? Steve starts muttering about value betting not long after our first taste of Gold Cup drama that eventful day in March 2000. He's been reading books. Dangerous. Actually, he's been devouring them, Raiding Basildon library for morsels of gambling good practice, crumbs of betting theory. He's already got the knowledge. In a few months since the boys came together for our assault on Cheltenham, Steve has turned into a steeplechasing encyclopaedia.

We are down the Willow Walk doing the usual 5pm - 6.30pm slot and Steve eyeballs us over his glasses and casually suggests a new departure.
"You know, I reckon there is more value on the flat."
Nick looks at Brynaldo who's nursing a pint. He can only squeeze one in before disappearing off to his sports club committee meeting. He gurgles to his frothy pint of 'guest ale', rather than to us.
"Yee-ees?"
Nick's a bit more direct.
"What? Bollocks!" he queries.
"Yeah, I think so."
Steve continues and we are a bit relieved.
"It's only early season, but there is definitely more value to be had in some of the conditions races and even some of the big handicaps". Nick is chortling.
"Value? What do you mean value?"
His tones are at once sceptical and mocking. Steve is laying himself open here, but he persists.
"Well, it's the idea that often in a race there is a horse, or even horses plural that are overpriced in the market. This is where you can beat the bookie. When you find this horse, well, you've found the imperfection in the market. The bookies have under-estimated that horse, in your opinion, for whatever reason. There's the value, so that's the horse to back."
Very eloquent, Steve. Even persuasive. But Nick's not having it.
"So that's the horse that wins then, is it? If it's so easy, why doesn't everyone do it?"
"Well, no, not exactly", comes back Steve.
"It's not always this horse that wins. All you have done is identified the value. It means you are backing a horse that has a better chance of winning than the market suggests. You are making the market work in your favour."
Nick despairs.
"So it *is* all luck really."

Steve's face breaks into a wide grin. He knows when he's got a serious argument. But more importantly, he knows when he's got an argument that needs at least another two pints. So he quits when he's ahead and disappears out into Victoria with Brynaldo. This leaves me scratching my head. I haven't got the tools to continue this debate even though I'd love to. So after a bit more banter about the horses and Steve's growing fascination with all things equine, we resort to the quiz machine and too much beer.

But the seed has been sown. Even through the murk of a Wednesday morning hangover I know my befuddled brain is hooked. I'm a mug punter after all. Here is another chance for me to shine!

I buy the Racing Post when there is some decent racing. It also helps with this bizarre tipping competition that me, Bryn, Steve, Nick and Paul, another mate from the office are indulging in: The Grand Annual. The rules are simple - fivers in, winner takes all for 25 events over the month nominated by each competitor. Some obscure sports are thrown into the mix. We've had speedway, greyhounds, snooker, rallying, spread betting on football shirt numbers, One Day International run make-ups and famously, Nick pulls a fast one with the Miss World competition. This marks the high water mark of my mug punting career. I'm almost ashamed. Have I really nothing better to do?

But reading the RP is starting to help me translate the unique language of the racing game. I mean, what does "he gets done for a bit of toe", or "this one likes to hear is hooves rattle" mean? And then we get silly. I open the page one day to see the headline "Doncaster Stallion Parade", and stranger still "Doncaster Breeze Up Sales". It all goes on in South Yorkshire apparently. I turn over the page to be confronted by Tony Morris's "World of Breeding". I'm sorry, but I can't take this seriously. It sounds like a spoof Viz might run on a dodgy *Farmers Weekly* story.

Maybe I should be taking this seriously. I'm not turning up many winners. I'm still backing second or third favourites and expecting them to win every other time. The same policy I've had since I was about 12 when Aldiniti did me a favour in the Grand National. I haven't really shaken off this cautious approach. I start reading a book called *Against the Crowd* by Alan Potts, a professional punter (just pause there a moment – a professional gambler. He makes a living at it. I'm not mentally equipped to deal with this concept). Some of it is really dull stuff, but on a very lonely train journey to the back of regional beyond, I pick up a few nuggets about identifying weak favourites, recording every bet, and being thorough in the research. Gripping. Well sort of. I'm spouting off to Helen, my wife, about this new idea of backing long shots. She just laughs at me.

    "Ha. And you took the mickey out of me when I won at Chester at a huge price! 'Fluke' you snorted. Now you tell me it's a theory, Ha!"
Oh I hate this. It's all pretty much true. Helen backed a complete outsider in the Derby trial at Chester a couple of years ago at 66/1 and it came 3rd. I bleat rather pathetically about the skill being in identifying an imperfect

market and knowing the form, and....and... It's no good. It doesn't sound half as convincing as Steve sounded in the pub the other night. I'm on a hiding to nothing. And in some ways she's right. I suppose *value* can often mean *outsider*. And the thrill of the big ones going in is (apparently) spectacular; far more of a rush and much more memorable than a winner by a street at bits-on. But I wouldn't know, would I? It's all theoretical.

Steve has some research, more of a thesis really - a statistically robust, analytical trend examination - on the boil which underpins the principles of value betting. I'm barely reading the Racing Post weekly, but I've already noted the tipping service of a journalist called Mel Collier who writes the regular *Pricewise* column. Steve has been following the fortunes of Mel's selections. Mel is taking a value approach; the long view; sniffing out the weak favourites and opposing them with over-priced alternatives. And by all accounts he's rather good at it.

Steve's project concludes that:
> "Moving straight to the bottom line, how well did Pricewise perform during the season? In all he recommended 59 bets in just 48 races. He found nine winning bets; on the face of it, a fairly modest strike rate of 15%. Yet he made a pre-tax profit of 66.35 points . If you assume a basic staking plan of £100 per point, Pricewise cleared a profit of £6,635."

Hmmm. I'm starting to see the attraction of the concept. Steve neatly sums up the approach when he asserts that "In a game where the art of breaking even is for many of us wholly elusive, 66 points is a no-nonsense, respectable profit. The ups and downs of the season, in fact, neatly illustrate the peaks and troughs of 'value betting'. The wins can be spectacular, but the methods of the value punter ("looking beyond the obvious" as Pricewise once put it) also dictate that losing runs, sometimes painfully long and confidence-sapping, are inevitable

Steve's detailed elucidation of the Pricewise theory remains insultingly and dismissively unpublished. I think he sends it to Mel - merely for information - but it does not even extract an acknowledgement. A travesty. Mel Collier leaves the Racing Post shortly after. Flushed with success and probably basking in Steve's expert analysis, he sets up his own subscription tipping service. Apparently a losing streak bit in shortly afterwards and anyone with a £1,000 bank at £100 a point would have lost it on Mel's first ten bets! He has spectacularly recovered in the meantime, however....

Steve's already been setting aside his dubious winnings from various Fantasy Cricket competitions over the Summer, not to mention his regular monthly fleecing of the rest of us in the Grand Annual to fund his onslaught on the bookies. He's doing pretty well too over the Summer. A couple of nice little earners come in on biggish handicaps at Ascot and Newmarket that Steve has targeted. Targeting the races. An alien concept that. It's almost a scientific process. What happened to pulling out the paper on Saturday morning on going long odds on gut instinct? I'm attracted to this value betting malarkey, no question. But I'm shallow. What attracts me is screaming home a long shot, the exhilaration of beating the market and the glee of collecting that fat wedge. Sometime soon maybe. My weaknesses are impulse betting, and following misleading cast-iron assured gut feelings. And that's before I get as far as putting in the leg work and doing the research.

## 7. WHAT'S THE CRAIC IN IRELAND?

*"There was half a million people there of all denominations*
*The Catholic, the Protestant, the Jew, the Presbyterian*
*Yet there was no animosity, no matter what persuasion"*
*"Galway Races"* Trad.

Stevo's been on about this horse all summer. Down To The Woods is one of the best two year olds in Mark Johnston's Middleham yard. Steve's mate's brother (with me...?) co-owns the beast and they have already earned some serious wedge from on-course bookies. The prize money, though quite tasty, is pocket money compared to the folding stuff they are taking out of the ring.

I meet the other half of Steve's mate's brother's partnership quite by chance in my local bookies one Saturday afternoon. Me and Nick are in there having a quick bet on Down To The Woods in a 6 furlong Doncaster event after getting the nod from Steve that he should be out to win. Indeed, he pisses it. This insider knowledge stuff is dead handy. I think me and Nick are a bit obvious about our success because a bloke I've seen once or twice on my commuter train taps me on the shoulder.
"How did you know about that horse?"
Maybe we just bloody well worked it out, I indignantly think. But we come clean.
"Through a mate down Basildon way who has connections to the horse"
I offer rather mysteriously.
"Oh really? My brother owns it!"
We eventually work out that we know the 'other' half of the owning partnership. Small world and all that innit?

So, come August, I'm telling Helen's Uncle Gerry about this in his local bar in Raheny, a decent enough suburb in north Dublin.
"Oh yes, it's running at Doncaster tomorrow. It's already won there, so it should go well." I've had a Guinness or two so the bullshit is beginning to flow quite nicely. "As long as the ground doesn't come up too soft it's a real contender." You would really think I knew what I was talking about. I frighten myself sometimes.
"D'ye hear this, Michael? We have a tip for the races tomorrow." The landlord leans over and pours us another smooth one.
"Ah, I like a bet myself on the horses from time to time. What's the name of yer fancy?"
I'm purring now. Seamlessly shifting though the gears like a Bentley
"Down To The Woods, Doncaster. Two-thirty. Can't lose. I know the partnership that owns it".
Can you picture the metaphorical wink and tap of the nose? I wince just to think about it.

Gerry is one of the most quietly spoken, gentlest and understated guys I know. We have a good banter in his local and he has a lot more to say for himself than anytime I have ever heard around his wife, the spectacularly generous and warm-hearted Aunty Carmel. She does like to talk, though.

Gerry sidles up at breakfast, next morning.
"Now David. Would you be thinking of having a little bet on that there horse you mentioned?"
So I nip out to buy a paper to check that he's been declared and in no time at all Gerry is whisking me down to the local Ladbrokes. Sure enough Michael from the boozer is in there exchanging knowing glances with Gerry. Gerry is playing it cool. I've no idea how much he and Michael put down, but I'm getting a tad nervous. My credibility is at stake here. Wish I'd kept my gibbering Guinness-loosened tongue still.

Me and the family are off to a holiday cottage in Wexford for the week, so I know I won't see the race. We struggle with heavy traffic heading south out of Dublin. Soon I realise why. We are passing Leopardstown. The place is mobbed with punters queueing to watch Giants Causeway edge another epic struggle in his glittering career. Today is Irish Champions Day. I can see the towering Grandstand from the car. My thoughts turn to Doncaster, but I can't pick up anything on the radio.

Hours later we see the other extreme of Irish racing as we pass the ramshackle Wexford racecourse perched on a rise overlooking the coast outside the town. The cottage is a few miles down the road and it is fantastic. It is set next to a ruined castle overlooking a perfect horseshoe shaped harbour. And the telly has teletext! Down To The Woods won at a miserly 2-1. But I am saved! "Pissed it", Steve tells me later. Sometimes the smallest victories are really the biggest. Gerry says I'm welcome back any time and especially if I've got any red hot tips. I expect there is a plaque dedicated to me in his pub and a free pint of Guinness any time I choose to collect.

I have to post my winning slip to Ladbrokes because I can't cash it in on this side of the Irish Sea. Still, worth it for the buzz. Down To The Woods sadly doesn't deliver on his promise, and spends much of his three-year old campaign on the sidelines with broken blood vessels and related problems. Steve's mate's brother's partnership eventually sells him on to a bookies consortium and he disappears into oblivion. I last saw him crop up in some bizarre race in Sweden. Shame.

I love Ireland. We return a couple of years later. This time enjoying a family holiday to end them all: the Mother, the Father, the Brother and the Mother-in law join four of us in a cottage in Cork. But, bugger me. It's working out a treat. Bliss. We are toasting on the beach in uncharacteristic, glorious Irish sun, drowning in the smoothest of Guinness and stuffing our gunnels on the finest, most delicate of seafood. Tonight we are nestled in a fantastic pub in a tiny West Cork fishing village called Glandore. The bar is called the Glandore Inn. No need for ceremony.

There is an enticing display of Irish Whiskies perched on a shelf above the bar. The pub is quiet as it's mid-week and Dad, Mum, Helen and me are enjoying a welcome tipple. Me and me dad have begun to have a little go at the Tyrconnells, the Bushmills and the Jameson's Reserve. Nothing serious, mind. But enough for Dad to start waxing lyrical about his gambling antics. And for me to encourage him. It's entertaining stuff, and frankly, some of it is a bit hair raising.

He tells me perfectly straight faced that he put an entire month's rent on a sprinter at York. My Mum was having kittens at the track until it completed the 6f jamboree in fine style at 2/1. I look at my Mum cupping a half pint of stout in her hands. She's taken to the black stuff like a natural.
"I could have killed him. Bloody killed him!"
"Yeah, but what about when it won?" I offer.
"No, it wasn't worth it. I nearly had a heart attack. We'd have been out on the streets".
Some exaggeration I think. Dad's just grinning.
"Double Jump it was called. I was never going to lose".
Jeremy Trees trained Double Jump and this was his first race as a 2 year old. And he delivered. A month's bleedin' rent!! Outrageous. I admire the balls. Even with the stable telling you it's nailed on would I do it? Nope.
"Jimmy Lindley was on him that day, although Joe Mercer picked up a lot of Trees' rides." Dad's in full reminiscent mode now. "Trees and Dick Hearn had been known to go right through a card at York and Doncaster. Peerless they were".

Dad was active on the horses in those days. He was part of a red-hot network of gossip when he worked in the ticket office at Malton Station close to where I was brought up in North Yorkshire. Malton and the surrounding fertile farmland and Wolds upland region was then, and still remains, an important horse training centre. It lies second only to HQ at Newmarket in terms of trainers and winners. Dad's telling me about Walter Binnie, one of the local trainers. He had his fair share of success, though he hardly competed with the big boys. Each year he looked to send out one his horses to collect on a big handicap at York or Thirsk to pay for his jolly Caribbean cruise during the dark days of the national hunt season.

During the 50's and 60's and before Beaching had his merciless cull of root and branch railway Britain, trains were the most effective way of transporting horses to race meetings. Walter Binnie raced his stock mostly at the northern flat tracks. His was a small operation and he and his stable team and jockey connections got to know the boys at the local station well through booking horseboxes on a regular basis. This is where Dad came in. Malton is a small station on the York-Scarborough branch line, though it was much busier then, with links north and south as well as the remaining east west route.
"We all got to know pretty quickly when he was sending his horse to collect the money for his Caribbean Cruise. Nine times out of ten, his holiday banker - usually a lightly raced, well handicapped sort for the season - did the business at York".

Inside info keeps the wheels turning. Not new then and still as relevant today. It's a question of knowing when the information is top quality, nailed on fact and when it's wishful thinking and half-baked rumour.

"Oh yeah, there was plenty of pretty dodgy stuff going on. None of it strictly illegal, maybe. More like, y'know, gamesmanship I suppose you'd call it. Stretching a point, seeing what they could get away with it. A lot of people knew what was going on."

Binnie had a string of half a dozen or so horses and was reputed to work the system. Poplin was his best horse and Binnie was frequently accused of 'working the horse in public', Thus the handicap mark was dropped until those in the know would plunge on him in a moderate race. The boys in the booking office would usually be in the know.

Horse racing is a big industry in Malton, particularly on the flat. In the late 50's and early 60's there were 7 or 8 yards all active to a greater or lesser extent, but all sending their horses to meetings through York and using the lads in the booking offices to make the arrangements. That's trainers, jockeys, work riders, stable staff and sometimes owners and managers all linked with the Malton booking office syndicate. Keeping the staff at the station sweet must have been a consideration for the yards as the railway occupied such a strategic position within the logistical framework. The mind boggles at the almost unrivalled quality of the information flowing down those red-hot rails.

Dad underlines all this with another nugget from the inside tracks at the booking office. We get another round of drinks in. This could be a long night.

"Pat Rohan was a bit of a bugger, you know". He had a runner called Tin Whistle, which pulled a fast one at the Ebor meeting in the Summer of 1962. This was apparently in the days before overnight declarations. Pat Rohan who had taken over the famous stables of Walter Dutton and was a gambling man from a gambling stable. The stables have gone now. Buried under a housing development. Anyway, Rohan was looking for a proper bet. Tin Whistle was an unexposed 2 year old whom the trainer thought was the business.

"Rohan wanted the best possible price for himself on his next outing. I think Tin Whistle was one of his favourites. Y'know, something he had been keeping for himself."

He was looking for a suitable opportunity. The colt was entered in a maiden at York, although the story goes, he was also entered in another couple of races at around the same time elsewhere. Rohan let it be known that he didn't expect Tin Whistle to go to York, but to one of the other tracks instead.

When horses were transported by rail, the horseboxes had to conform to certain requirements. One of these is that colts and fillies had be be loaded a particular way and that trainers would not share boxes. Rohan had already booked a box for York on the day of the race with the boys in the office at Malton. Come the hot and humid August race-day morning, the ticket office team, Dad included, realised what was afoot. Despite Rohan's apparent assertions that Tin Whistle would not go to York, his box arrangements had not been cancelled or changed. Moreover it was a box for a colt. Tin Whistle was available in the market for the maiden (having still been declared) and had drifted to 6/1. No stable money flooded to shorten the price because they didn't know he was running. Rohan had sneaked him to the track under their noses and made sure only he could take full advantage of an attractive price. But the boys from Malton station also got stuck in comfortably and sure enough Tin Whistle won the race hard-held by a couple of lengths in his Knavesmire maiden .

Presumably overnight declarations were brought in to cut down on these kinds of enterprising scams! But the stable staff caught up with Rohan.
"They were so incensed by his behaviour that they just downed tools. Ha ha. Nothing moved in the yard and Rohan was forced to settle up with them."
Dad revels in the story. What a scam. Quite how Rohan struck a deal with his staff is lost in the mists of time and to the wrinkles of the folding stuff. But the negotiations must have been pretty frank! Rohan eventually went to train in Hong Kong when racing became a fully professional sport there in 1971. The Protectorate was keen to build up the reputation at the Happy Valley track and a number of established European trainers settled there with some success.

Of course Dad never tells me about the days when he put down some serious wonga on horses that failed to deliver. But the outrageously successful gambles are always more fascinating. It's getting late now. The bar is fairly quiet, but there's no one moving us on yet. There are still a couple of locals up a the bar talking in hushed tones. Hope they're not from the Jockey Club! Me, Dad and Mum are nicely relaxed and Dad's still recalling the details of his glorious gambling career. I think he saves his warmest feelings for the Lincoln in 1961.

Brian Lee was a local jockey, apprenticed to Ernie Davey. He was passing the time of day down at the booking office knocking around with his mate Dad called "Lacker - can't remember his real name!" when he mentioned an upcoming booking.
" 'I've been asked to ride Johns Court for Ernie Cousins in The Lincoln' he said. The race was actually run at Lincoln in those days."
The lads at the station sat up and took notice.
"Lee went on 'He's a 7-furlong horse really, but I reckon if I drop him in he should get a mile easy enough' ".

He did. Dad and a few of the other lads got on John's Court early at 50-1. The horse scored readily enough over the mile and landed an SP of 25-1.

Brian Lee went on to be top apprentice that year, riding 51 winners at the same time as Lester Piggott and Scobie Breasly were fighting out the senior jockey championship. Lee was by then also riding winners for that season's leading owner, Major Lionel Holliday. Legend has it that when Brian left school he was faced with the choice of becoming an apprentice painter or an apprentice in stables. Soon after the Lincoln win he lost his claim and never seemed to turned that early promise into success at the very top level.

We call it a night at that point. The barman and steps down from the bar to unlock the front door and heartily wishes us farewell. He says he's looking forward to seeing us again. It's late, but I feel that we could have stayed all night and not been turfed out. It's cooler now outside and the ozone off the freshening sea hits our warm faces and we start to glow outside as well as inside. We all breathe deeply and congratulate ourselves on a good night out and a top holiday all round. Some times, for fleeting moments, everything seems alright with the world. We need to hang on to these moments. They matter.

That's enough sentimental guff for now.

## 8. ARCANE AGRICULTURAL ANXIETY

*"Harmlessly passing your time in the grassland away
Only dimly aware of a certain unease in the air."*
"Sheep", Pink Floyd, 1977

The cancellation of Cheltenham 2001 is a real kick in the teeth. We've already done the pub lunchtime sessions to pick out the ante post value. The Festival tickets are safely pouched. Steve and myself planned to step up the campaign. We were seduced by the prospect of seeing Istabraq attempt to take an unprecedented 4th Champion Hurdle, so we hatched a plot to take in the opening day of the festival from the luxury of the Tattersalls enclosure, returning home the same day to spend Wednesday in the boozer cheering home our festival favourites. Gold Cup day was to be a repeat of last year's expedition in the Courage Enclosure with the boys.

But quite early in the cycle of expectancy that I now recognise as part of the Festival build up, things are not going well. I'm hanging off the phone trying to get First Great Western to book seats for us on the Cheltenham specials. But the entire rail network is gridlocked in a post-Hatfield gauge-corner-cracking speed restriction zone. I can't reserve tickets for love nor money. I keep getting fobbed off with excuses about the use of rolling two-week timetables to cope with the engineering mayhem. Nevertheless, FGW have seen their way clear to offer a *First Class* Raceday Package! I'm appalled to see that I can book seats on Cheltenham Special with champagne breakfast and 'complementary' Racing Post for a tidy £150! Ha! (he rasped in a bitter and hollow manner).

I never get the tickets. This issue becomes a minor irrelevance as other events unfold. Foot and Mouth disease has gripped the country in ovine paralysis. The outbreak has quickly become an epidemic. It seems to grow daily as panic spreads through rural life and over-reaction through political life. We are exposed to media images of smoking pyres of burning carcasses. Sheep and cattle are being culled at alarming rates and in massive quantities. Sports fixtures are being culled equally dramatically amid jostling from sports administrators, politicians and pressure groups. Racing shuts down for a week or so to avoid spreading the disease. A limited programme soon resumes, but with the epidemic showing no signs of abating the decision proves to be contentious. Tracks can fulfil fixtures as long as they are not in an 'exclusion zone' surrounding infected farms. This effects many racecourses located in rural areas - the north west and south west are particularly badly affected. The restrictions seem crazy and yet the responses are ineffective.

A cloud inevitably hangs over the festival. The Racing Post is filled daily with multiple column inches debating whether the festival should take place. As the days of uncertainty pass, it is difficult to be confident about what sort of event would eventually come to pass. Already, the French trainers have said 'non' and refused to risk their horses travelling to

England. It soon emerges that the Irish-trained horses will not travel either.

Screeds of paper are dedicated to mulling over the issues. Finally, depressingly, but inevitably a case of Foot and Mouth is reported on a farm near Cheltenham and the surrounding exclusion zone breaches a small part of the Prestbury Park course. On that basis, the organisers feel they have no option but to cancel the event. "Silence of the Lambs!" screams the Racing Post in a 3-inch high headline over a picture of Cheltenham racecourse. Wry sentiments shared by many.

In some respects, maybe a clean break is best. A half-arsed, half-represented festival would have been insulting. What is the festival without the Irish? At least the doubting is over.

Well almost. There is a short-lived silly season where we get any number of crackpot schemes to host the showpiece on new dates, at different venues, or even to muscle in on other festivals. Arguments in the Racing Post and in the national press run themselves ragged trying to justify preserving the sanctity of the festival at the same time as demanding high quality racing action. In the end there is a nod towards compromise by including some additional Grade 1 races at Sandown's Whitbread Gold Cup meeting in April and on the Aintree National card. It's all a bit irrelevant really. I'm sure they will be interesting races when they arrive, but it's a token effort and not a replacement festival.

All this time, Steve has been sitting on some outstanding ante-post bets. During the build up to the festival we had both been perusing the ante-post market activity. My bets were hopelessly dead and buried before the year was out and long before Foot and Mouth intervened. Steve, on the other hand, had a lovely bet on Bacchanal for the Royal Sun Alliance Chase keeping him warm over those long, cold winter nights. He'd got on at a massive 25-1 early season and the horse had shortened up after some cracking performances. Henderson, his trainer, was keen on him and he was one of the market leaders. Steve also had Azertyuiop ante post for the Supreme Novice Hurdle.

No Istabraq four-timer to savour (he was nailed-on, surely), no Bacchanal/Azertyuiop ante-post swoop for Steve and no festival antics to report. Damn shame.

But no point in agonising any further. We decide that we can't let the newly constituted fantasy festival competition also fall victim to this agricultural madness. Steve recasts the competition for the three-day Aintree Grand National meeting. It's a good decision. This is a top meeting packed tight with quality horses in competitive races - many of whom had been primed for the now abandoned festival.

Well, it proves to be a glorious competition for me. I'm applying those theoretical value betting principles to live competition. Easy when it's fantasy. The going is heavy up at Liverpool. The weather has been atrocious. Gower-Slave plothers through the mud to land me a 14-1 winner in the John Hughes Trophy on Friday afternoon. It gives me a narrow lead going into the final day. We collect in the Willow Walk to analyse the standings. It looks like Vaughany is the only real threat, though Brynaldo is clinging to an outside chance too. It will most probably go down to the wire in the Grand National where the stakes are higher, literally. We give Steve - keeper of the sacred scrolls - our selections for the final day, and he reveals the choices with drama and respect befitting the occasion. Now I'm in contention for the trophy, I need to know the selections of my rivals. I'm frantically scribbling down everyone's picks on a tatty bit of A4, soaked with the dregs of Abbott Ale. This will do.

Grand National Day is always busy. I've got to get hold of my Sister-In-Law, Sue in Tenerife to get her selections. No bookies in Tenerife apparently. Then the Mother-in-Law wades in with an eclectic mix of each-way shots. Helen gives me her picks. And there's my own of course. So I'm off down to Johnson's in the High Street to get the wedge on. I'm greeted by a queue coming out of the door marshalled by Tweetie Pie and Sylvester handing out betting slips. Bizarre. I suspect this is the independent bookies' way of embracing the opportunities presented by the day. At least they have entered into the spirit. I can't believe the queue out the door though. This bookies is usually populated by half a dozen blokes escaping Saturday afternoon domestic bliss, together with the kitchen staff of the local Chinese take-away. But the National brings a whole host of once-a-year punters into otherwise uncharted territory.

I take my place in the line, ever so slightly resentful that I have to wait with these novices. Don't they know who I am? I'm a regular. I know what I'm doing. Let me through. But then I look at the slips in my hand. Seven £1 each-way bets and four £1 and £2 win bets. This collection would not convince anyone of my punting pedigree. I wait patiently for my turn.

The bets are down and I realise I'm in time to see the Maghull Novices Chase which is in our fantasy competition. It's a great race and my selection Ballinclay King hangs on by the tiniest of margins from Whitenzo, driven out by Adrian Maguire through bottomless ground. At 6-1, this must surely mean that I've bagged the fantasy trophy. I allow myself a small punch of the air and strangle a "Yesss!" as I remember where I am. The once a year punters are a bit taken aback, completely oblivious to the fact that there is more than the Big One on the card today and that some punters might be interested in those. I feel a bit sheepish under their gaze, but leave feeling that my punting pride has been restored.

The Grand National is a grim endurance this year through a mudbath. The ground is a quagmire and the race becomes a farce. There are only two runners with any sort of chance from about half way round. Red Marauder and Smarty slug it out through the sludge. Too many serious challenges crash out at the Canal Turn in an incident not far short of the Foinavon calamity repeated on Grandstand every year. It would have been abandoned had it been any other race. The suspicion remains that the fixture went ahead partly because the loss of Cheltenham and the Grand National in the same season might just have been too much for the jumps game to bear.

Red Marauder's stamina lasts longer than Smarty's and he crawls over the line in an exhausted state with his pursuer a distance behind. Blowing Wind who had been unseated at the Canal Turn is remounted by Tony McCoy to finish 3rd.. This just adds to the farcical nature of the race. That was about it. Vaughany's selection Beau unshipped his jockey following some mishap with the reigns. He was well placed and looking strong. It only occurred to me afterwards that had he won, Andrew might well have nicked the fantasy festival trophy. Beau was a healthy price. I had an each way bet on Smarty at 16-1, so a satisfactory day for me. Strange old race though. Hardly a great advert for the legendary steeplechase.

In the office on Monday, I'm expecting a few plaudits, maybe some deserved acclamation for my stunning victory in the competition. But no. Nothing was forthcoming, bar a modicum of acknowledgement that I had, indeed, won. Turns out that they are feigning disinterest because it's not the 'real' competition. Some old bollocks about Aintree being a poor substitute for Cheltenham. Miserable bastards, the lot of 'em.

Implications of the Foot and Mouth debacle run on for a considerable chunk of the year. In late Summer Helen and I are having a weekend in the Lake District. The weather is fantastic. We are staying in a pub called the High Cross Inn near Broughton owned by Andy, a colleague of Helen's in the music business. The pub is setting itself up as a live music venue and we are here to see a Canadian band that Helen's company are currently involved with. *Oh Susannah* deliver an impeccable set of country blues with some searing guitar work lighting up the ballads and Suzie Ungerleider's pure voice setting the room on edge, rising up over the mix like a cathedral choir.

This isn't a run of the mill gig. The stage is set up in a huge bay window of the pub's dining room with the rolling unpopulated upland of Broughton fell as a backdrop. It must present a strange view for the occupants of passing cars looking in. It feels surreal inside too. The L-shaped dining room is not ideal for live music. I resist the temptation to order steak pie and chips and sit round the corner with a pint of Black Sheep. But the room is full and its occupants enthusiastic. Encouraging, given that this is a pretty remote rural area. I don't suppose the band have played too many venues like this. Manchester Tramshed, Liverpool Apollo, Broughton High Cross Inn, Leeds Rotunda. Must get the t-shirt! The evening is finished off back in the main bar after the punters have gone home. We get an impromptu jam from the band joined by a couple of local musicians until the early hours.

So with delicate heads and fragile bodies, we set out next morning for a wholesome exploration of the village and hinterland. It turns out to be more of an amble than a ramble. A surprising amount of the countryside is still closed because of Foot and Mouth exclusion areas. Here we are about eight months after the first cases emerged and huge swathes of public footpaths and bridleways are still off limits. My cynical nose smells a decaying rat. I know from experience how many farmers and landowners resent the public walking across their land, even though they stick to the rights of way. I bet the landowners haven't been lightning-fast when it comes to removing no entry posters and other barriers across footpaths, even though the land has probably been released from quarantine. But there's no doubt that this part of the Lake District has been hit hard. Harder than most. Andy tells me about some big celebrations held in the village when compensation payments have come through for struggling farmers. Looks to me like many of the other industries in the region have been hit equally severely - tourism and its many visitor-dependent jobs must be the major contender. Tea-rooms, coach operators, B&Bs, pubs, arts and crafts, restaurants have all been slaughtered. I wonder how many fat, Government-sponsored compensation cheques they will get. The picture of winners and losers across the region will be very complex and will have repercussions long after we all start eating British lamb again.

I persuade Helen to make a detour to our journey home so that I can pay a visit to Cartmel, Cumbria's only racecourse. It too is a victim of Foot and Mouth. Currently it only hosts one fixture a year over the August bank holiday. And guess what. This year it was cancelled due to this infernal outbreak.

Cartmel is a beautiful Lakeland village hidden in a quiet spot away from the main tourist honeypots of Windermere and Ambleside. It's not that far from the M6, but a nightmare to locate at the end of twisting, single track, high hedged country lanes furnished with duplicitous sign-posts. The slate- and stone-built village is worth the wait, though. It shelters in the gentle southern slopes of the Cumbrian hills, barely a stone's throw from Grange-Over-Sands on the coast and boasts a perfect pub-flanked market square. So it is a surprise to find that the tiny interlocking streets and lanes are teeming today, almost gridlocked with visiting Volvos and Range Rovers who have crested the inaccessibility wave. Maybe tourism is awakening from its foot and mouth torpor. We take at least two full circuits of the village before locating the racecourse resting peacefully on its western edge. There is surprisingly little to see. I can make out a cluster of small official looking buildings in the middle of an uncultivated pasture. I guess that they are the stewards' and judges' positions because they have that odd tower-like appearance with sloping windows on the top deck that would not be out of place at a small regional airport. There is something of a modest grandstand and a few white rails indicating the finishing straight and that is about it. The rest of the track is empty save for a few oblivious sheep tending to the grass on the home turn, and the remnants of a recent car-boot sale that might also explain the busy village streets.

I close my eyes, breath in the sweet pollen-rich atmosphere, sneeze loudly and remind myself that this idyllic rural scene was once the subject of a notorious (and oft re-told!) ringer scam that sits high in the folklore of gambling gamesmanship. This was my secret reason for twisting Helen's arm to make the detour. Racing thrives on its history. The legacy of champions and the achievements of underdogs. But it is a sport built on wagers and chancers and risk-takers. Alongside the heroics of equine endeavour sit some audacious stories of scandalous punting plots and cheats. I swear the Gay Future Cartmel sting is one of the most entertaining I have come across. We head for home passing Morecambe Bay and Lancaster's ever expanding University, and I regale (or is that bore? I choose not to decide) Helen with some of the juicy details of that infamous day when connections of the Irish horse almost pulled off a £300,000 hit on the bookies at the August bank holiday fixture of 1974. The heart of this outrageous plan was to run Gay Future, a horse trained in Ireland by Edward O'Grady, in the Ulverston Novices Hurdle masquerading as another horse with the same name but of much inferior ability. This horse was to be run in the colours of Tony Collins who was well known at Cartmel.

The protagonists had representatives tearing round London lining up the horse in doubles and trebles with other Collins' horses that would be withdrawn before their races. It seems that one of the betting shop managers spotted a pattern and raised the alarm that something dubious was going on. The best bit of the story for me is where the bookies try to limit the damage by attempting to slam their office money on the horse to offset their potential losses. However, Cartmel had not been chosen on a whim by the syndicate. At the time the course had no 'blower' with London, so the bookies could not back the horse unless they got to the track with shed loads of wedge and put it on in person. Various accounts of the story paint fantastic pictures of taxis being despatched from the nearest Ladbrokes office with bags of cash stashed in hold-alls and jaguars jammed with bookies screaming up the M6 and getting snarled in bank holiday traffic around Birmingham. Whatever the truth, the horse was not backed down by the bookies and it won by 15 lengths at 10-1. But the coup was ultimately unsuccessful. Once the bookies had become suspicious it was not long before the true identity of Gay Future was revealed and the potentially brilliant plan foiled. Cartmel's place in history was guaranteed and it has enjoyed cult status since. The incident, if nothing else, prompted a revolution in the way that betting shops are connected to tracks around the country!

## 9. NEVER BET AT BRIGHTON

*"A happy pair they made, so decorously laid  
'neath the gay illuminations all along the promenade.  
'It's good to know there's still a little magic in the air – I'll weave my spell'."*  
Queen *"Brighton Rock"* 1977

The abandonment of Cheltenham is finally becoming a distant memory. Steve is getting stuck into the flat fixtures with alacrity; planning to do to the bookies in the rich half of the game what he had done to them over the poor. But I'm struggling with the Summer version of the sport. I can't get my head around the flat. I dunno. There's something about the longevity of steeplechasers that appeals to me. They are around at the highest level for much longer, barring accidents. I get fed up with the classic winners being sold to stud, sometimes before their classic season is over. It seems to me that so often their full potential is never realised in following seasons. The result of this is that I feel that I have nothing to get stuck into. It's always been like this, even when losing my pitiful pocket-money around the flat tracks of Beverley, York, Ripon, even - Lord preserve us - Catterick. No horses I recognise. No Desert Orchid to anchor my affection or Wayward Lad to sustain me each year. No obvious Championship meeting, the distances mean bugger all to me, and the classes of races are a foreign language. Back to the bottom of the learning curve, then.

We've all said that a trip to the races over the Summer should in part make up for missing Cheltenham. After much to-ing and fro-ing, we settle on a date in May for a trip to sunny Brighton. Graham Greene and all that. Steve winces. The quality of racing at the track is notoriously bad and it's a tricky little course with undulations and bends adding to the unpredictable nature of the spectacle. Excellent. Sounds like a laugh. Don't think we should take this flat game too seriously.

We collect below Victoria's graceful arches at the appointed time. Brynaldo's looking grey. He's had a few beers the night before and I reckon he's overdone it. He's a bit quiet during the opening fantasy cricket banter. Vaughany's last to arrive. Most out of character. We find him not at the appointed collecting point by Ladbrokes at all, but wondering in a seriously distracted manner in some obscure part of the concourse, looking most unconcerned about his late appearance. He looks distinctly ashen. If Bryn was grey, this is ghostly.

"Hello Andrew, are we in fine fettle this morning?"

He groans in response. I don't think he's ever looked so grim. Turns out that the office quiz night is to blame and he almost didn't make the train this morning. Someone made him team captain and his boys only went won the competition. A few well chosen and delicate celebratory single malts ensued, it appears. Disgraceful. Nick shrugs his shoulders in that 'only here for the beers' kind of way.

We board the ramshackle charabanc that is the South Central Trains service to Brighton. Bryn's making a decent fist of a come-back. That friendly man with the go-cart laden with beverages has made a welcome appearance so we polish off cappuccinos, frothy lattes and restorative fizzy waters. But not Bryn. He gets stuck in to the McEwens Export, whilst expressing mild surprise that he's the only one.

"Nick, mate. I thought you at least would be joining me!"

The South Downs scream by the window in a blur of chalk dust. A few moments later Nick declares,

"Bryn, bloody hell. We're pulling into Brighton".

Bryn shakes his can. There is a good 3/4 of the contents sloshing around in there. The come-back is halted.

"Bastards!" he declares in the face of disaster. Still its a good effort from the man with the raging hangover. "Didn't realise Brighton was so near", he mutters as we disembark.

It's not long before we are all joining him in some welcome alcoholic refreshment. We simultaneaously check out the shuttle bus departure times outside the station and the pub sitting opposite on the bright side of the road. There's a queue for the bus, but no queue at the bar. Pub. Bus. Bus. Pub. It's not difficult. Within moments we are settling into a round of nutty Ushers Ale and soaking up a few rays of glorious late morning sunshine. It's all hanging baskets and picnics tables in the heart of brash Brighton. The ambiance does the job for Andrew. He's starting to perk up. The ghostly pallor gives way to a pink, mischievous demeanour. He's reading the 'Spotlight' analysis of this afternoon's pitiful fare in the Racing Post. Steve was right. This is wretched stuff.

"Here we go!", says Andrew. There's a glee in his preface. "The 2.45. 'An absolutely horrific contest, which could put many punters off racing for life'. Ha Ha."

"I hear this down the bookies every time I have a bet." mourns Bryn.

" 'If anything does manage to win, it could well be Don't Worry About Me'. What sort of meeting is this, Steve?" chortles Andrew. He continues "Listen to this 'Snow Partridge - hasn't run on the flat for almost two years and wasn't exactly setting records when signing off anyway; Beckon - one of only a few going into this in good heart and that alone gives him a chance.' "

Andrew can hardly complete the sentence before he is convulsed in a spasm of mirth. This is the normally effusive, supportive Racing Post, defender of the faith against Fleet Street ignorance and TV scheduling; champion of the punter in the street in his struggle with the vultures in the High Street bookies. But here we see Lee Mottershead exposing the lower echelons of the sport to wicked scrutiny. The verdict delivered by a sarcastic quill is unequivocal in its damnation. There is no doubt about the day's most obviously facile contest:

"It gets better", continues Andrew, "3.40pm, Channel 4 handicap, 'A thoroughly miserable affair', in which Summer Bounty 'failed to excite anybody with moderate effort on return from long absence last time; should come on for that but certainly needs to!' "

It's fantastic stuff. This really is a shameful contest and Lee rises to the challenge with glorious deadpan delivery: 'Pekan Heights - only win came in an horrific Chester claimer; Mullaghmore - hardly a model of consistency, but could well pop up in a typical Brighton nightmare; Daniella Ridge - firmly on the downgrade and does not appeal, even in this admittedly weak contest; Victoriet - yet to really come close to winning in 17 outings and does not get the pulse racing on this occasion; Cedar Treble - hopelessly outclassed in two Kempton maidens.' It goes on. This is a wicked, yet searingly honest analysis.

It does the trick for Bryn. Whilst studying Spotlight's gruesome expose of the talent on offer in the 3.40, he has unearthed his nap of the day.
    "Kez, he pronounces.
    "Yer wha...?"I inquire. Steve's already there.
    "Could have a fair chance. 'shaped promisingly here on debut for current yard. Holds as good a chance as any.' Even the RP gives the thumbs up Brynaldo my son." Steve is enthusing.
Bryn reinforces his position.
    "That's the boy for me. Look at that form. There's a '2' there, and a '3'. Winning form. I'll be on Kez this aft." It's a proclamation.
    "First nap of the day. C'mon boys. Bryn's put up. Kez it is. I like the sound of that. Take the bull by the horns. C'mon. What has anyone else got? Never mind this RP negativity".
But no-one else puts up. We're on Spotlight's side. No amount of jollying along from Clarkey will change our view. Bryn's out on a limb. Steve doesn't follow through either.

I don't think Brighton needs running down any further, but my childminder's husband provided some extra background briefing before I embarked on this trip. John is a legend in Berkhamsted. Part-childminder, part-taxi driver, part-delivery man, part- house husband and d-i-y victim. Each overlapping element of his eclectic portfolio is accompanied by a mild-mannered but long suffering humour.
    "Awright Dave? Me, yeah, y'know. Surviving. Just waiting for 'er to give me some more grief, mate. Grief. All day long. Dunno why we blokes bother."
He nods inside at his wife, Sheila and looks back at me through world weary, half closed eyes. He's got all the medals going for endurance. Red Marauder has nothing on John. There's a wry grin on his lips, though. And the laugh lines stretching round his mouth are only partly obscured by three days' worth of white beard growth. He's a dry bugger when all said and done. Looking for his piece of the quiet life. Nothing wrong with that.

He's been a gambler in his time, too. Although Sheila put paid to his ambitions when the losing bets started to take divots out of the housekeeping. A particularly grim night at Wembley dogs involving a considerable punt on a short-priced losing favourite, a painful walk home in the persisting down and a half-hearted confession to Sheila seems to have marked the end of this era.

But his instincts remain. I'm collecting the kids the day before the Brighton trip and as I'm shoving biscuits in the hands of my grasping children, John is telling me about a horse that he witnessed enter Brighton folklore.

"You must have heard this one before". John's eyes are almost twinkling. "Myrtles Magic, she was called. Yeah. Good looking mare. Only had one eye." He looks at me for a reaction.

"One bloody eye? You aren't serious?"

"I am mate! It had never done anything special, but she was well thought of by the yard. The trainer fancied Brighton." Obviously one eye is less of an impediment than you might imagine! "One of our lot knew a bit about the game, y'know, and he reckoned this horse was a good thing for the maiden there. We were going anyway, so we made sure we got some money on this on-eyed mare."

John's enjoying the story. The gummy grin is still on his chops and his big hands are waving around his head and pointing at imaginary horses.

"We get close to the race and the price has collapsed. She's in to no better than 2-1, but we were still topping up, y'know, as you do."

I'm struggling with the straps on the buggy which are failing to keep my one-year-old restrained. John's oblivious.

"Anyway, the race got underway and Myrtle was fast out of the gates and in the lead." His mouth is all of a lather, but he's enunciating very clearly. "She was going well, mate. No worries. The jockey was sitting nicely on top and everything was fine. There's a bend at Brighton, you'll see it tomorrow. It's a nasty, tricky little downhill, left hand bend. Well the horses were going a fair old clip by now, see, and Myrtle, well, she didn't see the bend. She only had one eye, right, and it's the right eye. The jockey sees the bend, but the horse don't. He's giving her hands, heels, whips, kitchen sink - the works, but poor old Myrtle carried on straight as a dye."

John's laughing, but I know that his cash went straight down with pan with Myrtle. Wonder how long it took him to see the funny side.

"That was it! The horse didn't turn until she was up against the far rail. The rest were already well gone down by the finishing post. Trainer said he forgot which was Myrtles' good eye!"

My head is filled with a fantastic image of the horse pelting down the hill and heading like a dart out to the other side of the course. It must have been an amazing spectacle. The crowd probably went bananas.

"Unbelievable!" I express sympathy with John. "This game really is full of amateurs."

"Yeah, well have a good one tomorrow. Don't back any one-eyed horses."

This is a cracking yarn, embellished over the years with a bit of Brighton bad-luck exaggeration, no doubt.

So, fully steeped in Brighton mythology and steeled by another pint of Wiltshire's finest, we are ready for the ordeal ahead. The course looks splendid. It's baking in clear, undiluted early season sunshine. The compact stands are already well populated and we look up at the helter-skelter track falling out of the cliffs with a breakneck left kick. I'm still picturing Myrtle's Magic  - if she ever really existed - skipping down the hill and away to the stables.

The betting hall is newish and tidyish, the facilities clean and airy. I was prepared for a scene of near dereliction with broken windows, chipped plastic and peeling plaster board. But we sink into four pints of frothy nitrokeg in relative comfort and get to work. Today's joke bet turns out to be the Quadpot. It's Steve's idea of course. We don't bother with the Placepot today, instead there is a collective decision to pick horses to be placed in the 4 *best* races of the day. Ha, This fixture struggles to meet the Quadpot criteria!

No luck early on for any of us. We all draw blanks in the first three races, although I think a couple of the Quadpots are still up and running. It doesn't seem to be enough to sustain Andrew. He's starting to look grey again. Maybe it's the smell of the curry-slop and bullet-rice the rest of us are tucking into from the van behind the grandstand. The bright sunshine probably isn't helping him either. It's glorious up here on the downs. A prefect English early Summer's day. Never mind the quality of the racing, feel the environment.

So, re-fuelled, we are back for the highlight of the day. The 3.40 Channel 4 handicap (Class F) Div 1. Christ knows what Div 2 looks like. Bryn's already sorted with Kez. He spots a bookie down by the rail with one of these new fangled lap-top driven neon display pitches. All very flash. Except his name isn't clearly shown. Could be Racing Greene or Reckless Graeme or something. But it doesn't matter Bryn can see the odds lit up in glowing technicolour as plain as day. He's on already and back on the steps clutching his fancy printed bingo ticket, napped up for the day. "Nap crackle pop! Nap-a-doodle dandy, Brynaldo! Grins an insane Clarkey as the rest of us take our chances from the remaining collection of beasts.

They are off, up at the top of the track, careering out of the gates down the 1 in 3 gradient towards us. It's fast ground and the dust storm kicked up by the group is a more like a waggon train high-rolling across the virgin plains, rather than a handicap at Brighton. As if there weren't enough cowboys in town already.  The wagon train swings round the bend. All the horses make the turn. No wandering one-eyed nags today. Stitch in Time is leading them home, but Brynaldo's choice is sitting pretty against the rail, waiting for the break. Stitch In Time can feel Kez breathing down his neck, cruising along under a confident ride. Kez gets a glimmer of daylight and Tony Quinn up top needs no second invitation. He's through like a rat up a drainpipe and bolting for home. Brynaldo's urging him over the line.
       "Git in there!" he grunts.
Kez wins in easily.
       "Doing handstands" says an impressed Steve.

The RP agrees. Next morning's analysis is clinical. '...it only took a shake of the reigns to ensure a cosy win'. Top tipping Brynaldo. He called it early and put up the cash. Respect. He's delighted and goes of to collect his dues.

The rest of us are back in the bar, puzzling over the 4.10. It's another shocking contest. Lee Mottershead's again on form in his Spotlight verdict 'Waddenhoe - gone a long time without a win and nothing in recent performances suggests that will change today; Little Fox - connections look to be grasping at increasingly desperate straws'. I think we are getting the drift of his analysis by now. Another pint of gaseous creamflow bitter aids the thought processes. Me and Nick are mulling over the options. Neither of us have had a winner yet and we are looking for some serious value options. Lee's comments, though witty, don't really shed any light on the conundrum before us. I'm scouring the form details when the answer leaps up out of the page like a salmon on steroids. Flight of Dreams is the horse. It screams 'BACK ME DAVE, BACK ME. I CAN'T LOSE!' I'm hooked in by a simple enough statement, tucked away in the 'comments in running'. Sure enough, the casual observer may not have picked up Flight of Dream's spurned chances of glory in his last outing, but the RP's dedicated team of analysts picked up that in his last race FoD was 'hampered whilst challenging on the rail'. He also has some Brighton form from the previous Summer on this going. That seals it for me. It may be a threadbare clincher, but now I'm feeling good about the horse. This thin commentary is the missing piece of a jigsaw puzzle. It's the crucial big bit right in the middle that stops you making sense of the whole picture. Now I have it and my headache is gone.

"Nick, this is it. No doubt. Flight of Dreams for me. I'm off to get me wedge down."

"What do you mean, 'no doubt'? Of course there's doubt. Always doubt.".

"Well, I just mean I feel sure about the horse. Here I am struggling to make sense of a miserable little handicap with nothing between any of the donkeys on show. Now I can see that the form stacks up. There's a reason to back this horse and to leave alone the others. I am supremely confident".

Nick looks at me, trying to work out whether this a bit more grade 1 bullshit. He's waiting for the tell-tale cracks in my honest demeanour.

"I'm telling you" I add with a mixture of exasperation and hilarity, "this is the one. No doubt."

"OK", he concludes, "let's go and do it".

Bryn, Vaughany and Steve have their own ideas for the event and we split up to find the best prices. I get my notes down at 10-1. That seems to be about the going rate. We collect back in the stands and it turns out Nick's found 10-1 as well. The rest of the lads are on different nags at a range of prices and sporting increasingly risque or bad humour monikers such as Madame Jones, Stepon Degas and Dusky Virgin....... All set then. But no. Not all set. Steve's giving me some value betting grief in me lug hole. Gnawing away at me.

"Davoski, lad. See this joker at the end? EJ Mullins? He's pushed your fancy out to 16-1. SIXTEEN TO ONE."
He hardly needed to emphasise the point. I can see it too. Bastard, I've only got 10s.
"You know the theory about value punting, don't you? If you find the value, you have to follow it. If you're on the value horse in the field and its drifting, you need to keep backing it all the way out."
Stop it Clarkey, you're messing up my brain. I look at Nick. He's laughing.
"I'm not putting any more on, I'm finished for now."
The ball is back in my court then. Clarkey's on at me again.
"Go on Davoski. You can't let 16s go! Just think how bad you'll feel if he rolls up at that price and you're not on. You want to get topped up, lad."
He's a bastard. He knows he's got me bound up in an embrace of irrefutable logic, cornered in a value dark alley.

I wander over to Mullins' pitch with the lads' guffaws ringing loud in my ears. I scrabble around for some change in my pocket and lump on a whole three quid. What the hell, eh? I rejoin the group and turn to see the bookie wiping off 16s and chalking up 8s! EIGHTS!! Ha ha. My £3 has tipped him over the edge. He can't take me on. Punter power prevails. What a glorious moment. Confirmation, then, that this really is a joke meeting.

I'm still chortling away as this 1 mile contest gets underway. I lose track of the race a bit from my vantage point and it's only as the group is close to home that I realise Flight of Dreams is in the lead. Madame Jones and Dusky Virgin both appear to be reeling her in to my tired old eyes. Me and Nick have our hearts in our mouths as she flashes past the post, still 3/4 of a length up on her rivals. Ecstasy! This is a victory to savour. There's a roar from me and a slap on the back from Nick. It was never in doubt. "Won with something to spare" says the RP the next morning. Didn't look like that from where I was standing. I take particular satisfaction from looting EJ Mullins' satchel of his forty-odd quid. More so than the 50-odd we both take from the other bookies who offered 10-1. It feels like we bust a bookie today! It's the Brighton sting. Steve re-reads the form. "I don't know where you got that from lads. I just don't see anything here to give a clue about that sort of performance." I'm not sure either. It's a question of interpretation.

But still the well is not dry. I collect a surprise Quadpot payout. Complete bonus. I've not been paying attention! I take my spends from the nice lady in red sitting in the Tote booth. "There yoo gur, sunny." Long way from the Tyne, I muse, as we make for the nearest exit. Nothing for Vaughany today and nothing for Steve, but three of us leave the fabled South Downs track with smiles on our faces.

The entertainment hardly lets up, though. This is Brighton after all. We are in London-on-Sea where the cosmopolitan atmosphere is supercharged by the brash pink pound and crusty Bohemian wholefood. We are still revelling in Spring sunshine and our next stop is the seafront. Proper fish 'n' chips seem the logical progression. I'm trying to square the shack we buy the grub from with my image of the seafront cafe in Graham Greene's Brighton Rock and the girl that Pinky meets there. This is light-years away. Don't know what Pinky would have made of neon glitter and "have a nice day, Sir" Big Mac sham, but he would have approved of the scam we've just pulled at the races.

Nick's already clocked the funfair at the end of West Pier. We are there before the chips have gone cold. There's plenty of activity. The sun has brought out a good crowd. First up is the waltzers. The good crowd must be on the dodgems because there's no one else on this ride. So me, Nick, Vaughany and Bryn get the less than welcome attention of Mr Waltzer who decides he's going to have a bit of a laugh with four lads down from the Smoke who should know better. This is the ride that never ends. I swear we hear 'Reach for the Stars' about 6 times as we are hurtled round the ride with laughing-boy giving a nice extra tug on the back of our car everytime we pass him. S Club 7's obscure b-side 'Reach for the Sick Bag' would be more appropriate as we career past Steve and his smug 'I'll leave this one to you, boys' smile.

I'm a wreck by the time we get off. Wobbly legs and spinning head. It's like the 4.10 all over again. Bryn doesn't look much better and I really fear for Vaughany. Nick, on the other hand, is grinning like enamel is a rarity. "That was fantastic, what next?" Steve's made his way over to the end of the pier and is waiting for us in the shadow of the big dipper. We join him. We can see the cliffs from the end of the pier and just about pick out the racecourse perched on top.

Nick's eying up the ride and I'm looking at some kids hanging over the railings below us wrestling with big sea-fishing rods hurling fat, green lines into to the spray. There's a good dozen or so of them with the full kit: rod rests, bait boxes, fold up seats, keep nets, sandwich toasters, surround sound tellies. Expensive business these days, a bit of fishing.  Meanwhile Steve reaches deep into his own keep-net. There's a bit of clinking and chinking and then, like a rabbit from a hat, he's produced a bottle of wine and five beakers. In a minute, he's whipped out a bottle opener and is pouring out healthy glugs of claret for each of us. What style! Here we are sipping a fine red wine bathing in the warm evening sunshine amid the throng of the funfair at the end of the pier. This is quality entertainment. Good call Steve.

Nick gives in to temptation and has a go on an Arabian Carpet ride that gyrates its poor unfortunate passengers in a huge arc, backwards and forwards over the end of the pier. I've had enough of that thanks. I can't find my keys. I didn't notice them falling out, but I guess that they've been ripped from my pockets by the centrifugal whirl of the waltzers. Nick climbs down from the ride, still grinning insanely. We follow that with some ridiculous shenanigans on the dodgems. Christ, boys. Grow up. Steve displays a piece of particularly vindictive driving  and thinks its hilarious to give me a broadside as I'm trapped in a queue of bad drivers behind Nick. We decide to call it a day before it gets really nasty in the Quasar arcade.

Brighton is buzzing like a chainsaw. We pass at least four stag and hen parties on their way down to prom. Nothing like a bit of branding on your big night on the town: check out the Hawaiian shirts, Cleopatra-a-likes and enough Village People to populate a large London suburb. Time for a swiftie in the pub by the shuttle bus. The Ushers still slips down well, but the character of the pub has changed. We've got the big-it-up Friday night disco. Gone is the charm of the hanging baskets and pre-race anticipation. Instead we get a full on dose of glitter-ball acid house, neon r'n'b and sticky carpet funk. Except the place is nigh on empty. All dressed up and no-one to go. Party animals though the five of us are, I don't think we quite fit the bill. So we head off for the train.

But there is one more unexpected treat in the day. We are slumped across bench seats on this rattling Thameslink train, contentedly mulling over the day's highlights. Bryn is getting some deserved plaudits for his outstanding up front call on Kez, nap of the day, when he too digs deep into his nap sack. Out pops a half-bottle of Laphraoig single malt whisky and five glasses. This gets better and better. He had planned to have a drink on the pier, but Steve beat him to it. So we finish off a top day rolling peaty malt whiskies around the bottom of plastic cups and trading highlights from a day at the seaside.

Ages afterwards I am reminded of this classic outing at a different sporting venue. A few of us are enjoying a day at The Oval watching England give a rare, but outstanding thrashing to the South Africans in a One-Dayer. It's another glorious day. We are melting under a June sun almost as scorching as Trescothick's searing pulls through the on-side. The Oval is a proper cricket ground. It's largely open to the elements. None of the stiff formality of Lord's here. The house is packed and determined to have a rip-roaring time in this corner of Kennington.

Me, Bryn, Nick, my brother, plus a few other mates are passing round the party eggs and Pringles sat behind a bunch of lads who have come to take the piss. There are maybe 6 of them, late 20's - early 30's with sleek haircuts, designer sunglasses and streamlined cool-bags. There's always a bit of piss-taking and wise-cracking at the cricket, but these lads are experts. Seriously. We are in the presence of greatness. Anything that moves is subjected to a volley of incisive and hilarious abuse. The grief they inflict is merciless and all pervasive. No-one is safe. As the beers flow, the abuse still stays on the witty side of offensive and its impossible not to join in. Resisting simply invites more abuse. One guy with long grey hair is christened "Whitesnake" and is greeted with the opening bars to 'Europe - The Final Countdown' every time he stands up. Quality stuff. "De-de-der-der, de-de-der-der-der" every time he goes to the bog! He looks up at the crowd with increasing perplexion as if to say "What? Who? Me?".

We strike up a healthy banter, but like I say, no-one is safe. We are passing pork pies and pasties up and down the line when Bryn makes a fatal mistake. He starts unpacking a small egg-based tart. "Is that a quiche, Bryn?" enquires Nick in a sufficiently loud voice. "Quiche?" spits one of the lads in front, taking the bait. "Quiche!" replies his mate. Three or four of them look round in mock horror. Bryn sees his mistake immediately. His head is in his hands. But a grin adorns his face. The unravelling is only just beginning. "Real men eat egg and bacon pie. Quiche is for wussies". The chorus goes down the line. "'Ere, this blokes got some quiche. Hope it's got a nice bit of gruyere cheese or maybe some sun-dried tomato. Yah." Bryn offers up his quiche to the guys in front. "You're welcome to a bit. Plenty to go round." But this doesn't save him. "My God", says the recipient. He's on a roll. "This isn't any old quiche. This is *Iceland* quiche. 69p a slab! No expense spared boys. If you are going to do the quiche thing, do it in style!"

The quiche becomes the star of the show. "Anyone want quiche? Nice fresh *Iceland* quiche anyone?" "Pass it to Whitesnake!" someone shouts. So that's it. The quiche begins a journey from hand to hand 10 rows down and 20 seats to the left. By now we are all standing up shouting "Left, left. No, no. Left. Pass it to Whitesnake." The TV cameras must be picking this up. "Who?" people keep looking up at us. I'm pissing myself. This is surreal. Unbelievably, the quiche actually arrives with Whitesnake and we all give a cheer. A slightly bemused Whitesnake looks up at the lads, gives the thumbs up and breaks out into a broad grin. This prompts an even bigger cheer. He's not perplexed or slightly offended anymore. He's entered into the spirit of it. Or been dragged kicking and screaming, more like!

In the middle of this melee, to return (rather distractedly) to the theme, Steve sends me a text. He's at the wedding of one of his mates this weekend, otherwise he would be here at the Oval. I flogged his ticket to my brother. "Davoski. Just been on Brighton beach. There's an old lag here still talking about the Flight of Dreams Brighton sting of 2001". Ha ha. Legendary.

## 10. GRIM, DULL AND FRUITLESS

*"I went to Hell and to the races*
*To bet on the Bottle of Smoke"*
The Pogues, *"Bottle of Smoke"*, 1987

My college years - the gloriously tasteless mid 80's - were reasonably active betting years. Mug punting was rife - a little knowledge can go a long way, it can be a dangerous thing. Most of my betting was done in the summer holidays, at flat courses back home in Yorkshire. There used to be banner posters outside many of them clarion-calling 'Go Racing In Yorkshire!' The alliance of Yorkshire race courses were no respecter of boundaries. Redcar was in Cleveland and Beverley in Humberside. But this is no time for local authority pedantry. Proper Yorkshire, ie, the pre-1972 Ridings, was well endowed with many glorious courses.

The majority of them specialise in flat racing. Thirsk is a decent track close to the centre of a pretty market town. Ripon is an even lovelier town with a good track at the gateway to the Dales. Beverley is the epitome of charm and character, whilst Doncaster hosts the country's oldest classic, and neatly bookends a great summer of racing with two magnificent betting spectacles: The Lincoln in March and the November Handicap.

So why did I end up gambling away the stipe end of my student grant at the armpits of Yorkshire courses: Redcar and Catterick? The sun never shone at Redcar races. There was always a slicing wind cutting across from the coast nearby. We could leave home in the midst of a blazing high summer day and spend an afternoon swathed in a Redcar races sea fret with only the ICI factory belching out orange pollution to break up the grey aspect. The track itself didn't offer a lot of comfort. It was surrounded by housing estates that seemed to cramp up the circuit in a vice like squeeze and force it through some tight little bends. My 'Aerofilms Guide to British Racecourse from the Air' describes it as a 'singular course'. I think that is generous.

Catterick was worse. The track was surrounded by towering piles of unwanted spoil from the adjacent quarries carved disrespectfully out of prime Yorkshire moorland. An ugly, crusty and polluted lake covered much of the inside of the track which served to encourage the feeling of dereliction. The scene of industrial decline was completed by a flaking concrete trunk road embankment passing close by the circuit. It was a hole of a course with no facilities to speak of. I stumbled across a gem of a book called 'Cope's Racegoers Encyclopaedia 1962'. Leafing through its mottled pages I discovered that 'in January 1961 Catterick Bridge opened a £30,000 new stand which provides facilities previously undreamed off at this small Yorkshire course'. That must have been the twisted pile of rusty iron and crumbling grey brick that I could see across the track. The intervening 27 years had not been kind.

We used to populate a brick outhouse construction in the silver ring where we partook of fizzy keg bitter, traditional for the time (long before widgets had been thought of) from a dirty old temporary pump. The only food to be had was a hot dog/burger van outside the bogs. I had had enough of burgers one desperate Friday afternoon so I asked the bored 'sales assistant' for a cheese sandwich as advertised. The guy took one of his burger buns, slapped in a sliver of plastic unmelted dairylea and charged me £1.50 of my hard-granted wedge! I was appalled.

There was no way of seeing the horses all the way round the track from where we were herded. The quality of racing was always as miserable as the course. At least there was the outside chance of a decent race every so often at Redcar. I never, ever had a winner at either Catterick or Redcar and I never, ever want to go back there. Lee Mottershead would recognise them as experiences that 'could put you off racing for life'!

Ah, but York. The jewel in the Crown. The Ascot of the North. There is nothing that matches the grandeur of the Knavesmire during the Ebor meeting. Packed, pristine stands overlooking a perfect horse-shoe course of carefully manicured turf providing top quality racing on one of the fairest tracks in the country. Uninterrupted sightlines and an unpretentious welcome.

My memories of youthful Summer days on the Knavesmire are less about the races themselves, and more about the chance to top up the paper round/odd job money, and enjoy the spectacle. Magnet Gold Cup day on a Saturday in July was a hair-raising experience. A lot of the social clubs, pubs and factories in the area used to target this day for their annual outing. Coaches of beered up, lairy, once-a-year punters would descend on the Knavesmire via half a dozen pub stops, to wreak merry hell in Tattersalls and over in the Course Enclosure. No matter what the weather, blokes would be exposing vast plains of hairy, tattooed torso, swilling cans of pale ale at an alarming rate and backing favourites with uncontained zeal. Fantastic stuff. If this is the Ascot of the North, then Magnet day was about as far away from Ladies Day as Nijinsky was from steeplechasing. And I'm talking about the ballet dancer.

By the time I return to the Knavesmire the place had changed incredibly. The 15 years since my last visit have been filled by a massive rebuilding programme, still not finished, and an overhaul of the facilities. I don't know if Magnet Day retains its earthy, populist charm, but the track is now firmly aiming at corporate dollar as well as factory wedge. Two spanking new stands have been built, one where the old Tattersalls used to be and one in the Members enclosure. Me, my Dad and my brother are in the new Tatts. Bit pricey I thought to get in – certainly compared to other tracks. But the views across the vale from the 1st floor of the grandstand are exquisite and no one is complaining about the marble-floored betting hall downstairs with it's gleaming Tote booths, endless bars and up-market food outlets. Outside, the views are equally good. The new members grandstand is a glass and steel affair with 1st and 2nd floors given over to restaurants and corporate boxes. The track at York swings left shortly after the winning post. To accommodate this, the new stand has a kink in it so that if you are in the top deck clocking the action through binoculars it will feel like the horses are running straight at you. The whole effect is one of being wrapped around the course, close to the action. A bit like Upton Park……..

This is a Saturday meeting in October, the last of the season at York. I have a shocking day. By this time I'm giving the old value principles a bit of an airing. Neither Dad nor Paul know Steve and his theories and so I take this as licence to wax lyrical and embellish with abandon as if I have come by a new system all by myself. Trouble is, I don't properly understand it yet and I have no inkling of how or when to deploy such threadbare tactics as think I have developed. I am fully exposed as yet another sham mug punter. Dad is sceptical anyway. Listening patiently as I ramble on about big priced winners and what a thrill it can be. "Hmm. He says. Has anyone ever got rich on these tactics? How long have you gone without a winner? Won't you be better off backing these long shots each way?" I had no answers. I am, frankly, backing long shots with the subtlety and reason of a steam hammer. "Yeah, you've got to go each way, Dave" Up chimes little brother Paul. "That's your best bet" Jeez, what does he know! "Do that, then pick something with a good name and you are laughing…" I'm exasperated and he loves it. I've just handed him a bit more wind up material.

Nearly every field on the seven-race day is at least 15 runners strong. There's one decent listed sprint and a clutch of absolutely impossible late-season cavalry charge handicaps. I realise later - much too late - that this is not a good day to apply value principles to full effect. So, having set myself up, I get well and truly murdered. Worst of all, Paul and Dad both pick up a couple of spawny each way returns, much to their chortling and childish glee. My, how happy I am for them.

I really fancy Polar Kingdom in the last mile handicap. It's a shit or bust moment and I up my stakes to a cool £10 and lodge my bet at 9-1. The race is a belter. We are all three down on the rail and I'm screaming my head off as Polar Kingdom flashes by in the lead by a fraction. Is it a trick of the light or does the jockey stop riding, thinking he's got the race safely pouched? On the stands rail, Abbajabba is finishing strongly and to my utter contempt has apparently stolen the race by a short head on the line. I am mortified, spitting blood. How did Polar Kingdom lose it from there? I look at Dad. He's ashen too. "Thought he had that Dad, I couldn't see him losing as he came passed us. D'you reckon the jockey didn't see Abbajabba on the other side of the track". "Yeah, could be. I was on him too….. each way!" He gives me one of his uncontrolled belly laughs. Paul's up for it too. "Didn't you back it each way Dave?" Bastards! I think. Each-way thieves, the lot of 'em. It is a long way home.

Revenge, a dish best served in newspaper and smothered in brown sauce, comes 18 months or so later, when Paul and I return to the Knavesmire.

I've had a busy time on the horses in that window and I'm in the middle of a patch almost approaching purple. York has had a busy 18 months too. The building works on the course are now complete and the course is sparkling. We marvel upon verdant early Summer turf, blooming hanging baskets and a belligerent crowd. 28,000 are packed into the Knavesmire's first Saturday meeting. It feels special, certainly, but in a way that I have not encountered at Cheltenham, Epsom, Brighton or anywhere else, in fact. Maybe it is that curious mixture of Royal Ascot and Magnet Cup.

The streets between the railway station and the track are a river of racegoers. A lithe, vigorous stream of punters pulsing towards the track. Many of the blokes are in suits with blue members badges hanging off button holes; there are gaggles of girls looking spectacular in short Summer dresses and headwear not out of place at Newmarket. The stag parties advertise themselves with regulation Hawaiian shirts, but there are also the country casuals in corduroys and check shirts, and of course, the combat trousered, tee-shirted and unshaven are generously represented. At the turnstiles I can feel a characteristic anticipation. I'm getting that familiar but intangible well of emotion and sense of occasion. I slap Paul on the back.

"It's going to be a top day. This is fantastic!"
He's grinning too and can't take his eyes off a girl with a see-through white lace dress and high heels. He's a filthy minded sod. Me? I hardly notice.....

We go for the Course Enclosure today and a berth very close to the winning post. I slope off to the bog: the great leveller of all human life. Here, in a nutshell, I see this Ascot/Magnet Cup cross section I keep talking about. There's a chap – well turned out, smart grey suit, clean shaven with a racecard tucked tidily under his arm - waiting his turn at the urinal. Whilst around the corner a there's a youth - reeking of lager, sawn off jeans and not much else - having a piss in the hand-basin. The queue for the bogs is clearly too big an ask.

Indeed, it proves to be a belter of a day. There is a gentle start that sees Paul and I demolish some adventurous noodle and chicken curry concoctions, down gassy bitter substitutes and lodge ambitious placepots. The last named, despite my many-layered multi-permed, minimum stakes approach still crashes and burns at the first race. Bollocks. Paul has secured early and generous odds on Mister Sweets in the first and is visibly gutted when he is out of the frame, despite the horse putting in a good performance. The second race is a similar story.

Next up, the William Hill Trophy, is a classy sprint handicap. I've already exchanged texts with Steve who, understandably to my mind, recognises what a good day he is missing. He tells me he's on River Falcon at a decent price. So is Paul, but at a different price and for different reasons. He gives a game run, briefly threatens and almost looks likes he will sneak the race until the favourite, Dazzling Bay, emerges from the pack, lurches alarmingly right to the stands rail but still eases home a quality winner.

Paul momentarily got excited. At least he got a run for his stake. I was nowhere.

But my moment of vindication is nigh. The next race is a 7f handicap. Me and bruv have both decided that Golden Promise can't be beaten. He's already a short favourite, the form stacks up and it's easy to pick holes in the credentials of his rivals. Paul thinks he's a good thing too, presumably the enunciation of his name, once rolled around the mouth like a gobstopper has the right tone for this kind of class B event. The nuances of picking a horse by the name are beyond me. So I introduce Paul to the subtle intoxications of the reverse exacta.

"Oh yes, when you reckon the winner is nailed on, all you have to do is find the next one past the post, and combine the two selections, just on the off-chance your second pick nudges out the obvious candidate. In fact this is the ideal scenario because the pay out is much superior."

Paul is convinced and likes the sound of Lucayan Beauty in a poetic couplet with Golden Promise. I'm left scratching my head. Despite advocating the exacta, I can't find anything to go with the Golden one. I scour the RP, looking for inspiration. Remarkably I find it buried in the form, but crystal clear in its way. Channon's horse, Black Falcon has won off a higher mark on good-to-firm in reasonable company in a biggish field. The RP verdict is to dismiss him on the basis of a poor showing in a better class next time out when he was tailed off. But he was only tailed off in a four runner field and its easy for the jockey to step off the gas and get beaten a long way when there are only three rivals - particularly if the horse likes to come off the pace. No protection in a four runner field! The trip probably didn't suit then. And here's the clincher. Channon, in the trainers comments on page 5 gives a hefty clue and he's hardly beating around the bush: 'I'd like to think he could win off that mark'. It's a dismissive comment about his horse's weight allocation. He's almost derisory!

So I strike the reverse exacta and as I walk back to meet Paul, I'm checking out the bookies. They've chalked him up at 16s! Unbelievable. Even the RP reckons 6-1 tops! I even find one offering 20-1, so I'm on - minimum stakes though. But I'm pleased with the bet.

I tell Paul about the intricacies of my selection procedures, but he looks as bored as you probably feel right now. No matter. The race is in the bag. Black Falcon leaves it late, oh so late, to mount his challenge. He's had to weave in and out of traffic like a shunter across the points at Willesden Junction, but he's found room now inside the final furlong and he's screaming up the far rail like a freight train across the Prairies. That gorgeous black beauty has stolen the race by the width of a cow-catcher.

The reverse exacta is down. Golden Promise flops miserably and I hear an announcement inviting the trainer to visit the Stewards. Too bloody right. Getting the exacta up would have been sensational. But I am delirious at having beaten the bookies and glowing from that illusory, seductive feeling of having worked it out myself. I try to buy Paul a beer whilst crowing insufferably about value betting. The queues are too long though and we settle for sausage and chips, with a healthy splash of brown sauce. I didn't expect the taste of burying the Abbajabba affair to be so tangy.

The day is capped off for me in the lucky last. Paul is desperate to get some of his money back and commits what I blithely inform him is a classic mug punting mistake. Safe in the knowledge that I have already bagged my value winner, I offer some advice.
    "Chasing your losses on an odds-on favourite is gonna find you out. Classic mistake."
But he's indignant and he returns after a few minutes having secured 11/10 about Hawk Flyer. With Fallon aboard in the final race of the day, Paul is lucky to find anywhere offering odds against.
    "See, it's not odds on. I've doubled me stake because I didn't have a bet in that last but one race, so I'll be going home OK."
I'm still healthily sceptical and offer to show him how it's done. I make a big show of unfurling the RP, smoothing out the wrinkles and getting to work on the form. It's a brash show of smugness and it deserves to end in disaster. But, remarkably, it doesn't.
    "Look, ignore the favourite, he's far too short and unproven. What have we get elsewhere. Hmmm. There are only 8 runners in this dodgy maiden and there is bound to be some value with this Fallon-factor making the market." Paul's smirking, like he recognises overblown bullshit when he hears it. "Look here at this Johnston horse, Wessex. Forecast to go off at 8s. Well bred, it says here, and a mile should suit. 6th last time out in a reasonably competitive event, but on soft ground. So maybe he needs it firmer, like today. And look - it's all here. He failed to stay the last 2 furlongs in that 1m2f race. He obviously needs today's trip!"
Paul does not buy my crystal clear dissection of the form.
"We'll see", he mutters as I slope of to get my 8/1.

We watch them canter down to the start. Fine beasts, all of them. And we roar them home going the opposite way. At least I roar. Wessex is 2-3 lengths clear having dismembered the field in a slowly run race. Paul's incredulous. I really had set myself up for a big fall, all in the name of good old fashioned bullshit. But it all came off and suddenly I'm starting the think that maybe there is a key to this game.... But I can't allow myself to go there. I just savour the moment. I collect my winnings, shake my fist-full of dollars at Paul and let out a rankerous bellow.
    "Ha ha!"
A lady queuing up for her dosh is grinning at me. Beating the bookies twice in a day. It's the stuff of dreams.

We head back into town and I buy Paul some beer and we watch the straggling remnants of stag weekenders and Corporate Boxers meander up and down Micklegate like lost sheep. York is back on my A list.

## 11. UNFANTASY CRICKET

*"Some people say that life is a game, well if this is so*
*I'd like to know the rules on which this game of life is based*
*I know of no game for fitting than the age old game of cricket*
*It has honour, it has character and it's British."*
The Kinks, "Cricket" 1973

Whilst my mates and I are not quite as alcohol-soaked as these recollections make them sound, it is true to say that most of our anecdotes and inspirations have their roots in some good old fashioned public house banter. Like the day a discussion within the imaginary combat zone of fantasy cricket becomes a plan to tackle the real combat zone of actual sporting conflict. It's an early season lunch-time session. Early enough that there is still much to be won and lost in haggling over subtle rule changes and dodgy transfer deadlines. Today however, we recklessly talk ourselves out of the realms of fantasy and into the steaming cauldron of the Department's 6-a-side cricket competition: The Lesley Grimmet Trophy. Jules Rimet eat your heart out!

In no time at all we have rustled up a healthy team of misfits, half-fits and half-wits from the fantasy league managers and we are in business. As sports day approaches, our enthusiasm grows. We have a bottom line of course. We don't know the strengths and weaknesses of the opposition. So ultimately, our fall-back position is that if we get knocked out in the first round, we can proceed to the bar, get trolleyed in an orderly fashion and pretend that was the plan all along. We choose to hide behind this simplicity. But the reality is that each of us is secretly taking it seriously. Three or four of the team get in a bit of decent practice down the park over a lunchtime or two. I join them. We all remember vaguely how to hold a bat the right way up, and chuck down a few half volleys. Mildly encouraging and damn good fun.

Come the big day, we gather down at the Civil Service Sports Ground in Chiswick in the vicinity of the bar. It's a quality line up:

Dave 'mean seam machine ' Atkinson: venomous opening bowler unleashing meteors of red death from a full 8 pace run up and from a height of, ooh, about 5 foot 8 with a
big jump. Captain by bad luck.

Darren 'I'm opening' Cooper: opening bat, opening bowler, opening fielder. All round super cricketer. A legend in his own lunchbox.

Steve 'steamin' Clark: Stylish bat from the classic school. Precise and organised. Motivator and motivated. Less stylish but effective spin demon.

Nick 'Jonty' Jenkins: Pugnacious and authoritative batsmen. Powerful and punishing. Deceptive medium pace/spin bowler. Fearsomely competitive and committed in the field.

Philip 'Sledger' Glide: Aussie ringer. Batsman with silken poise and timing. Accurate ripper of wrist spin. Hawk-like in the field.

Chris 'Stendo' Stendall: tidy wicket keeper, strong, whirlwind number 11 batsmen in a team of 6, organiser, kit man, time keeper, photographer.

There's a loyal supporting cast giving it some serious pom-pom cheer leader action from beyond the boundary rope too: Brynaldo is there. He'd love to play, but picking out a small red ball in Chiswick's green acres is regrettably, not amongst his sporting talents; Johnny Underwood is there too. He's a man with a deep knowledge of the game and a genuine love of its grace, charm and poetry, as well as cheap classical CDs. John has a leg injury which restricts his mobility, although he is officially down as our 7th man; Vaughany of course. Unfortunately, no sporting ability whatsoever, but gives the proceedings an air of country charm; and Di. Di. She's a personal friend of Courtney Walsh, Ed Giddens and countless other international cricketers through her links with Sussex CC. Her support alone should be worth a good few runs. However, she likens my smooth, classical almost Chris Old-like delivery strides to a pissed Phil Tufnell. The legendary Yorkshire all-rounder would flinch at the comparison.

The day is a stormer. Prior to the first game, there's an air of expectancy pervading the team. We limber up in understated manner by knocking a ball around the outfield. The scene would conjour up the image of a stylised English Summer's day: team warming up under azure skies; tented pavilion buzzing with expectancy; beer warming nicely in the sun; Nick having a slash up against the wall. Beautiful. Stendo captures the moment for posterity on his Kodak.

The moment I pull on my whites and lace up my cricket boots, I feel like I'm in uniform. Whilst we've all entered this competition primarily for a bit of a laugh, none of us want to disgrace ourselves. I don't want to let anyone down, that's my bottom line.

In theory I'm captain. Wrong place at the wrong time and all that. I attempt to sort out the batting order.
    "Darren, mate - your our best bowler". He plays decent club cricket for a side in Kent, "so why don't you open the bowling and I'll put you in Number 4"
He looks at me blankly.
    "No mate, I'm openin'. Yeah. I'm-I'm-I'm openin'."
There goes my authority.
    "Oh, alright then. Fine by me."
I can see Nick sniggering. Steve goes in next, then Nick and Philip. Stendo and I fight over the last man berth. I win.

Our performances are staggering. We absolutely breeze through the first two or three games. We probably have a stronger team than any of us thought. Darren is brutal on the bowling and clearly his best position is opening bat. I'm glad I insisted on this. One of my better decisions. He's a big chunky lad and the blade is like a matchstick in his paws. Darren gives anything short and wide the big heave-ho. Maybe there's not too much style, but there's plenty of good effect. He has an excellent eye and the timing is spot on. And there are plenty of juicy long hops on show at this level. When he's out, it's usually because he's missed a straight one. Then we get the chuntering. He takes it all very seriously.

"Did you see that umpire? He wouldn't give me middle. I was asking him for middle and he wouldn't give me middle. Did you see that?" He goes on. And on. On one occasion he's run out by the bowler because he's backing up too far. I sympathise with Darren as it's a cruel way to be out. The bowler could just have given him a friendly warning. Nevertheless big D whinges away so much about his dismissal that we lose all patience with the moaning sod.

"That's the way it goes Darren. No point moaning about it now." He's been chewing the ears of both umpires too. They've told him to piss off as well.

It's not all Darren though. He's our best player with bat and ball, certainly, but Nick and Steve have an excellent series of games too. Once they are comfortable in the middle - not that there is long in a 5 over game – they both shows signs of real quality: plenty of authentic cricket shots, useful improvisation, hefty drives and maybe a couple of slogs. When Nick comes off the pitch, he is absolutely shattered. He's not done this much running since junior gymnastics at his dodgy Catholic boarding school. He's sweaty, breathless, red faced, gasping for a fag and bursting or a beer. We are all true athletes today.

Philip, the Aussie ringer, is probably the biggest surprise. He's in at 4 and so not as much opportunity to show his skills as the big boys at the top of the order. But in our semi-final against a decent team, we are gathered on the boundary rope aware that we probably don't have as many runs to defend as we would like. Philip's been running up some good singles and twos - plenty of space on the ground with only 6 fielders. There's a fair amount of vocal encouragement for him and his partner, Nick.

"C'mon Phil. Show 'em what your made of. Show 'em some of that famous Aussie grit."
Next ball he swings an imperious six clean over extra cover with barely any back lift at all. It's quite simply the most extravagant shot we've seen all day. We are on our feet, screaming our adulation. He pops a couple more boundaries that over too, just for good measure.

Our bowling is probably not as strong as the batting, man for man. But up to the semis, we've always managed to be sufficiently frugal to carve out a winning position. Darren is clearly a very good bowler, but the rest of us are all able to do enough, one way or another, to put together a string of sound performances.

And Nick is an inspiration in the field. During the semi, he is bowling his little tweakers and slaps a ball down short of a length, inviting the batsman to swipe him over mid-wicket. The batsmen eyes light up like Bonfire Night and he plants his front foot down the pitch, heaves the bat in an ugly leg-side smear, but succeeds only in skimming the ball off its top edge. The ball zips up almost vertically. Now its Nick's turn to show the fire in his eyes. There's a caught and bowled opportunity here. Nick accelerates from the end of his follow through (about two paces past the bowling crease) with such ferocity that he kicks up a dust storm. He hurls himself full length down the pitch, flings out his arm and catches the ball at full stretch a nano-second before it would have hit the pitch. He leaps to his feet with an insane grin and gives an almighty roar directed at the batsman. Nick is holding the ball aloft, gripping it so hard that he's popping the stitching out of the seam like pips from a melon. Johnty Rhodes has nothing on this performance. The batsman looks bewildered and a touch disgruntled as he trudges off the square. This fielding tenacity encapsulates our performance.

During that semi I look round at the other boys. They too sense that we can win this little trophy. Etch our names forever into the annals of Civil Service cricketing legend. Well, you know. Big fishes and little ponds. We all want our 15 minutes..... But there's a problem. It's been a long afternoon. In truth none of us really thought we would get this far. Turns out that we won't have much of a team for the final. I'm due to get back home to meet my wife so we can head north for the weekend. Steve has to shoot off home to babysit his kids and Philip has got £55 seats booked at Covent Garden Opera House. He's due to hook up with his wife and friends in about an hour.

We've cruised through to the final and it is with bitter regret that we realise we can't field our full strength side. Wretched planning. Steve's already gone to catch his train - he is already late. I reckon I can stay for the final and still be back home in time for a reasonable start up the asphalt carpet. Phil wants to play, but he's really into time added on by now. I have a word with the opposition and the umpires. They want a game, of course. So we agree that what ever happens at the toss, we will field so that Philip can bowl his over. We play our 7$^{th}$ man, John, which means we can at least have a game. John's mobility clearly hampered by his damaged leg and hip. I hadn't realised how much until I saw him moving around the outfield.

Philip's mind is probably already in the dress circle and he throws down absolutely the worst six balls he's delivered all day. It's stinker of an over and goes for shed-loads. He knows it too, and he shrugs at us as he takes his cap and departs for The Mikado. We will miss his mercurial batting talents later. John, too, gets carted all over the place. Though he's been put in a very difficult position and if he hadn't agreed to play we couldn't have competed in the final at all. The rest of us perform reasonably with the ball, but we have a mountain to climb if we are to overhaul the opposition score, particularly as we are two batsmen down. So it proves, but Darren and Nick give it the kitchen sink and a couple of dishwashers too. We are far from disgraced, being bowled out in the 5$^{th}$ over. I even get to make a rare appearance with the bat. Once I remember which way to put the box in.

I disappear before the presentation with pangs of regret about what might have been.

We hook up in the SD early the following week. Time for the post mortem. Nick dishes out the runners-up trophies. Only he and Darren were left at the end of Sports Day and Nick went home with 5 of these cheap and cheerful gongs clanking away in his kit bag! Picking over the bones of the day is painful business. We realise that those of us who had departed early to honour other commitments needn't have bothered. Steve didn't get far at all.

"The bloody train broke down outside Liverpool Street. It was a proper break-down too. We were stuck there for over 45 minutes. I had to borrow someone's mobile phone to get through to Debs. It was like one of those mobile phone ads! She ended up leaving the kids with a friend up the road. She wasn't too happy with me though. Said I should have made sure I was home in good time. I wouldn't mind, but I was making an effort. It could have been a lot worse! In the end, there was no point leaving."

Worse was to come. Philip didn't get to the Opera House until half-way through the first performance. He wasn't allowed to his seat by the militant ushers until the interval.

"Yeah, not only was I fuming that I had paid £55 a ticket for something I wasn't bothered about seeing, but then I don't even get to see half of it anyway. And what a shocking last over too."

There's no doubt that we were utterly, completely robbed. With our original line-up we would have competed well and, I have no doubt, won the final. I am convinced of this. The knowledge that the early departures were all empty gestures merely deepens the scarring. I'd like to be a winner really. Just once.

Arnie once said, "I'll be back". We went back too. Year after year. But we never get this close again.

## 12. BRANDY CHASERS

*"They say chances on the outside  
Are looking very slim  
I've been so lucky on the inside  
I feel I'm going to win."*  
Thin Lizzy, *"Cold Sweat"* 1983

I still haven't got my punting sorted. But I'm becoming a lot more active down the bookies. And now Steve is telling me that bookies are a thing of the past. What's this?
"Betting exchanges. The emerging force in gambling and gaming. Punting on the net, lad."
"Eh?"
"It's fantastic news for us value backers, Davoski. Especially ante-post. Just think. You can get about your fancy early doors at a big price. Later when the price comes crashing in, you can lay the bet off at a fraction of the odds and build in a tidy little profit."
It seems that at least a couple of new betting exchange sites have become established on the web recently. Their key feature is that punters can lay a horse to lose as well as back it to win. So now everyone can be a bookmaker.

Steve has checked out the sites and is evidently impressed. Betfair.com is promoting its revolutionary services with a tipping competition at the 3-day Cesarewitch meeting. Steve had only just set up an account with them, having already been well pleased with the product offered by flutter.com. He's entered the tipping comp. We collect down the Buckingham Arms one Friday lunchtime and I almost choke on my home-made Buckingham burger when Steve reckons he's in with a big chance of cleaning up. He's excited, on-edge. His foot is doing that instinctive tap-tap-tap again. Like he's playing bass drum at a Cozy Powell tribute. A sure sign of excitement. There are three eligible races this afternoon and he knows what his nearest rivals have gone for. Steve has applied value principles, so he knows that if one of his selections comes in, he will have a very good chance of topping the tipping table. Or something.

I get a phone call from Brynaldo early on Monday morning.
"Bloody hell, Dave, have you heard Steve's news?"
"No. What?"
"He's cleared a cool grand on that tipping competition. No joke."
This is sensational stuff. Worthy of a couple down the WW at lunchtime to get the full SP. It's true. Munir won handily in the Group 2 Victor Chandler Challenge Stakes at 20-1 on Saturday. Steve had a pretty good idea that the money was in the bag. But in these circumstances he was a cautious soul. Who wouldn't be? Never count your chickens and all that. He waited for the phone call. We get a blow by blow account of the nip and tuck, the to-ing and fro-ing with his competitors in the crucial final few hours.
"My 'lucky horse' was Munir. This one-time Guineas prospect hadn't fulfilled his promise. But on this particular day he got very similar

conditions (a straight 7f on easy ground) to those he encountered when slamming the Greenham field at the start of the season."
The call duly came.

"Congratulaions, Mr Clark. It gives me great pleasure to credit your account with £1,000."

Brynaldo is the first to ask.

"So what are the plans, Steve. Presumably you will be treating Debs to a nice holiday somewhere posh. Or maybe finish off that long-standing DIY commitment?"
The answer surprises no one.

"Fat chance, Brynaldo. Debs isn't getting her hands on this little lot. Not sure if I'll tell her yet! I might take her out for a slap up meal. A bit of a treat. But this is the break I needed. This is my launch pad to get out of this place." Steve lays out his strategy. "Value bets. Every time. 1 point equals £10. I have a balance of 100 points. I aim to double that in a year. The pot is then worth £2000. So then I up the ante. 1 point equals £20 and so on. That's the theory. Stick to the principles, maybe tweak the system as I review my progress, but keep doubling the money. And maybe, eventually, one day, I'll be out of this dump."

Stirring stuff. It's a great speech and we are with him all the way. I'm convinced by the theory now. But I haven't got a bean to show for it. I'm still awaiting my first genuine value win. I am gradually banishing those days of Lucky 15s and Yankees and each way bets on 2nd favourites to the dustbin; consigning them to memory banks marked 'experience'. These are mug punts. I'm a value better now. I think. The only way to test this out is to get stuck in. 'Value' as a concept is an imprecise term, a subjective view. In essence it is a moving target. My idea of value will be different to Steve's and to Bryn's. Balancing those twin criteria of potential and price to unearth the value is key. But how do you use it? In handicaps? In big fields? Focus on a particular distance or discipline? Maybe just Grade 1/Group 1 events? Or novice hurdles? Inevitably, I start off with a scattergun approach, dipping my toe in the water here and there but unsure of how it should feel. I need a win to point me in the right direction.

This is the topic of conversation when we are down the pub of course. Another Cheltenham is only just around the corner. Brynaldo is on fire at the moment. He's blazing quite a trail. Last Boxing Day he got stuck into the King George VI Chase at Kempton and had an inspired moment of success. He had already snapped up some shortish prices about one of his favourite horses, the French raider First Gold. But another horse emerged during the season to court his betting wedge. Bellator from the sumptuous Venetia William's stable had already rewarded Bryn with a nice little win in the Haldon Gold Cup at Exeter back in November. Now he saw the Williams' gelding on offer at a startling 50-1 for the King George. He availed himself each way, as they say.

Helen and I were driving up the motorway to Mum and Dads for a post-Christmas family get-together. Jammed in heavy Boxing Day traffic I have my nose stuck up against the side window salivating at the thought of Burger Kings as advertised outside Woodhall Services. It was a grim journey. I don't drive, so was able to check my text messages when the phone jingled-jangled in my glove compartment. In a manner of speaking. It was Bryn. 'Bellator You Beauty. 3rd place at 50-1. Thank you very much' screams the text. What a result. That was a handsome payout, and I concede, a genuine value win. The SP was actually 33-1, so Brynaldo did a top job in getting on at 50s. What an outstanding call. He was careful not to tell me who won the race because he knows my Dad was taping it for me to watch when I got to Pickering. Turns out First Gold has romped it at 5-2 and given Bryn a double pay day. I needn't have bothered with the secret squirrel stuff. My Kempton selections were no-where.

Bryn's love affair with Bellator runs out of steam about two months later when the moody gelding, carrying a substantial Brynaldo stake at 5-4 favourite, refuses to start at Ascot in a decent Grade 1 event. Carl Llewellyn is aboard Bellator for the first and last time and the camera catches him in a helpless moment watching the rest of the field receding from view. He shakes his reigns at the beast underneath him and does a bit of urging, but the belligerent Bellator is unmoved. Llewellyn is hardly a windmill of encouragement, but even if he had been more animated it is hard to see Bellator is going anywhere except back to his cosy warm box for the afternoon. The assured tones of the delicious Clare Balding inform us that "…for those of you who backed Bellator, you've just lost your money." Bryn is incredulous on Monday down the pub. Bellator goes in the black book of horses to avoid. There is no way back from those dark pages. Indeed he doesn't win another race.

Some months later Bryn is still having considerable success. A horse called Irbee from the Nicholls yard is doing the business. He wins after wearing blinkers for the first time, or "Reggies", as Bryn refers to them after Reggie Blinker the legendary (not) Tottenham and Belgium striker.

Plenty happening for Steve too. But still nothing for me. I'm watching and learning though, and my general awareness and knowledge of the game is starting to develop. It's a slow business. A bit like trying to turn round a super-tanker. You need lots of space and time, it's hard to see any change with the naked eye, and you get covered in seagull crap. The first two points are more relevant than the last one. Obviously.

There are some early season highlights to the 2002 jumps campaign. After a slow start I've taken in some of the bigger races and I'm trying to work out where my angle is. Best Mate absolutely scorched home in the Haldon Gold Cup at Exeter, Sackville romped away with the Charlie Hall Chase at Wetherby. On the same card Irish raider Boss Doyle won the John Smith Hurdle. Just like he seems to have done for the last half-dozen years.

The first of the season's classics is upon us. The Mackeson Gold Cup meeting, rechristened 'The Open' at Cheltenham kicks off the business end of the season. We take the opportunity of a closer look at the action when on the Friday Nick, Steve and Bryn and me take the afternoon off. We split our time between the Jugged Hare and Ladbrokes next door. This is better than working. No winners yet again for me. Gun n Roses II nearly breaks my heart in the opening amateur jockey's chase. He stops up the hill like he's run into a brick wall. I can hardly believe my eyes as GnR's massive lead at the final furlong marker is eaten up and the race is thieved from him by Samuel Wilderspin. GnR was a 7-1 shot. It doesn't help that Steve has backed the winner. This is as near as I get all afternoon Gutted is not the word. "Welcome to the jungle, it gets harder every day" as Axl once said.

If nothing else though it rams home the significance of that unforgiving up hill finish at Cheltenham. I will never underestimate the importance of stamina at the track. Later, we are all studying with appropriate reverential respect the form for a very decent conditions 2 mile chase featuring some smart second season chasers (see how smoothly I am slipping in to the appropriate terminology….). Steve announces that he has already secured a very nice price about a recruit from the flat game called Latalomne. In the bookies he tops up with a bit more. The horse wins like an express train. The rest of this respectable field are blown away in backdraft. Latalomne explodes up the home straight like he's polishing off a 5f sprint. Stunning performance. Steve is cock-a-hoop, landing a three-figure profit. Bryn is on him too and continues his fine form. Not long after this Steve plunges on the ante-post markets and takes an inviting price about Latalomne for the Queen Mother Champion Chase. This is the start of a three-year love hate relationship.

Shooting Light is the star of the feature Thomas Pink Gold Cup on Saturday. This is Nick's fancy for the race and, like Steve, it marks the start of a similar, though less intense three year love-hate thing with the beast too.

The Hennessey Cognac Gold Cup is next on the seasonal highlights agenda. It's a cracking handicap run over 3 miles 2 furlongs at Newbury in late November. I'm looking forward to the race. I'm in The Feathers near St James' Park on the Friday before the race with my new work colleagues having a swift beer. Start as you mean to go on, I say. But they are not big on race banter. Nick and Bryn wander down a bit later on. Even without Steve, we manage to sustain a decent discussion about the Newbury event. I'm busy nailing my colours to the mast. "I'm going for What's Up Boys. He ran up a string of wins in novice events at the arse end of last season. And look at his price. You can still get about 16s." We indulge in some welcome Friday night wind-down banter and head off for home at a respectable hour.

I still feel good about the selection next morning though. I've looked at the form and it stacks up. He goes well fresh, his jumping has come together and he fits the profile of 2nd season chasers. Against the choice is a slight doubt about the going which will probably be on the soft side and some old bollocks about him being a spring horse. This is plainly nonsense. He's only 7 and hasn't been racing that long. Out of his eight wins up to this point, four were in November and December. It's just that he got his jumping together over fences in the Spring last season. I can feel myself getting all indignant about such short sighted punditry. But of course this time it's working in my favour. This is why he's such a big price. Hallelujah! I've discovered value! I think he's got a better chance of winning than the bookies, so I should back him. It's so simple! So I'm on at 16-1.

The race isn't quite so simple. I'm sat on the edge of my sofa at home staring at the tiny telly in the corner. Normally the telly's fine. I don't like big screens that dominate rooms. But today it's too small. I did contemplate disappearing off to the bookies to watch the race, but they can be such soulless places. I stick with the homely feel of the cosy living room which is being torn apart by my rampaging children. Helen is in the dining room. There is a decent field of 14 runners and they're off. "They're off, Helen." No response. Not vocal anyway.....

The pace seems pretty solid to me. What's Up Boys takes handy order in the middle of the pack as Grey Abbey and Monifault lead them round the first circuit or so. Grey Abbey falls and suddenly the race kicks on a gear. There's a mile to go and the soft ground/decent pace combination is already taking it's toll. Frantic Tan, Jocks Cross and Hindiana are all dropping away. Turning out of the back straight, What's Up Boys, easy to pick out as the only grey left standing and with jockey Paul Flynn resplendent in red and black silks is on the tail of the leading three - Behrajan, Take Control and Lord Noelie. I think he's going to be right there in the mix.

The pace is hectic now, all the horses are off the bridle and jockeys are rowing away like it's the Head of the River Race. Two out and What's Up Boys is in the picture, but there are still two ahead of him. I think he's closing but it's not fast enough. At the last fence Flynn asks for a big jump and the flying grey lunges over the fence like he's leaping cartoon-style off a rocky crevice. Except he's over-balanced. For a moment I think he's going to tip over, but the horse somehow finds a lovely stride. "Come on the grey, come on". I'm off the sofa now, edging towards the telly. There's a long finishing straight at Newbury and I'm willing What's Up Boys to make use of every yard. He catches Take Control who is being driven strongly by Tony McCoy. Behrajan in front is not stopping though. What's Up Boys has found that extra gear and is tearing along now. It's a magnificent sight as he eats up Behrajan's advantage. But the jockey has to pull him round the leader to launch his final assault up the stands rail. Has it broken his momentum? I am on my knees. Literally. Genuflecting in front of the screen with my nose about six inches from my horse's flowing grey mane. I'm screaming at him. "Come on the Boys" And he is. Like a bullet. Where has he found this speed after a 3 mile slog? Is it too late? I can see the finishing line. One last effort. I can't hear the commentary any more. Too many competing voices in my head. But I call the result as both beasts thunder past the post. What's Up Boys by gossamer thread. "Yes. You absolute beauty!"

What a finish. He was like an Exocet up the home straight. I'm palpitating and hyper-ventilating. "Mummy what's wrong with Daddy?" I look round and my eldest daughter hugging my youngest as if protecting her from some horrible monster that has invaded the living room. Does she mean me? I pick them both up and swing them round the room. "Woo-hoo. Daddy's horse just won!" I'm not sure how much this reassures them! I rush in to Helen. "Feel this, just feel this!" I put her hand over my ribs. My heart is pumping like Tom Araya's bass at a thrash metal frenzy. "Exciting is it dear? Did it your horse win". My chest swells and I half turn away and say "Too bloody right. 16-1. My first value win!" Cue the stirring music and quivering top lip. I settle for a couple of generous congratulatory texts from Bryn and Nick. Glad I was so bullish in the pub last night. I might never get this chance again.

So, my first genuine bona fide value result. This is nerve-jangling hard work, though. Value punting is starting to feel like a long and sordid journey. It is the circuitous route to success, but it is pot-holed with self-loathing, recrimination and frustration, and signposted by isolated victory, illusory perfection and fleeting superiority. Mug punting is a road to nowhere with no A to Z and too many pit-stops at expensive motorway service stations.

I want to move from the latter to the former. I want to be a punter with a plan, a backer with a road map. I'm sick of printing money for the bookmakers chasing mug bets.

Glad I got that off my chest.

The What's Up Boys moment is a bit of a landmark, then. I'm always going to have a soft spot for the horse now. I follow his progress quite closely and he has a mixed season really. He runs well enough for 4$^{th}$ in the Welsh National over Christmas, but is pulled up in is next outing and is a bit outclassed in the Gold Cup at Cheltenham, although he stays on gamely for 5$^{th}$. His trainer Philip Hobbs surprisingly enters him for the Grand National and as the great day approaches, I see the value in this at 33-1 each way. He runs such a game race and jumps like a stag. He looks to have the race won after the last. But so many races have been won and lost between there, the elbow and the post. What's Up Boys is pursued by the relentless Bindaree who has a 10lb pull. Johnson on board Boys is flailing away for all he's worth. Carl Llewellyn switches Bindaree to the inside and grabs pole position on the rail. This is a good move and seals his victory. What's Up Boys never gives up all the way to the line. But Bindaree sneaks up inside a tiring WUB and takes the National by a length or so. Later, I heard that both trainers had been stood next to each other watching the dramatic events unfold. After the last, Bindaree's trainer Nigel Twiston-Davies turned to Philip Hobbs and offered his hand in congratulations. Only for the offer to be reversed 90 seconds later. I like what I see on the telly and in interviews of Philip Hobbs. Seems an honest, straightforward trainer on the upswing. Bryn is ecstatic. He had backed both Bindaree and the grey each-way and simply didn't know who to cheer home first. What an enviable position.

But I'm getting ahead of myself. This Aintree meeting is merely a post script to the main event of the National Hunt season. Steve, Bryn and I have another Cheltenham experience to savour first. This year we have cranked up the commitment. After the farcical foot and mouth disappointments of 2001, we are licking our lips and plotting up ante-posts for a full-bodied full-force three-day extravaganza. Going the full distance at the festival is hard-core behaviour and I pinch myself to think that a little over two years ago we were festival novices. This is truly a revolution.

Bryn's mate John lives not far from Cheltenham and is happy to put the three of us up for the duration of the event. I don't realise at the time what a peach of a break this is. I'm half-wondering whether we shouldn't find a B&B somewhere so that we don't impose too much. The briefest of squints at the sorts of prices charged by unscrupulous landlords who advertise in the Racing Post very quickly persuades me that John's offer is as sound as a pound. Tewkesbury it is.

There is plenty of ante-post activity of course. Steve is trail-blazing the route to glory. Bryn has a look and I dibble and dabble at the big chases and the Champion Hurdle from about Christmas onwards. Nothing excessive but I do love the idea of wading in to some of the fancy prices chalked up about the outsiders. Getting on Foxchapel King and Japhet at big odds and then seeing the prices collapse when they do the business next time out is almost as satisfying as backing a winner. Almost. What I should be doing is laying off the bets on this new fangled betting exchange wheeze. But I'm not there yet. Steve is uncovering some off-beat theories whilst investigating the murky waters of gambling texts and treatises. He comes up with an angle on the Tote. He e-mails me.

> "Came across this info which I thought you might be interested in:
>
> Here are some stats for the SP versus Tote obtained from the winner of the flat turf races from 1993 to August 2002.
>
> All winners: the average SP was 6.45-1, the average Tote odds were 7.63-1.
>
> But break this down further. Favourites: average SP 1.92-1, average Tote 1.78-1

This is more revealing. The Tote has long been the betting tool for the newbies, grannies and impresarios who back the favourites. And this is why the Tote is paying LESS than the SP on favourites.

The bigger the price, the more value you will get with the Tote. So for instance, where the SP is 10-1, the Tote is paying 11.58-1 and at 33-1, the Tote is dishing out almost 50-1.

More or less confirms what we thought.

PS. What is your deadline for the cricket transfers?"

With only a few days to go I am awash with information. I drift aimlessly through it - tipsters views, Sunday broadsheet supplements, 5-day handicap declarations. It's all spread out before me on the floor and I hastily jot down form notes, trends, the weather forecast - anything that might be a scrap of use. I feel like I'm cramming for an exam. "Don't forget to enjoy yourself!" teases Helen, clutching our youngest who has just exploded in a nasty outbreak of chicken pox. I'm starting to feel guilty.

No turning back now though. Accommodation, tickets, transport, punting wedge, fanciful strategies and the hip flask are all ready. Big breath then. Time to go.

## 13. THE CHELTENHAM POSSE

*"I put my money in a suitcase*
*And headed for the big race."*
Thin Lizzy *"Cold Sweat"*, 1983

Maybe there is a hint of nerves in the air as I hook up with the other hombres on the stroke of high noon. Rendezvous at Paddington Station Burger King seems appropriate, but the collective appetite is not for junk food.

Steve 'town & country' Clark looks the part - almost. Gentry corduroys, Barbour jacket and dapper brown felt trilby. He could be a deadringer for Nicky Henderson if only the PVC holdall, circa 1982 borrowed from his son Dom, had been ditched. Brynaldo Reynaldo is up for it too. He's looking pretty casual, despite being weighed down by half the contents of a well stocked Superdrug. Acid attacks in the night are to blame apparently. And I am in a Glastonbury frame of mind, shockingly spurning my parental duties and running away from Chicken Poxed children.

Here we are: three hotshots ready to take on the good, the bad and the Barry Dennis's of the Cleeve Hill mob with nothing more than a fistful of ante-post bets and a loaded Racing Post. Du-dulu-du-dulu doo. Wah-wah-wah. Three days at the glorious Cheltenham Festival are ours for the punting.

Burger King brekkies duly scoffed, we ride shotgun aboard the Cheltenham Pony Express, which remarkably departs on time leaving the hackneyed Wild West analogies back on Platform 7.

There is a fairish measure of quick-fire excitable conversation on the train: shallow, largely pointless and fairly undignified. We burn out quickly like cheap rockets on Bonfire night and revert to our Racing Posts. I reveal my grand scam which is the product of those days cramming like an exam-addled student over the analysis of the trends boys in the Racing Post: the result is the 'Cheltenham Matrix'. A system, by Jove, to beat the bookies. I haven't been wasting my time in the build up to this event. Not me. It is a bit embryonic, mind. It's a sort of a triangle thing with horses, trainers and races down each side. It all hangs - this system - on the subtle interplay between correctly weighted circumstances and conditions. Once those precious variables are fed in (and this is the skill), then hey presto, the winning horse will reveal itself. Steve and Bryn are a bit skeptical. They offer polite noises and inquiring grunts, but clearly prefer the more conventional 'form' route. Pah. Luddites.

We are making smooth progress through the contents of the buffet car and some rather genteel Cotswold countryside….. but we need the declarations! How can we get any serious study in if we don't even know which bleedin' horses are turning up tomorrow! I'm on the text to Nick back at the office who can check out the Racing Post website. He's busy.

"I'm busy" he texts. We are left to wait few shakes a gelding's tail before he comes up with the runners and riders for the first three. I'm striking off the non-runners in the RP as Nick barks 'em out. We get to the Champion Hurdle and Nick has not mentioned Istabraq. So all the gossip was true! He's a non-runner. The markets will go crazy. I am incredulous, and on the point of announcing this sensational news to the rest of the train...
"Ha! Not really!"
A perfectly timed blinder. It's a wind up. Slipped me a crippler.
"Eee-fucking-aawww!!"
Then Nick's gone. Back to being busy.

The Oirish are getting nicely tanked.
"So boyz, what's yer tip fer the Festival", inquired a swaying raider as the train arrives in Cheltenham.
There's no time to answer. Indeed a response was not really sought. The advice is to lump our mortgages on Like-A-Butterfly and In Contrast on Tuesday and Colonel Braxton on Wednesday. Simple really. Bryn takes careful note.

Final decs are safely pouched outside the station courtesy of the Gloucester Echo. We are to become very familiar with its front and back pages. And not just to keep the chips warm.

There's not much sign of the fabled Cheltenham 'craic' in these quiet, though admittedly splendid Regency streets. It's a good 15 minutes (feels like a lifetime in a beer desert) before eagle-eyed Steve spots a Hogshead looming oasis-like at the end of the street . John our host for the next two nights arrives after a hard day at the office and we crack on with a few beers before hatching a plan to take the party to Tewkesbury.

Tewksbury - Bryn, displaying a startling lack of basic Civil War knowledge, insists on calling it Tweaksbury - is an ideal base camp, just a short journey from Cheltenham. We strike out for the local chippy and a bit more ale. We are in good company. It's only the BBC s sporting utility man Johnny Inverdale in the corner, sipping half a lager and tucking in to a steak pie and chips. There is a host of media types thronging around him giving it large about rubbing shoulders with minor celebrities. Someone pops Inverdale a hot tip for tomorrow - Frenchman's Creek, we overhear and take note. Blimey, we are collecting tips like Stig of the Dump. Bryn has some shoulder rubbing of his own to report. He is claiming he clocked the ravishing Clare Balding that very morning as she purchased whatever medicines Bryn had left on the shelves at his local Superdrug.

The media circus moves off to its hotel bar and shortly after we slope off home. Steve and me are already knackered and beered up. Brynaldo has been on the GnTs and John is wondering when Bryn's rock 'n' roll mates from London are really turning up instead of these jessies. England's Test v NZ has started and Bryn who has the lounge sofa berth is taking in the action on Test Match Special. After lights out, those listening closely would have heard the dulcet tones of Blowers and Aggers accompanying a less dulcet but much closer rumble as I decorate the inside of John's bog with some pre-festival 6X fuelled apprehension.

I emerge from slumbertown feeling none the worse from my bathroom exertions. Hussain has bagged a ton, Brynaldo has flu and Steve is on the Racing Post run. It's all happening. Brynaldo, fast as a shark and twice as deadly, is in with his accusations. He's guessed it was me churning up my guts last night. Damn. Steve's back, laden with freshly laundered Festival Rps joins in the general piss-take.

Soon it's like a library in the living room.
    "Anyone fancy a brew?" chirps Brynaldo.
Silence.
    "I'm definitely opposing Like-a-butterfly" I state.
Steve nods sagely, but suggests that the first race is in fact wide open. A bundle of contradictions. An enigma wrapped in a conundrum. More collective nodding and chin-scratching.

I jump up decisively.
    "Who fancies a tea?" I offer heartily.
Bryn responds with a stream of abuse. He has had the kettle singing in the kitchen for the last five minutes. He doesn't seem to have grasped this opportunity of some serious revision. Anyway, several teas later, McCrirrick is winding it up on the Morning Line and I have narrowed down the 1st race to a short list of 12.

All set then and off to Safeways for some top brekkie scram and a bit more research. But no, not all set. Brynaldo has left his ticket back at the house! This campaign has been planned with military precision, its been the topic of conversation for a year, research has been done, preparations made, restaurants booked, pubs scoped, bags packed, trousers pressed, foot spa warmed.... and Bryn forgets his ticket!

Still, time is on our side. The rogue ticket is pouched and we catch the bus to town.

Brynaldo checks out the form on the bus. And sorts out his horses as well. Ho Ho. There's a nice festival atmosphere now in the town centre. It's a pleasant mild Spring day. After briefly checking the post-race watering holes (Dawn Run looks favourite) we wend our way to the course. Fantasy Festival selections are dribbling in. There are some devilishly convoluted plots afoot. Just the cool and erudite Vaughany left to play his fantasy cards. And as Cleeve Hill looms into view they are all in. Vaughany late but canny as usual....

We are all in too. Tatts is packed, mobbed, heaving. Absolutely thronging. Steve gives Brynaldo and me the slip somewhere near the 1 furlong marker. Half an inch of reign and he was gone! We see Istabraq's trainer Aiden O'Brien looking a bit shifty and later on, it emerges Steve has seen owner and legend JP McManus dodging about. I think there is an Istabraq scam afoot. Never too late for scare stories. Placepots are placed and we reel Steve in by Barry 'Bismarck' Dennis's pitch for the opener.

And they're off... as they say. The tape goes up and two years of pent up frustration gives rise to a belly roar which raises the roof, shakes the floor and tingles the spine. The Supreme Novices Hurdle is a belter to begin with. Adamant Approach falls when looking well set. Like-A-Butterfly and Westender are absolutely hammer and tong up the hill. Both jockeys give everything to the post with Charlie Swan holding on by a whisker. A Fantastic race in a pressure-cooker environment. It's breathless stuff, I'm giddy with emotion. I don't think I've been injected with such an instant rush of adrenalin since I stood in the Kop at Leeds for the first time.

All Ireland is singing right in my lughole. My wedge was on In Contrast who has a splendid race to finish fast in 3rd. I thought he was closing on the front pair for an over-excited moment. But I've only backed it on the nose. I needed that Like-A-Holeinthehead. Brynaldo, though, is off and running. He's backed In Contrast each way. Top result. My Cheltenham Matrix goes in the bin. Embryonic yesterday, still-born today.

One bookie said that they had waited two years for the festival and had been cleaned out in the first 10 minutes! Great quote, but we don't believe these canny buggers. It's Steve, Brynaldo and me versus any bookie in the ring. Cooommmeee ooooonnnn!!!!!

Next up, the Arkle. The Arkle. I draw a reverential breath of respect. It's another top- drawer race. We all get a run for our money, but don't bag the winner. Moscow Flyer looks sublime, the business and at a tasty price too. Seebald, Armaturk and Fondmort are all in the Flyer's wake and he absolutely hoses up that hill. Another one up for Ireland. I swear this bricks and mortar grandstand is doing an Irish Rover jig under my very feet.

Champion Hurdle. Check the emotional wiring for burn out. Istabraq and all that. The betting ring is going crazy. Dennis is laying Istabraq at 9-4. He is taking the piss! He isn't giving a price on the other contenders. He won't close his bag until he has taken 10 grand. Bloody nerve. Steve toys with the idea of having some of that, just to wipe the smug smile off Dennis's drooling chops. But thinks better of it. 9-4, though, is at least a quarter of a point better than anywhere else in the ring. This is Istabraq we are talking about. The legendary Istabraq. There is a scrum of punters desperate to have a pop at Dennis's smugness. Steve still wavers. I can see that sentiment is creeping in. We would all love to see Istabraq claim that precious 4th Champion Hurdle victory. Steve's thinking is getting cloudy. He wants to cheer home Charlie Swan one more time and have a slice of Barry's wedge to boot. But it can't happen. Last year was his chance, surely. Foot and Mouth put paid to that. Steve dallies and in no time at all Dennis has closed both his bulging bag and his fat gob.

Istabraq remains the star of the show though. He's treated to a touching ovation during the parade past the stands and is applauded every inch of the way to the 2 mile start. The jockeys seem to be taking an age to sort themselves out, horses milling around for far too long. It feels a bit tense over there. Or is it here? Finally, the tape goes up to that familiar roar. Before the field is properly settled, Istabraq has taken up a position at the back. Down the home straight, concern amongst the crowd is palpable, rising like flood water as Istabraq sends out distress signals. He is not moving well. Something is clearly amiss and not much later this great champion is pulled up having 'lost his action'. An over-used phrase at this festival. It's a huge disappointment. Disbelief is tangible. Groans roll and bounce around the stands as if an echo in an empty cathedral. But the place is packed and no-one wanted to see such an anticlimax to a stunning career. Well, maybe only Barry Dennis.

Worse is to follow. Valiramix, favourite for the race since early in the year, now has the the title at his mercy. He is travelling beautifully, up with the pace. But between hurdles he appears to trip. We can't see what's happening from where we stand, but it's clear that the horse has fallen and jettisoned McCoy who damages his shoulder.

Before I've digested the consequences of the two best horses being lost to the race, Hors La Loi III has stayed on and taken Istabraq's crown. Whilst I have been sneering at Dennis, it emerges that Brynaldo has sauntered over the rails and blagged a piece of Hors at 10/1, collecting a tasty each-way wedge on Marble Arch into the bargain! Brynaldo is on fire. I didn't even hear him screaming them home. This man has ice in his veins!

Not long after the race it's announced that Valiramix has in fact come off much worse than McCoy. He has had a horrible fall and has been put down. Desperate, tragic stuff. This must be almost impossible for McCoy to deal with. He may be hard as nails, balls of brass. But coming after the tragedy of Gloria Victis last year, the Champion Jockey could be forgiven for wondering what the hell it's all about.

Despite Brynaldo's win, it's hard not to feel a little hollow. Hors La Loi is a fine horse, but battle was never really joined in a race that appeared to have had all the juiciest ingredients. Two of the principals didn't fully participate and neither will be seen on a racecourse again.

But the show must go on. Three good races follow. Frenchman's Creek catches the valiant Carbury Cross in an excellent William Hill National Hunt Chase. Of course none of us backed it. I bet Inverdale resisted as well. He is, after all, the horse-owner well known to Martin Pipe who turned down the opportunity to buy a share in Make A Stand in the year he won the Champion Hurdle.

There is amateur mayhem in the 'Fluke' (as the electronic information board describes it) Walwyn Chase with horses up-ended, unseated and tailed off right left and centre. Horses and jockeys litter the track between every fence down the back straight. The Bushkeeper navigates a true line through the carnage and lands the spoils. We don't. I'm on a Pipe horse in the last of the day, the Pertemps Hurdle Final. But he's not having a great festival so far and Ballysicios under performs. Freetown takes the piss to the evident delight of two jocks bellowing "Go on Tony, Go on myeee son" two rows behind us. I was looking down the track for Tony McCoy's horse. They were talking about Tony Dobbin on Freetown! At 25/1 or so they went home happy.

We push off for a pint.

There is a brief period of respectful mourning on the way to town for our heroic losers. At least I'm being respectful. The other boys are voraciously tucking into the Gloucester Echo Wednesday declarations. Bryn's had a top day, but Steve is as potless as me. Have some pity lads! Don't we need some space here? But I succumb and it's not long before I'm talking up the chances of Japhet and listening to some pissed blarney in the Dawn Run about lumping on Florida Pearl for the Gold Cup. Haven't we been here before?

The pub is heaving with post-festival celebrations and recriminations. We spill out to the pavement. John joins us for a beer flashing a winning Bilboa e/w ticket. Bilboa for Thierry Doumen was almost the forgotten horse in the Champion Hurdle and finished a gallant 3rd. We make for Montpelier, the classy part of town, so the locals have it, for a few Guinnesses. Bryn thoughtfully suggests that those of us with parental responsibilities might tactfully touch base with those left at home. Oh yeah, good call!

By the time we check into the Berkeley Arms back in Tewksbury for the remainder of this frantic day, Bryn and I have already been distracted by the bright lights. The kebab shop had proved irresistible. It does a job, you know, but as doners go it's a distinctly *regional* experience.

So on, then, to the scene of the week's greatest triumph. We've stumbled upon the Berkeley Arms Quizzz Niyte. Too good an opportunity to miss is this. We are wired and live, and for the first time today, there is a whiff of victory in the air and it's blowing our way. Our Festival Posse takes up position by the bar and the locals are already checking us out. Steve has a bit of needle going. There's an eyeball confrontation with a heavily bearded anorak-type from the Tewkesbury Inbred History Society on the next table. And a terse exchange takes place behind us with a hairy tub of bollocks from the Rural Obscure Musical Appreciation Society. Mr Casual Quizmaster steps up to mike. Centre stage. He loves it. Neatly pressed faded denims, tan cowboy boots and a roll-up lodged in his beard where his gob should be. What is it with facial hair round here?

We rise to the competition. We are hot. Incendiary guess work, scalding long-shot recollections, steaming inspiration. And we are cold. Ice-cool, precision-tooled team work, chilling cheating. Brynaldo burns through the media round with a stunning display of TV trivia and an awesome grasp of

Simpson's chronology. It gives us a head start and somehow we always feel that we are in with a shout. Then comes the music round. Bloody hell, it's bits n pieces! Where's Nick when you need him?! But we pull it off with an eclectic mix of good fortune, broad based knowledge and *Action Man* eagle eyes. Steve spots '1968' on the answer sheet for the year of release for a song which we know neither the title nor the artist! Outrageous. But it is enough. The Festival Four swing into town, tweak the tails of the Inbred Boys and scarper with the prize money before the raffle is drawn! We sleep contentedly.

You know how you stroll to work on a morning and as you pass the supermarket you shake your head sadly at the people who are already waiting in the car park pawing their steering wheels and staring at their watches? And you think 'get a life'. Steve crashes into the flat with a fist full of Racing Posts as I emerge from the bog. "Late opening the doors", he says. "Shoddy, unprofessional behaviour", he moans as he settles down with a mug of steaming tea to unpick the secrets of the SunAlliance Novice chase. No chunder incidents to report, I'm pleased to say. But Bryn is looking green. He gingerly fills up the hip flask. We interpret this as an encouraging sign.

It's bleeding freezing outside. A chill easterly blowing out of a steely sky has replaced the warm spring-like glow of yesterday. A test of the Tewkesbury grass verges confirms that the overnight rain has turned the going Good to Soft.

Still, a hearty breakfast warms the cockles. Nick is first in with his studied fantasy selections, followed by Paul and Sharon's intricate trifecta, reverse forecasts and odds-on favourite doubles. Steve holds the phone in one hand, a calculator in the other and his head in another. Is this the spirit of the game? Bryn and I set about our selections on the bus. My phone goes. It's the boys from the office checking they have the spelling correct of my tip for the Gold Cup tomorrow.
     "B-E-H-R-A-J-A-N" I say. "Yeah, plenty of ale! No not a winner in sight.......Stu, you still there?"
Was it only last week I was telling them to lump, lump and lump again on Behrajan? Well it appears they have. They've had a whip round and raised £36. That sort of pressure I don't need.

Weeks later I'm on a training course talking to someone who works in my building but whom I'd never met before. The conversation turns, with some gentle prompting on my part, to racing. She mentions that she had been given a good tip, allegedly, for the Gold Cup and had parted with good honest cash to an office whip and the "bloody thing" didn't even finish!
     "Oh". I say in a weak little voice. "er....is that Stu over there....?"
Wish I hadn't prompted.

Only a few hardy souls outside the Dawn Run this bitter morning. Vaughany weighs in with his cute selections for the fantasy festival. The course is mobbed. Just like yesterday. There is a bit of placepot activity and a frantic bout of texting from Nick who is worried we have misinterpreted his fantasy selections. Sorted though. He's sloping off home to catch the races on the telly. Nice one.

First up, the SunAlliance Novice Hurdle. The same bone-shaking roar announces the start of Day 2. A maximum field of 28 horses bolt for inside rail. It's all over in a flash as Galileo comes from out of the clouds. This victory from the Eastern bloc fulfilled a charming prophecy from Nicky Henderson at a festival preview evening when he said "We love the Irish, we tolerate the French and now they tell me a Pole will win the SunAlliance Hurdle!" You better believe it! Some Fantasy Festival wedge has also been earned on the back of the Polish raider. But nothing for us boys so far.

I'm fairly confident that the French raider Japhet will go close in the Royal and SunAlliance Chase. And he does. He's just being asked for a bit more at the business end of the race when he takes a tumble at the second last. Our combined wedge on his back was the straw that finally broke the camel. It's a strange old race all round. Hussard Collonges is the unexpected winner at a big price and one of my old mates Chives finishes in the frame.

Then the showpiece. The place is hotting up for the Queen Mother Champion Chase. I sit out the cauldron of the betting ring, happy to see what my ante-post punt, Knife Edge can deliver. Steve has Latalomne and Bryn is in amongst the action wheeling and dealing his way to a decent price on Edredon Bleu and Flagship Uberalles. Flip-flopping favourites as the bearded freak from Channel 4 will have it. The tightly knit field of elite chasers arcs past the grandstand, streams up over the hill and purrs down the back straight. Magnificent sight. This is why we are here.

Next time we see them, it's hell for leather. Cenkos is setting a blinding pace out in front, Flagship is under pressure, Tiutchev is flagging, Edredon Bleu is beaten and Latalomne is gathering himself. He looks well set. Steve can't help himself "Gooo ooon La'alomne". Too late. He clatters the second last. The race commentary is fractionally ahead of the video pictures and he's called a faller before we see him hit the deck. Jockey Vinnie Keane knows he had the race for the taking. He cuts a pitiful image. The camera lingers on him beating his fists on the turf in frustration.

Flagship rallies under a superb driving ride from an emotional Johnson and he pours his mount over the line, beating Native Upmanship into 2nd and a game Cenkos in 3rd. Brynaldo is flying. He's berthed the Flagship. Quality call once again. Knife Edge disappoints. Not quality. That was some race. My heart's still pounding.

Steve is distraught. He's as convinced as Vinnie that Latalomne was cruising up to take the race. He's feeling flatalomne.

No time to draw breath. These races are relentless. I've studied the Coral Cup, so I'm feeling confident. Hard to Start is the boy for me from out of the handicap (whatever that means). But it's a tough 2m 5f and the slog does for many in the field. Not Ilnamar though who scorches home unopposed. Pipe's 3rd string. Not for the first time this festival McCoy has picked the wrong one.

Steve needs some space. I, too, need time to reflect. Brynaldo takes a look at me and thinks I may be gutted, an empty shell, a broken man, wrecked, all washed up. He's only partly right. I'm also hungry. I stomp off in search of a large pork and apple sauce bap. Comfort food at a time like this is a basic requirement. The plan is to give the next race - another amateur hatchet job with plenty of scope for disaster - a miss and meet by the Guinness enclosure. But I can't get within twenty yards of any of the superior junk food emporia. They are mobbed. My mood darkens. So I sidle off to the parade ring and watch the horses emerge for the National Hunt Challenge Cup. Rith Dubh, a gelding as big and dark as my mood skitters onto the track with an aloof air. The jockey wears JP McManus's famous colours. I swear the horse winks at me on his way past.

Right then. I can take a hint. Real or imaginary. That junk food failure has sent me over the edge. I'm all steely determination and bloody mindedness now. I find the best price on offer and slap down double my maximum win stake at 10/1. This is no time for strategy. I go off in search of the lads by the last fence and swallow hard. Can't find them in the melee. I'm on my own for this one.

It's a marathon 4 mile trip and plenty begin to drop away. But Rith Dubh is held up in mid division. He's jumping like a stag. As he flashes by me with a circuit to go, he's picking off his contenders one by one.

Coming down the hill for the last time, there is barely a fag paper between three or four very tired horses. At the last, Rith Dubh is there, he flies it and challenges for the lead. I can't breathe. I catch the finish on the big screen. It's bloody close. Rith Dubh is a canny old bugger - a shocking idler in front. JT McNamara is aboard and asks him for more. He doesn't want to hit the front too soon. But is it too late? They stretch over the line. Looks like Rith Dubh to me from a furlong away. But the commentator calls a photo. More agony. I switch from scanning the crowd for the lads to fumbling for my race card.
"Come on 19, come on 19."
Christ I am really shitting myself. Here it comes - (the photo result, not the bowel movement).
"1st number 12, 2nd number 7."
"What? WHAT?" I politely enquire of my neighbours. Rith Dubh not even in the first two? I think I've spotted Steve's ten-gallon hat and I move towards him.
"Correction. 1st number 19, Rith Dubh. 2nd number......"
"Yeeeeaaahhhh. You fucking beauty!"

I hurl myself at a rather surprised Steve in spasms of ecstasy. He deals with it very magnanimously. Safe to say I'm rather pleased.

I try, but can't wipe the insane grin off my chops, especially as the bookie is counting out those juicy tenners in to my hot little mits. My jaw is starting to ache.

But it's only my mits that are warm. The rest of me is perishing. It is as raw as a butcher's window over by the Guinness enclosure, and twice as busy. We have our going-out togs on and they don't offer much protection from a bitter north-easterly. The Mildmay of Flete is to be our last race of the day. We plan to shoot off before the Bumper to fulfill an appointment at a rather superior eating establishment. Bryn and I lump on Mr Baxter Basics who is doing well on the first circuit until the jockey, Brian Crowley, drops the reigns. Bloody hell, there are only a few things you need to get right as a jockey. Holding the reigns is one of them. Tosser. Mr Baxter Basics is pulled up. Steve's punt, Gower-Slave under-performs too. We take that as a cue and make for the exit.

There is a spectacular view out of the taxi we hijack as it motors up Cleeve Hill. The sun is dipping behind the main grandstand radiating warm feelings over the track and half of Gloucestershire. I'm flying already and this sets the seal on it. Winchcombe is a glorious village of soft Cotswold stone and we sink into three of Flowers' finest pints in a cosy boozer on the High Street. The ozone has got to us all and we are glowing with the healthy outdoors. Some more than others. I look like a beetroot.

Time to tot up the winners and losers. Out comes the Schedule of Shame. Before Rith Dubh I was £98 quid down. But now I have a £2 profit to take into Day 3. Bring on the dancing horses.

John and Louise arrive from Tewksbury having cunningly avoided the festival traffic mayhem. We decant to the restaurant and gather by the fire clutching small apéritifs and large menus. The Maitre d' makes his outrageous entrance. He's a bit flamboyant.
    "He's in the right place. Bent as a butchers hook", someone mutters out of the side of their mouth.
    "More like Bajan Bandit!" responds Bryn, quick as a flash. Lenny Lungo would be mortified at the comparison with his top chasing prospect.

The Maitre d' talks us through the menu and specials with such verve, passion and enthusiasm that he immediately wins us over.
    "The duck sirs and madams, is slow roasted over daringly spiced red-hot embers for many hours (pause to lick lips in provocative manner), so that the flesh, pink and sssssssucculent simply drips off the bone into a quivering, tender mound on your gently warmed platter", (or words to that effect).
Well who could resist such a vivid description?

We are ushered through to the main room of exposed beams, subtle lighting and cosy tables. The food is top quality, the service impeccable and the conversation even better. This is what its like to be a grown up, then. After plundering several quivering ducks, an ocean of Chardonnay, a trio of strawberry syllabubs, two enormous cheeseboards and a partridge in a pear tree, we heave ourselves into a taxi home. A very satisfying evening.

The final day of the Festival dawns grey, cold and breezy. We are meeting the rest of the gang on the course. They can only summon up the enthusiasm for one day of the festival. Not hardened vets like us. Looking at Bryn I think he could use a vet. He was green yesterday. Today he is yellow. The boy is not well. Matty Hoggard's 7-fer down under against the massed ranks of the New Zealand hordes got him through the night. I pick up some emergency supplies of wipes at the Supermarket. It's going to be a long haul.

We pack up the kit bags and scoff another top brekkie. Insulating bacon fat is a requirement. Conversation turns to last night's Festival highlights which confirmed that Steve was robbed in the Champion Chase. Latalomne was going supremely well and gunning for the lead when he came down.

Bryn wants to go home. The raw easterly is ripping him to shreds. The bus is late. His nose is running like a drain and no-one stands down wind of him. He's taken Sudofed, Paracetamol, Lemsip, Vitamin C, Nurofen and Preparation H (you can never be too careful). He rattles when he walks. If he was a horse he'd be put down.

When the bus arrives, John and Louise are already aboard, having decided to take on the touts to sample the delights of Gold Cup Day. We agree to regroup by the bar in the Courage end. But before we can get in, Steve is fleeced and has to surrender his bottle of single malt whisky. Nightmare. This is the Bust the Bookie Fantasy Festival prize. Surely the narrow-minded stewards must understand this?! But he is forced to secrete it in the bushes outside, to be retrieved after racing. Or more likely a warming treat for the Stewards as they rifle through the undergrowth as soon as our backs are turned.

But the lads have arrived. It's good to see them and they are already into their second pint. Nick is looking frisky and edgy. He's been given a tip in the Triumph Hurdle, first up and he's looking to lump. Vaughany is dapper and aloof. Perfectly turned out. £100 to his handler. He claims once again not to have studied form. But this is a bit of a pantomime. We nod, touch our noses and flash wry grins. We know Vaughany of old. He will be there at the final reckoning. Gunner Goodwin and Sharon both appear calm and collected. They are sitting pretty in the fantasy comp, along with Bryn and Vaughany. Nick has an outside chance but Steve and me are looking for long shots.

John and Louise arrive. They passed the Tout Test, having forked out £20 for the Courage enclosure. Could have been worse - face value is £15. One of our number couldn't make it on the day and his ticket had to be sold. So Nick, the closest we have to a bona fide tout went into battle with the Cheltenham hardcore to dispose of the burdensome voucher. After a bit of tactful window shopping, he struck a deal with an unruly looking bloke outside the course. He thrust a 'ching' into Nick's hands and stalked off.
"What the bloody hell is a ching?" we chorus.
£5 apparently. Jokers. Still, Nick's done the knowledge now. He's got the lingo and another career option.

The banter is good. Bryn's spirits have picked up. We fan out for our assault on the bookies. First race optimism and all that. I have targeted this race and I'm putting my eggs in one basket. Jonjo O'Neill or bust. I sniff out the value on both his charges, Quazar and Giocomo. I also have an ante-post token still alive on Live the Dream. I watch all my selections fail gloriously from my vantage point on the rail as Scolardy, an Irish raider takes the field apart. He could be called a winner from the top of the hill.

There is more room to move down here by the rail, but it's more exposed. It's bleeding freezing with nothing to break the wind except my glowing bonce. I seek solace in a tasty 'barbecued' chicken baguette. But bloody hell, talk of breaking wind...... Nick's Irish connections have paid off big time. He's only gone and backed Scolardy on the nose at an outrageous 14/1! Top call. The bloke on the train had put him on to it.
"Charlie Swann's yer boy today in the Triumph. Can't lose"
This had sent Nick scurrying for the Daily Mail's race card to find out whether Swann was the name of the horse, owner, trainer or jockey!

But what else do you need? Nick's done the business, bagged the winner he needed and in the first race to boot. And this where he delivers his alternative strategy: 1) secure an early winner, thereby guaranteeing a successful day and relieving the fear of failure; 2) Get shit-faced on the proceeds 3) Have an interest bet here and there; 4) Still turn a healthy profit at the end of the day and roll home wankered! Perfect!!

There is some serious fantasy festival action unfolding. The Triumph has levered Andrew into contention after Scolardy proved to be an inspired selection for him too. Gunner and Mrs G are manoeuvering into striking distance and I have hauled myself into the frame with a 33/1 e/w return on 3rd placed Diamond Joshua. Brynaldo is not out of it either. If only Steve's pentium III 150 gigabyte mental arithmetic processor could handle the bet permutations to fractions of pence then it would be quite exciting. It emerges later that someone - was this you Brynaldo? - someone talked Louise out of backing Diamond Joshua e/w at 66/1. Ouch.

I'm plotting up some value in the Stayers Hurdle. Steve scoffs at my intention to back Boss Doyle, the Wetherby specialist, at a truly shocking

50/1. So I back him anyway. An act of rash spite. I pay the price as he is predictably and hopelessly outclassed.

This is one of the best races of the festival. Baracouda is held up in rear for the entire first circuit, eventually nibbling away at the contenders. As Bannow Bay leaves the pack behind to push for home, Baracouda emerges and starts to reel him in. In a faultless, patient and classy ride, Thierry Doumen stalks his prey and ruthlessly pounces on the run in, taking Bannow Bay comfortably. Baracouda is the genuine article. Another success for JP McManus who was so convinced by the arguments of Bannow's trainer Christy Roche that he didn't even back his own horse.

More Fantasy Festival activity goes down before the Big One. Hushed tones, secrecy and furtive glances accompany the staking of tiny fractions of profit margins on short priced favourites by the main contenders. Meanwhile Brynaldo and I blow all our fantasy wedge (bar a minimum last race saver) on Behrajan and the Florida Pearl. Nick has sentimental, real and fantasy cash on Pipe's Shooting Light.

We gather by the rail. Me, Vaughany, Brynaldo, Nick and Steve. This really is something special. Months of research, keen anticipation and hours of pub talk all culminating in this moment of tight-lipped, breathless expectation.

The tape goes up and 18 of Europe's finest chasers set off at a cautious pace in a wide- open renewal of the premier event at the Steeple Chasing Olympics. As they roll past us to descend the hill with a circuit to go, Shooting Light is already struggling. AP McCoy pulls him up shortly afterwards. Nick's hurling abuse and scowling all over the place. Otherwise it's nip and tuck.

At the top of the hill, the picture suddenly changes. In a few short strides, the race is over for such luminaries as Behrajan, Shotgun Willy, Sackville, Florida Pearl, Foxchapel King, Bacchanal and Lord Noelie. That old lag See More Business is charging down the track like a four year old. And here comes Commanche Court, but Best Mate is playing with them. Biding his time. With the hallmark of true class he picks off the leaders, surges to the lead and is away. It's a defining moment in the chaser's career. Can't argue with that result.

Steve is beaming. Earlier he had promised to launch his headwear into the stratosphere if Best Mate trotted up. The sombrero is duly hurled in celebratory fashion high over the thronging mass (or should that be a massing throng?). Though it was quickly retrieved! For Steve, this was the Great Festival Saver Stakes. A sweet ante-post moment. His first and only successful punt of the campaign. But Bryn is in a different league. Best Mate delivered the 3rd glorious leg of an elusive and stunning Triple Crown. What a performance as he adds the Gold Cup to his other gems, the Champion Hurdle, and The Queen Mother! A remarkable achievement.

Nick is oblivious by now. He's taken refuge in the bar from the wind screaming off Cleeve Hill. I seek sanctuary too. I need to lick my wounds and consider how I can ever face the boys in the office after the Behrajan debacle. I subsequently discover that he injured himself during the race whilst jumping. Frankly, this was never going to be enough to save me! Why am I such a gobshite? Answers on a (small) postcard.....

The rest of the afternoon is a blur. I get a top spot next to the winning post to see Joe Blake give me a good run for my money in the Foxhunters. Me & Bryn sit out the Grand Annual as I stuff my face with further offerings of Festival fayre. Fadoudal du Cochet upsets the Pipe top weight handicap scam. Another victory for Ireland. Bryn is buoyed by the Triple Crown tucked away in his kit bag. But he ain't well. The drugs and adrenaline are wearing off. He's looking forward to his bed now.

It's Cathcart time and the Fantasy Festival is peaking with a three-way struggle between Vaughany, Gunner Goodwin and Mrs G. Steve is having trouble holding the ring as bets and saving bets and counter-punts at tiny stakes fly in from all quarters. It's getting a bit tense.

Steve's brother-in-law, Dave, appears. He's lumped big-time on David's Lad after consulting his Superform subscription. This is proper betting! How refreshing! But the RP prognosis is not good which seems to deflate Dave a bit. Looks like the horse is being saved for the Grand National.

The race is a procession. Royal Auclair pisses it. In style, mind. McCoy's 1st winner of the Festival and it comes in the penultimate race. Who would have guessed. And it means that Sharon has landed the fantasy trophy with some shrewd punting. Vaughany is bride's maid yet again. And I don't think this is the appropriate point to sully his reputation with potentially tarnishing allegations of 'choking', 'bottling it', etc. So I won't.

The last race is upon us. So soon already. But the betting action from our group is now down to a minimum. We are winding up and ready to head off home. Not for Dave, though. The Superform analysis suggests a wager on Fiori may be rewarding. Infact it is Rooster Booster who provides a memorable win and the Top Jockey gong for Richard Johnson. The Courage Best end is decorated with a million shredded pieces of Superform advice cast to the four winds. Dave heads of home skint but smiling.

A windswept John and Louise head off home after an unsuccessful day. Miraculously, Steve retrieves the bottle of 10 year-old oak-matured malt from its grassy knoll hiding place. The stewards missed it! We walk back through Cheltenham via O'Reilly's Bar, stopping only for Nick to relieve himself amongst Cheltenham's Regency flower beds. The 20 minute bladder-repeat syndrome, well known to all blokes of drinking age.

The Montpellier Massive are out tonight and it's party time. Me & Nick are a bit disgraceful in the pub, but it is like a shop window in there. What can you do? Don't think Mrs G is too impressed by our laddish behaviour. And me a New Man and all. Shocking. Time to cool off in the evening air.

The party continues on the train home. Steve breaks out the whisky and Nick is licking his lips. We are being caroused by a pissed Irishman who knows every miserable, maudlin ballad from 'Fields of Athanry' to 'A Pair of Brown Eyes'. Andrew is sat in front of this half-cut crooner and is doing a sterling impression of snoozing ambivalence. He even declined a tot of malt! I can't believe he's sleeping through that racket.

Meanwhile, there are a bunch of London lads behind us who are determined not to be outdone and launch their own repertoire of classics such as 'Roll Out the Barrel and, ooh, 'Doing the Lambeth Walk. Oi!' Nick has found his second wind and joins the smoking club at the end of the corridor in between polishing off Steve's whisky, and uttering "Denise will kill me!", and other epitaphs. But the excesses of the day are taking their toll on him. The eyebrows are knitting together. He's like a tinderbox. One spark and he'll be off like a firework.

Eh up, there's some developments over here. We've all clocked the classy filly sat across the carriage. All leather trousers and simpering accent. And she's up for a bit of sport. Steve's whipped out his Schedule of Shame, recording his Festival bets in his big glossy ledger. I can see she's registered this and she's pointing to it and whispering something to the lump of upper crust lard opposite her, sporting a Rupert The Bear waistcoat. She starts gesticulating and grinning. Quick as a flash I whip out my own Schedule of Shame. But it's not the same. Mine is thin. Steve's is thick. Mine is clean. Steve's has masking tape. Mine has pen. Steve has...... highlighters! Two colours. And a system. There's no competition really. Gunner vacates his pole position next to this highly strung filly and Steve slides up on the rails, opens the bible and settles himself in.
    "You see, I keep a record of all my bets. Would it help if I explained the colour-coding system.......?"
    "Oooh, Steve. This is fascinating! And do you win very, very often?" simpers the leather-trousered temptress.

Steve plays a blinder. The train journey goes on forever. This is a top class staying performance. The whisky is flowing and there's even a cheese board pulled from the depths of Rupert The Bear's nap sack! Sensational stuff. The temptress is getting off on the crack and she's up for a bit of a laugh.
    "Give us a song, Simon....er, Steve. Go on, you know you want to...."
    Steve tactfully demurs.

Even the best bred fillies need room to canter and she makes excuses to shimmy past Steve in search of the ladies cubicle. As it happens Nick is in search of the Gents. His twenty-minute syndrome taking full effect. He stands up at the same time and can't help but run his eyes up and down her perfectly presented fetlocks. He is unsure how to deal with this close encounter. If he had been wearing a monocle it would have popped off his face. If he was Terry Thomas he would have said "I say!" But he's Nick and he said "Christ I need a piss"....

Rupert the ponce is engaging Steve in some post-race chat. He comes out with a classic.
"I say Steve, if you don't like your bladdy job and London, and you simply larv the hawse game, well you should bladdy well get yourself a nice hice in the cantrey. Why not? That's what I say...."
You silly old upper class twat. Bet he doesn't get a shag tonight. Steve might...... Oh but too late, we've arrived at Paddington.

We've said our sad goodbyes and gone our separate ways. There's just me and Steve left waiting for the Eastbound tube. That melancholic feeling is beginning to kick in. The end of a great adventure, back to normality.

But hold up. There's Nick on the other platform. Blimey, he really is the worse for wear. He hasn't clocked us yet. Nick is stood right on the edge of the platform, lurching to and fro, legs akimbo, groin thrusting out, hands buried inside his crotch pockets. And there is an evil sneer on his face. He's chewing a piece of old gum, jaws working on it like a steamhammer, eyebrows joining in the middle of his scowling fizzog. He doesn't know we are here yet. A couple of likely lads pass within a couple of yards of him. The scowl intensifies and he burns a stare deep into their backs. It says
"Don't fuck with me unless you want your legs broken."
...right out of the Clash City Rocker manual, circa 1977.

So Steve and me try to attract his attention . Out come the remains of Rupert the Toff's extra-churned Somerset mature Cheddar and we start lobbing bits at him. After a few near misses, Nick catches sight of a block hitting the platform nearby. He follows the trajectory back across the tracks and stares at us. Blankly. For an eternity. As we wave at him maniacally, a glimmer of recognition spreads across his face. He explodes in a blaze of emotion skipping lightly through confusion, joy, irritation, humour and fear. We don't get any more sense out of him before he boards the tube. The last view is of Nick giving us the finger and the Vs as he disappears down the tunnel.
The next afternoon as I am reflecting on three excellent days at the Festival, I get this text message from Nick:
"Fell asleep on tube & ended up at Aldgate East. Trains stopped running. Night bus home - in bed by 3"
It was that kind of Festival really. Roll on 2003.

## 14. ACNE IN HACKNEY

*"And the hare upon the wire
Has been burnt upon the pyre
Like the dog that once raced
Out of Trap Two"*
The Pogues, *"White City"*, 1989

Time for another dose of nostalgia. Harking back to my student days, I had some early mug punting practice beyond the delights of the bitter North East. It was kick-started down in London. My best drinking mate, Simon, had got a top job in the 'big smoke' (we blunt Northerners like to think we could sneer with the best of the rest). Si was working for William Hill, Esq at a range of his betting emporia in SW London. When I say 'big smoke', I betray a glib Northern understanding of the concept; Simon had actually moved to his Sister's gaff in Guildford. Simon's patch had bookies fighting for survival amongst the smug suburban affluence of Porsches, Pimms and Abigail's Party: Tolworth, Surbiton, Leatherhead. Hardly West End.

It was the Summer holidays by the time me and my mate Tony got ourselves sufficiently organised for a visit. Simon was sharing a fantastic house in Greenwich owned by Manfred Mann of '60's pop fame; '5-4-3-2-1' and ' Do-Wah-Diddy' amongst his articulate repertoire. His flat mate, Helen, worked for Manfred and was doing some house-sitting for a while. So Tony and I waved our Student Railcards and were spirited away to taste a night on the town, Greenwich style. Next morning, with thick heads, thicker tongues and heaving stomachs, we hatched a multi-nodal, spatially-challenging (I was still a geography student after-all) gambling experience.

We planned to meet up with another mate of ours, Liz who had also pursued a career-developing southern slide. Her patch was more the sort of thing my Geography degree was telling me that I should see in big cities: urban squalor and deprivation. Liz was living in Hackney and studying Occupational Therapy at Homerton hospital. Another mate, Dave was coming down from Stafford and so we were 5 Yorkshire exiles taking on the camel-coated, sovereign-ringed geezers in residence at Hackney Dogs and Kempton Park Races. Bring it on.

We met Liz and Dave in town and cabbed it out to the 'London Stadium' from some obscure North London line station, the name of which is now lost to me.

Dog racing was a completely new experience. I wasn't expecting what I got. The stadium was grim at best. We were peering out at the bare track from the only covered stand. It had a corrugated iron roof, peeling red paint and a soulless bar. There were a few red plastic, damaged, classroom chairs arranged around 1970's vintage, fag-burnt Formica topped tables, littered with empty crisp packets and half finished drinks.

This was about as far away from glamorous gambling as it is possible to get. The greyhounds have always been the down-at-heel poor relation of horse racing: a working class sport run for small purses and producing few household names. Except Ballyregan Bob. Er, and Mick The Miller. Bizarrely, I met these two animals in the flesh - well almost - years later when I was taking my kids round Tring Zoological Museum. The girls were haring (no pun intended) up and down the aisles ogling at stuffed lions, zebras and eland deer. We approached the last glass case in the room and I was mortified to find these two legends of the oval circuit peering back at me. I had to check the little information board to be sure I wasn't being take for a ride. Ballyregan Bob and Mick the Miller, taxidermied and preserved forever in a dusty collection out in rural Hertfordshire. What an ignominious end. I was in shock all day.

But I digress. I suppose the dogs reached their zenith in a post-war Britain where inexpensive, round the week entertainment could be delivered to a sport hungry urban dominated population. Every city had at least one track, London was awash: White City, Wembley, Wandsworth amongst others have gone since the sport's 1950's peak. It seemed to be a sport in decline that day in Hackney too. There were not many punters around, maybe explained by the fact that this was a morning meeting (and we had already missed a couple of races on the nine-strong card). There were a few people dotted around the perimeter of the track and a few more outside wrestling with the half-dozen or so bookies' on their pitches.

Emboldened by a pint of gassy lager, I went outside for my first bet. I was soon back with my tail between my legs. I explained my plight to Si.
    "Bloody hell, this isn't the place for my little two-quid bets. It's like a gangland get-together out there."
There I was with my £2 ready to invest in the stripey trap, when the guy in front of me peeled of a string of twenties, grunted a number at the surly looking bookie and thrust the dosh into his big fat mits. This is a different world to my little each way bets. I looked at the pound coins in my hands and buried them deep in my pocket.
    "Yeah," responded Si with a chuckle, eyes narrowing against the bright day as he shot a glance down to ring, "It's a different world out here. This is hard core gambling, serious money, no prisoners taken".

Bloody right is was. Scared me to death - it wasn't for the likes of innocent college boys like me out there. I had these bruisers who spat expletives out of the corner of their mouths marked down as money launderers, pimps, drug runners and due-payers. Si nodded to the Tote windows at the other side of the bar. So I trusted the nice lady in the red jacket (thought I detected a Geordie accent) with my carefully saved student grant and watched dog number 6 get skittled over at the first bend by the 5-dog. Went down like a nine-pin. Limbs everywhere. Not pretty.

We had a few beers and had Simon explain the racecard info to us. Complete mystery to me. Liz offered some homespun wisdom.

"A bloke on the ward I'm working on said you have to watch the dogs and their handlers as they go down to the traps. Whichever one has a wee or number twos, well that's your puppy. Carrying less weight apparently. That's the key to it."
So we watched the preparations for the next race with an unhealthy interest in canine bowel movements. It got pretty silly, as well as futile. None of us won and we left before the last race to get down to Kempton Park for the second leg of our double header.

No regrets, then, about leaving London Stadium. The track was a hole and resided in a run down part of East London in need of significant regeneration. The sun was out and was beginning to draw a heady stench from the urine soaked litter piled up in doorways and alleys around the perimeter of the track. It was a bizarre place. On one side was an expanse of open ground bordering the stadium, presumably once the site of a factory; and on the other was an array of traditional businesses: taxi cab firms, kebab shops and junk emporia, as well as a smattering of empty and derelict two-storey, flat-roofed shops and terraced housing. The intimidating rubbish strewn urban jungle on this side of the road provided a brief, surreal counterpoint to the factory site on the other with its savannah of tall grass waving lazily in balmy mid-day sunshine.

No surprise to me that a few years later the dogs had gone and the had stadium closed; further rationalisation of the sport in London. And then, a few years later still, I read that the area has been chosen as the hub of Britain's Olympic Bid for 2012. Hackney dog track will be the site of an 80 000-seater flagship Olympic stadium. Ironic indeed. There's a picture on the back of The Independent showing the track littered with skips, sundry ironmongery and rubble. And there is the rickety enclosure we occupied with once proud letters proclaiming 'LONDON STADIUM, HACKNEY ' emblazoned below the holed roof. Only some of the letters have dropped away and HACKNEY is now _AC_NE_. Appropriate. Actually, I seem to be plagued by this theme of landmark buildings in my life closing down and manifesting into something else. The hospital I was born in is now a mental institution, my first school became a working mens' club, my first student flat share was in a condemned tower block now demolished and my first proper private sector flat share turned into a brothel. My first dog track becoming an Olympic stadium sits quite well compared to that lot.

Kempton Park was a different proposition. Well appointed facilities, proper bars, low minimum bets and high quality racing. Kempton's best fixture may well be the King George VI boxing day meeting, but it had a good flat programme as well. I immediately felt more at home. We arrived just after the 1st race, but there were a further 5 decent races ahead of us.

None of us had had much of a win at the dogs. I was a bit more confident that on common ground, I'd win some back. Alas. Mug punting was to be my downfall. Those 2nd favourites just didn't seem to go in. Dave, the canny bugger, landed a couple. Always played his cards close to his chest, did Dave. I never even found out how much he won. How he could spurn such an obvious gloating opportunity is beyond me. I bet they were each way wins though. Tony didn't have much luck either. But he was even more skint than me and slightly more sensible, so didn't have as many bets.

Apart from Dave, who slyly pocketed some notes, we all took a wallop. Si was taking his gambling fairly seriously then and I think he ended up losing some proper dough with a magnanimous shrug of the shoulders. There would be another day for Si though, starting tomorrow.

It's a fair old trek back to Greenwich and we were pretty jaded after tracing a convoluted route around London. Just one more call was left. Local landmark, The Cutty Sark was calling us. Glorious though the Tea-Clipper is, that night it was no match for the Cutty Sark pub further down the wharf. We five Yorkshire exiles combined to slag off Southern beer, whilst drinking copious amounts of it. The local ale Young's tasted like it had been hauled straight out of the Thames through a trap door in the floor of the boozer. Thin, pale and sour, we were soon slaughtered on the stuff. More irony. Five years later, I was living in the shadow of Youngs Wandsworth brewery, drinking regularly this quintessentially London ale.

It wasn't long before we were meandering our way back along the wharf and down the steps to check out the Thames, offering a little of the Youngs back as a mark of respect (Liz excepted).

So we all landed back at Simon's expansive pad rat-arsed, lairy and mud splattered. Helen's reaction on this invasion is unrecollected. But I do remember her turning up a few bottles of her home brewed red wine, which we downed whilst exploring her immense record collection. Fine woman I thought. I guess she made an impression on me. We were married ten years later.

## 15. BOUNDARY BOYS

*"If I didn't have bad luck I'd have no luck at all"*
Albert King, *"Born Under a Bad Sign"*, 1967

By late 1988 I had left college and moved to London to start my first proper job. The Summer just ended had been funded by working at the local Trout Farm as a fish gutter. It doesn't count as a proper job, but I'm sure I learned some useful skills that help equip one for life at large…..and if I'm ever stuck by a trout stream with only a razor blade for company I won't starve!

I'm still doing a bit of punting. A bit of interest here and there. I'm messing about with Lucky 15s, sometimes each-way Lucky 15s and placepots. These are all multiple and accumulator bets loved by the bookies because they require a whole series of results to drop the right way to cash in on the stake. Most things seem to be dropping out of the frame for me. I very rarely get my money back on these mug bets. I'm lucky to get one winner a meeting, never mind two, three or four to make some serious dough.

I discover that the office is a great place to ramble on about stuff in general. Betting gets an airing at about the time the 1990 Cheltenham Festival was kicking off. The festival is a cracker, of course. I have my lucky, lucky 15 on Champion Hurdle day, picking some obvious horses. I call my mate Simon who is still serving time for Billy Hills. He was in Leatherhead that day. I'm anxious to know how I've got on.
"Hello Dave. Be quick."
Polite as ever. It's one of his busiest days, needless to say.
"Who won the Champion Hurdle, Si?"
"Kribensis", he barks. "The favourite went in."
Excellent. One up, anyway. There's a bonus on single wins where the odds are doubled. So doubling up 95-40, well that's er, over 4-1! Phew.
"What about the first race and the, er, Arkle is it?" I continue falteringly.

The names of the three championship events to kick off Cheltenham were not yet seared into my grey matter. Bitter experience of subsequent years would lock the sequence of Supreme Novice, Arkle, Champion Hurdle into my consciousness.
"First race is the Supreme. Forest Sun won the Supreme at 7-4, another favourite and Commandante took the Arkle at, hang on, yeah, 9-2" confirms Our Man at the Bookies.

Well, I'm in business. I tell Si the details of my bet. It turns out that's the lot. Nothing for me in the Coral Cup.
"Yeah, marvellous Dave. Shame about all those favourites, otherwise you might have had a pretty penny today. 'Bout £40-odd quid, mate. Look gotta go. There's grannies queueing up with 25p each-way bets for the handicap finale. Laters, yeah?"

I don't know whether to feel elated or downcast. As Si was reeling off my winners I was floating on air. But then he says 'shame about the favourites' and I'm left feeling cheated. Still. This feels like a big win. If the fourth leg had come up I really would have been in the big time.

Of course I'm giving it the full works in the office the next day. It's a competitive office. Me, Rupert and Keith. All graduates in our first jobs in the Civil Service and all with very different ambitions. I collect my winnings and tell the boys it's like falling off a log. I don't have a bet on the middle day of the festival, but I still haven't stopped going on about it by the Thursday.

This time I'm pointing out the outrageous amount of money that went unclaimed on Wednesday's placepot. It's up around the £500 mark. I'm telling Keith & Rupert that all you have to do is pick a horse to finish in the first three or four in each race and you land the placepot. Piece of piss! So they are both up for it. My advice, based on years of thorough research, detailed analysis and hard won experience (I'd done placepots at least three times in the last 6 months!) was that picking the favourite or 2nd favourite in each race was a sure fire nailed on banker. Oh, and to double up in races with big fields. So we are off. Pen chewing and stewed coffee inspire a range of interesting selections. I inform the boss of our Cheltenham swoop, request the afternoon as leave at ridiculously short notice, and hare back home with £6 of placepot lines each. Marvellous.

We don't make it passed the 1st race. The Sun Alliance Novice chase with a field of about 25 does our dough. The favourite, Regal Ambition, romps home. Horses we've picked like tombola tickets, Fort Noel and Tinryland are nowhere to be seen. Probably never heard of again.

Of course I had to ring the office and relay the bad news. No internet provision in those days of information underload. I was not flavour of the month.
       "You wanker, Atkinson!" is Rupert's standard response in these circumstances.
He still claims I owe him 300 notes. I'm dismissed as a " 'Kin joker". Glad he saw the humour.

The office was a fantastic introduction to the work culture. We got away with long lunchtime leaving drinks, office cricket and mindless banter. In addition to Keith, Rupert and myself there was Viv, a glamorous 30-year-old vixen, and Marianne our psycho-analyst boss, as scatty as a Cleo Lane impersonator. I remember Marianne's wise words when Keith got a transfer elsewhere in the Department, in doing so breaking up the dream team.
       "Enjoy this set up. Milk it for all you can. Because you will be hard pushed to work in such a relaxed, laid back office again. You'll be lucky to find people who get on this well and you won't get the freedom or lack of responsibility any where else."

Rupert sat opposite me and would perpetually lean back on his chair against the window which framed an exquisite Westminster skyline, and muttered things like "Mmm, tricky Heathrow boundary issue". Or went to extra-ordinary lengths to avoid being drawn by Marianne's devilish and increasingly desperate plans to get him to wrap a timetable around his proposal papers. My Mum rang up one day and Rupert answered the phone.

"Dave? No he's not here." He leant back on his chair, craned his neck round to look at Big Ben and then said "'Spect he's having his mid-afternoon dump by now!"

My Mum loved Rupert, cheeky git that he is, and was almost sorry when I was there to pick up the phone. She missed him when I moved jobs!

Rupert was a wiry bloke of Malaysian decent. He was a climber by instinct and a lazy git by choice. He spent most of his days staring out of the window, hands on hips scowling at the weather and saying,

"Bloody top bouldering weather, this. What am I doing here? Those useless forecasters have got it wrong again. I could be down at Tunbridge Wells getting stuck into a couple of v.diffs."

Keith would typically riposte something like:

"Rupert, you are approaching 30. You must be the only trained geographer I know who still believes the weather forecast!"

Roo was seriously obsessive about his climbing. He would ramble on about it all day and disappear on the leave at the slightest break in the weather. We all became experts on the terminology of climbing. We had no choice. Difficulty ratings like E3s and E4s would trip off the tongue; we all felt compelled to discuss the merits of pieces of kit like cramp-ons, rubberised climbing boots and dodgy lycra trousers; and we knew exactly on which part of Lundy was home to the formidable Devils Lime Kiln route. This was a series of sea cliff climbs on the obscure bird-watchers paradise in the Bristol channel. It was Rupert's nemesis. He had identified a new route on this complex, had 'cleaned it off' and was ready to climb it for the first time and claim naming rites. This last point is the crux of climbing. Naming a route is about as good as it gets in climbing mythology. Apparently. Circumstance and bad luck meant he never completed his mission. But I've rarely encountered such hardline enthusiasm. Like all the best diseases, it was infectious.

Hard life though, climbing. He tells a classic story of near disaster in Hathersage when climbing in the Peak District. He had pitched up on the Friday night and downed a good few beers before rising early to tuck into a climbers breakfast at the local café well used to satisfying demanding climbers' appetites. Not long after he and his mates were ready to make the first ascent of the Matterhorn without oxygen (or something), when he felt serious rumblings.

He jumped out of the car and into the local public lavs near the bus station. The world was dropping out of his bottom in a potent mixture of Stones real ale and sausage fry-up when he noticed that there was no bog paper. Too late. Rupert was in the middle of a nasty incident for which only a small bale of blotting paper would suffice. He was horror struck and powerless. He rifled through his coat and managed to find a pocket diary. He started ripping the pages out one by one to attend to his needs.

"I got to November before I could stem the flow!" he said in his own illustrative way.

A close run thing.

Keith, a ginger-haired Scotsman with big alcohol consumption and small bladder capacity had a fantastic football bet the year before. Keith has impressive sports knowledge and was flaunting a comprehensive grasp of American football long before any real popularity surge in England with the arrival of joke has-beens like 'The Fridge'. For all his derisory comments about England and the English game, he also knew his domestic football inside out. In early January he spotted that Liverpool had drifted to a whopping 20/1 for the double. He had a speculative fiver's worth. Arsenal were strolling to the Championship at the time, but as the season wore on Liverpool clawed their way into the frame and it became a two horse race.

Eventually, the Scousers stole a march on the Gunners and were title favourites. The office monitored the progress of this bet closely. 20/1 now looked an absolute steal. Liverpool cleaned up in the FA Cup and in the final match of the season they met Arsenal, their only rivals for the League, in an Anfield title showdown. Liverpool would win the title and land a first ever back to back doubles unless Arsenal beat them by two clear goals. Away from home. Unlikely.

Ho Ho. Keith thought the money was in the bag. So did we. So did his girlfriend. Telling Alison that he was about to collect on his inspired gamble betrayed an uncharacteristic and surprising over-confidence in Keith. She was no fan of punting, but was quite happy to liberate the profits for a down-payment on a new carpet. She was pretty sick when Michael Thomas slotted the second goal between Bruce Grobelaar's legs in the final few moments of that knife-edge thriller. But not half as sick as Keith. Gutted is not the word. Neither do the culinary terms shish-kebabed, filleted, skewered, flambéed or spit-roasted adequately describe his feelings.

The money was almost in his clutches, only to be ripped away in the most dramatic of circumstances. I was horrified for Keith. 20/1 was a fantastic price. Bold gambles like that deserve to be rewarded. Roo on the other hand roared with laughter. He absolutely howled when the final whistle blew. I know. I could hear him from the other side of London.

This was a mid-week game and the troubled Scotsman was visibly shaken when we saw him at work the next day. He struggled to speak.

But this was a mere ripple in a North Sea gale when compared to Scotland's humbling at the hands of Costa Rica in the World Cup at Italia '90. Even by Scotland's standards, their meek capitulation 1-0 to the

Central American minnows was a horror show. It immediately extinguished any serious hopes of the Jocks progressing through a group which also featured the mighty Brazil. Keith was seriously affected. He literally did not utter a vowel to anyone in the office unless it was bona-fide boundary business.

This lasted for three days. On the third day, we had a fire alarm and had to evacuate the building. Ironically, the London Fire and Civil Defence Authority were located in the building next door. They didn't see the funny side of sending out their shiny helmets about three times a week to our office. Building works on the top floor were playing havoc with the fire alarms, apparently.

So we all collected on the pavement, shuffling around and making small talk, as you do, whilst awaiting the sour faced fire-boys to turn up. But not quite all of us were doing the polite conversation thing. Keith was alone on the other side of the road, looking blankly into a grey and listless River Thames. He had his back to us. Rupert and I were pointing and laughing, but he failed to respond. He didn't even look away from the river, preferring to contemplate his doom in splendid isolation. Viv was running out of patience.
    "What *is* he doing? Is he mad?"
She had gone past humour and run headlong into frustration. This was true of Alison, Keith's other half too, it transpired. She rang up during these silent hours to ask if he was speaking to anyone in the office
    "….because he certainly isn't at home!"
It was hilarious to see Keith stone-walling Rupert's outrageous jibes. The dam finally burst later that day. The first trickle appeared after finishing a purely business phone call. He replaced the receiver, focused on something in the middle distance and said quietly,
    "Every time. Every bloody time…."
This was a surprisingly restrained and understated way to express the bottomless exasperation brought about by the repeated crushing of expectation.

Keith claims he has got better at dealing with defeat over the years. He's had plenty of practice. Ha Ha. In his new job everyone in his team knows that he is a huge Hibs as well as a Scotland supporter. Hibs reached the Tennents Scottish League Cup Final earlier this season. Keith had got hold of tickets for the game at Hampden Park and returned home for the game. Hibs succumbed in a dreadful game to Livingstone. Even in the fairly shallow pool that is Scottish premiership football, Livingstone are absolute tadpoles. This was a bad day for Keith. This feeling was not lost on his team back at the office.

Despite his efforts to emphasise his approachable and engaging manner, the next morning his office door was closed to the rest of the team. His demeanour might not always re-inforce his approachable nature. Indeed he candidly admits that people have observed that he 'could smile a bit more' and that he 'seems to frown a bit'. So Keith was ensconced within.

Nothing sinister - perhaps a personal phone call needed to be made - when the door opened a tiny crack. Just enough for a hand to squeeze through and place a box of chocolate digestives on the table. And for a voice to float through the opening.

"We're all really sorry about Hibs, Keith".

Then the door closed.

He tells me that he can even be gracious in coping with his team's defeats. No matter how intense the pain. I'm not entirely sure he's convinced everyone......

## 16. THREE BLOKES AT THE OAKS

"It makes you wonder. It makes you proud
To play for England. And hear the crowd"
*England World Cup Squad, "This Time", 1982*

"Seen this?"
Steve proffers today's Racing Post. Next to the Daily Naps competition and just below the Ripon Top Draw info (esoteric reading) is an advert for the *Punters' Package - The Oaks at Epsom Downs*. Me, Nick and Steve are toying with the idea of a day at the races, if not a night at the opera. Brynaldo, though, has counted himself out of the running.
   "I don't do the flat," he claims.
Ah, but we remember Brighton.

Steve, no surprise, is keen as mustard. He went last year and had a stonking afternoon. He's no stranger to classy afternoons at the races. That same Summer he gained access to the members' enclosure at Ascot on the back of his mate's racehorse-owning brother. The occasion was the King George VI and Queen Elizabeth Diamond Stakes. It was here that the season's wonder horse, Ballydoyle's Galileo famously trounced Godolphin's Fantastic Light, the leading horse from the previous year in an epic encounter. The duel ran on all Summer and the two met again at Leopardstown. Fantastic Light prevailed in that heavyweight shoot out. In the analysis of that gladiatorial race, the Racing Post began by saying, 'It seems almost a pity to have to analyse this race in dispassionate terms. A truly heroic battle deserves to linger in the memory as a magnificent spectacle between two outstanding racehorses.'

Steve had seen a blinder. What a quality affair when you get to hang out in the parade ring in your best bib and tucker, watching the cream of Europe's fillies turned out to perfection. The horses are game too; it's a Group 1 meeting after all. I remember Steve describing how he saw Aiden O'Brien carefully giving out last meeting briefings to his jockeys only a stones-throw away. It doesn't get much bigger than that. Apparently The Queen brushed passed later.
   "Wotcha Clarkey!" she is rumoured to have uttered.

Back to Epsom. The day has all the hallmarks of a cracking day out. Nevertheless, we are on the horns of a dilemma. The 2002 World Cup is moving into full Japanese swing and England are due to play Argentina at the Sapiro Dome on the very day of the Oaks meeting. The punter's package includes entrance, beer vouchers, food tokens (two very persuasive arguments), a bet at the Tote, and free RP and racecard, fondue set and cuddly toy all for the knock down price of £15. The small print is even juicier. "Giant diamond vision screen showing uninterrupted coverage of England v Argentina before racing starts." It's a Noon kick-off and the first race has been put back 40 minutes to accommodate this rival sporting attraction on the other side of the globe. Enlightenment at last! We are up for it and Steve takes himself off to acquire the said package.

It's an early start for me from the leafy byeways on the other side of London. A bit like the expedition to Cheltenham, I end up catching my normal work train. I have the advantage of being in civvies and I feel smug about it as I check out the *commuters*. They are a breed apart, and today I feel a couple of notches up the evolutionary ladder. Now boarding at platform 5 are the Hemel Menopausal Maidens, a gaggle of 5 or 6 stony-faced middle-aged women gossiping and moaning and criticising whilst caking make-up to their craggy features.

In front of me sits a dead ringer for Richard Pitman. Honestly, I do a double-take whenever I see him and have to restrain myself from asking how it felt when Red Rum robbed him and Crisp of the 1974 Grand National. Today, he's even wearing a Pitman-esque Navy blazer with brass buttons and a pair of grey flannels. He's probably more rotund than our TV race-day host, but he sports the same over-size glasses, balding head and signet ring on the little finger. He's accompanied by a youth with a case of bad body language. Looky-likey turns to the youth and in a voice far more plummy than the real thing, says,

"So what lessons are you missing out on this morning Robert? Damn shame. Loved school m'self. Golly yes."

The youth does the full Kevin Teenager act, wriggling in his seat, pulling a face, mumbling a vowel-less grunt and burying his face in *Skateboard Stunts for C....* magazine (couldn't see the last word).

Nick and Steve jump on at Clapham Junction as I'm polishing off a Burger King brekkie. They wouldn't expect anything less. I've managed to scribble down this week's fantasy cricket scores in between tearing lumps out of a bacon and sausage bap. The scores easily provide diversionary conversation until we hit Tattenham Corner. It's still early season and despite Steve's blistering start in the competition, we all still think we can win. The idyll of early season optimism. Sometimes it's all some of us have to cling to.

The grand old Epsom Downs are sheathed in low cloud. A hint of drizzle, rather than the answer my friend, is blowing in the wind. The route from the station to the main entrance takes us past the 5f sprint start on a spur off the main track. There is a considerable drop down to the winning post from here and the famous sweep of Tattenham Corner is really obvious too. This course has traditionally posed a serious challenge to the thoroughbred who is asked to run over constantly changing gradients across an adverse camber and frequently at a break neck pace. The fact that the World's best known race is run over such a testing track has caused concern on plenty of occasions since Lord Derby and Lord Bunbury inaugurated the blue ribband in 1780. Henbit won the 1980 Derby in stunning style, but was found to have cracked a canon-bone and tragically never raced again. There is a risk attached to racing at whatever level and in any conditions, whether it is the helter skelter of Brighton in a dust bowl or a 3 mile slog round Towcester in bottomless ground. I'd hate to see uniformily even and fair tracks at every course. Racing would lose something. "Come racing. You always leave richer for the experience." mutters Alistair Down in his laconic style from inside my telly most Saturdays. As if to underline my sentiments. Alistair is right. You never leave the races any poorer. Horse racing has an intrinsic value beyond gambling and prize money. Tracks like this embody that notion.

Steve is busy explaining the bias of the draw advantage, the location of the freshest piece of ground close to the stands rail and the soft ground.
"Anything with a wide berth here as no chance in tomorrow's sprint. You need to be factoring in low draws."
Nick is distracted by something else to be factored in to the day's proceedings.
"Seen this fair? Fantastic. Sorted for later then."
He's eying up the big wheel and this bizarre spinning cage affair, still being attended to by some dodgy looking mechanics. Steve is halted in full flow.
"Yeah, you need to be against that far rail as early as possible. That sprint is going to be a cracker, but looking at that ground........yer what Jenkins? Hmmmm. I'm not a big fan of these childish rides."
He's going a bit green. Think I remember this from Brighton too.

It takes us ages to get in. The Punter's Package may represent good value, but pompous stewards are not as easily impressed. Our down at heel value tickets do not warrant us entrance through the badge holders' moated, ballustraded, bannered and doric-columned gateway. Instead, we are ushered with gloved hands through a side turnstile, hidden from the view of the main entrance, at the base of the grandstand and past the junk food sellers (behind a door marked 'beware of the tiger', as Douglas Adams would have it.) You get the picture.

We have plenty of time to check out the best view of the track from the Grandstand, recce the best food franchises, and even lodge our placepot selections. Probably most important of all we set up camp in front of one of the two giant screens which will show the footie. We are sheltering from the interminable drizzle under a temporary marquee where a covers band of Abba-likes are belting out a series of 70's and 80's crowd pleasers. It's just like the Clapham Grand on a Saturday night; only the crowd are more interested and worse dressed. There's a nice atmosphere building. We've exchanged beer tokens and are well into the second round of widget-smoothflow-no-nonsense-traditional-Irish-cream-ale froth. Whatever, it slips down a treat. All the talk is suddenly of football. The big screen is showing soundless big match build-up snippets and there is a huge roar of approval to a Mohican-ed Beckham interview with "Dancing Queen" overdubs courtesy of our house band. Appropriate.

We are not the only ones necking frothy beer like there's a run on carbon dioxide. The crowd is building as fast as the TV hype and there are plenty already bladdered. We've got some renditions of "Vindaloo" emerging from the rowdies at the back, giving "With A Little Help from My Friends" from the band a serious run for it's money.

Close to kick off now and the volume has been cranked up a few notches. I'm experiencing that comfortably heady cocktail of alcohol, anticipation and adrenalin, leaving me tingling and wired. And, by now, pissed. Nick and Steve are the same. They are glowing and we exchange insane grins and battle cries at every new face on the screen. Football may be my third choice sport these days, but there is no denying the sense of occasion that a big World Cup game, with buckets of ancient history and recent controversy, can bring. The game has been set up perfectly by England's stonking and, frankly unexpected 3-0 demolition of the quietly fancied Danes. This is a World Cup of upsets, of turmoil and this is the nation's biggest game for four years.

Epsom has the atmosphere of an intense football mad pub, only we are out doors and there are thousands here. Just before kick-off, the telly does its 'the day the nation stopped for football' slot and we are treated to scenes of crowds up and down the country waiting for the off. Bugger me, there we are! Almost. There's a shot from the air of Epsom Downs with its throng of punters gathered in front of the screens. The place goes wild and the massive cheer is only surpassed by the gritted-teeth call to arms of the kick-off.
    "C'moooooon!"

We've moved outside to get a better view of the screen, despite the drizzle. It's tense stuff. England look composed with no early scares. But the sound is atrocious. No one can here Motty's patronizing alliterations and pointless observations. Someone eventually finds the remote control, but the commentary is drowned out every time Simeone gets the ball.
    "Booooooooo. Cheating bastard."
He got our golden boy Beckham sent off in France you know. Or when Owen shimmies and shapes anywhere in the Argies' half. Beers are still slipping down and maybe that's to blame, but to my cynical old eyes, England seem to be making a fist of it. They are taking the game to the opponents and all playing well. Sinclair is inspired down the left flank, and there goes Danny Mills with some intelligent runs down the right, putting in some decent crosses. Even Heskey fizzes a breathtaking volley passed the oppo's upright.

I'm at the bar ordering refills when Beckham threads the ball through to Owen on the edge of the box. He's on a jinking run across the goal-face inside the box and his dancing feet do everything asked of them. The defenders can't resist and are suckered in to the challenge. A little nibble at Owen's feet is enough to precipitate a crashing fall and a penalty to the boys in red. I'm half way through collecting the beers, but the World, even drinking, stops for a few moments. Beckham, looking lost in this massive indoor stadium, tries to collect himself. He's as nervous as hell, I can feel him shaking. But at least he's taken the Captain's responsibility. He steps up to the ball as I step up to the front. It's a crap penalty, down the centre of the goal and at a nice height for the keeper as Big Ron is probably saying somewhere. But it doesn't matter cos the Keeper is infact sprawling away to the left chomping turf. The place goes bananas. Fantastic stuff. By the time I've collected the ale and picked my way through a few more dancing feet, it's half time. Celebration time. Time to relive the moment with the boys.

I get a text message from Hughesy who's somewhere in deepest New Cross with Stu and a few of the other boys from the office.
  'TAKE THAT BECKHAM BOMB AND HAVE SOME MORE ARGEY BARGEY. HEYHEY!'
I think he's happy. This is not the moment to consider the profound effect that text messaging is having on our communication skills.
  "For God's sake, I hope they don't come out and play like pansies in the second half", implores Nick.
  "You know like England do. Time after time, we try to sit back on a lead and defend deeper and deeper. We invite the opposition on to us and think we can play like the Italians do. We can't defend like that. It's not our natural game."
Agreement all round.
  "And look at the way we ran the game in the 1st half. We should be looking to make the game safe, but I bet we end up sitting on it and giving everyone heart failure", adds Steve.

Never was a truer word spoken. A few glimmers apart, we watch a nerve wracking, tortuous 45 minutes of grim football. To be honest, Argentina never came close to scoring and we heartily cheer their increasingly desperate substitutions. The final whistle is greeted with an almighty roar. The euphoria of Beckham's goal is still fresh and we are intoxicated. The goal cements his reputation and completes a neat circle of rehabilitation after his sending-off exactly 4 years ago.

We've all got those beaming faces and cheeky expressions that say:
  "Well that was ace. What next?"
Well, next is the Princess Elizabeth Stakes, Class A (listed) 1m ½ f £22,750 to the winner. Steve has no trouble switching his attention and ploughs into the RP with the voracious appetite of a man on half rations. Me and Nick are a bit more circumspect. I'm still wrapped in an indulgent wallow, so the hustle and bustle of the ring doesn't appeal as much. And I don't get an adrenalin-fuelled rush of excitement when the 6 declared beasts crash out of the gates on the far side of the track. I think I'm suffering adrenalin deficiency. All my reserves have been used up during the game. My body is going
  "Sorry, Dave, but me and the other glands have had about enough. You'll have to wait a while and watch the next couple of races with an air of detached cool and academic observation."
Which is what I do.

But Steve doesn't. He's on Kootenay. She's a soft ground specialist and lands the Princess Elizabeth easily (4 lengths) at a useful 11/4 from an under-performing Golden Silca. It's a top start, Steve has played the soft ground card to perfection and he's well set for the afternoon. Kootenay led from flag to post and absolutely reveled in the conditions.

The Coronation Cup is up next. The meeting's Derby for older horses. This is a good race and I'm coming out of my torpor. I'm on Storming Home who almost, but not quite, does. One for later in the season maybe. The soft ground is causing all sorts of grief and the races seems to be about getting to the Stands rail off the camber at the final bend. Tactical maneuvers to get the best out of a strip of better ground in front of the corporate boxes seems to be deciding some of the races. The German raider Boreal wins in good style at 4/1, with a healthy string of top performers in his wake. All Conquering Godolphin's Kutub, sent off favourite, trails in a desolate last.

Time for more refreshment before the Oaks. Chicken baguettes do the job nicely, as we shelter from the drizzle inside. Everyone else has had the same idea and we can't get to the rammed bar. This is no barrier to Clarkey though. With that devilish look in his eye and employing silky skills first seen when mopping up discarded chicken and chips at the Great British Beer Festival, he's rounded up three abandoned pints of fizzy lager. Way to go! Nick's laughing is head off at the bare-arsed cheek of it. Steve's grinning too, but indignant. "Well if they can't be arsed to look after their ale, they deserve to lose it!"

I've been studying the Oaks a bit. Checking the form against the classic trials earlier in the Spring, some of which I'd seen on the telly and I'm watching the market. I've had a little ant-post bet on Aiden O'Brien's Quarter Moon, so has Steve. But I'm also looking at two outsiders who came through earlier races with credit: Snowflake and Spinette. There's a question mark against them over the state of the ground, but that's reflected in the price. I have a little dip. We go down to the rail for this race.

The soft ground seems to mess them up again, as what looks like a strong Oaks, in terms of the quality on offer, becomes more of a slog through the testing ground. It's Kazzia, under a strong ride from Frankie Dettori, who burns off her nearest rivals, most notably the well-touted Islington who appears to hate the cloying conditions. Quarter Moon comes late to give Frankie a fright, getting her nose right up Kazzia's hindquarters, and finishing with a bullet. A sight for these sore eyes at least. But the post comes too soon and Kazzia lands an impressive 1,000 guineas/Oaks Classic double. My outsiders prove to be just that in this mire - 10th and last.

There's some Class C 3-y-o handicap next, which doesn't trouble me too much. Keiron Fallon romps home on Lingo against the stands rail. We are back in the grandstand bar admiring a craftsman about his business. Steve is coming back to our perch with full cans of unopened group 1 bitter, liberated from an array of careless owners. It's a top performance. We polish off the round and with encouragement from Nick and Steve, I go off in search of replenishments. But it's no good. I don't have Steve's panache. I'm loitering around tables, trying to check out who might be leaving an untended beer and after a few ums and aahs, I return empty handed. Nick is scathing of my efforts. Rightly so. And Steve is even more forthright.

"Diffident bastard", or some such he mutters as he strolls, brazenly around the bar, shamelessly lifting fresh cans of John Smith's as if he's doing the cleaning up at the end of the night.

Dumaran, another soft ground specialist takes the next handicap. I'm beyond caring by now. My phone rattles a merry tune. It's Stu, trolleyed and lairy, tearing up some south London pub.

"Dave, Dave. Fuckin' hell, Dave. Mate. Never in my life, not ever in my living memory, have we beaten them bastards. But today we did. We fuckin' did it. We done 'em!"
His voice is cracking with emotion, or too much shouting. Not sure which.

"What a day. Fuckin' give that ponce Beckham his due. He did it today. Have any winners yet you old bastard....?"
But he's already long gone before I can answer. The phone has probably disappeared down the toilet, or down the barmaid's front.... I dread to think. He's happy. The World Cup is big event for the boys in the office. No one has seen them since the middle of May.

Next up, the 7f Surrey Stakes. I've had an adventurous exacta on red-hot Red Liaison with Oases, whom I note is jockeyed by Pat Smullen, resplendent in the fine powder blue colours of Gallagher Equine. Odds-on Red Liason screams home by 2 ½ lengths and I'm cheering on the blue of Oases into second. Yowzer! A penultimate race saver. Fav and 2nd fav in an exacta won't make me rich, but I'm already working out how many stakes I'll recover as go to see those lovely ladies in red.

Nick and Steve see the replays and realise I've been cheering on the wrong bleedin' nag. Terfel at 6/1 whose jockey also sports natty blue silks, has taken 2nd spot by half a length. The ladies cast me sympathetic smiles as they hand back my Tote slip.

"Sorry darling, this is a losing ticket." They say, each in Geordie accents.
I try three windows before I accept that it's not their mistake. It's mine. I must cut a forlorn figure as I head back to the bar to be received by Nick and Steve's howling laughter. Steve decides it's worth another beer. But he's getting reckless now. He saunters up to a table populated with punters checking out the replay of the last race on a nearby telly. The artful dodger edges in, spots a tinny and casual as you like picks it up. Only his eagle eyed-neighbour has rumbled him and takes it from our intrepid hero's grasp.

"Oh, sorry", says Steve, nice as pie. "I thought that was mine."
So then he stands there for a few more minutes bold as brass, with me and Nick roaring abuse from two tables away. Steve's passing the time of day with the bloke he's just tried to rob.

"Thought Kinane should have pressed the button earlier."
"Red Liason won the German 1000 Guineas I see."
"Good effort from Terfel, stepping up."

Balls of steel. Cheek of iron. He returns beerless but unscathed. Lucky he didn't get a twatting.

It's the lucky last. A 7f handicap is as lucky as can be. Nick lumps on Johnny Ebeneezer who pulls out a scintillating display to take the race by the scruff of the neck and stamp his presence all over the opposition from 1f out. He eases home a comfortable 3 lengths clear and Nick's delighted. Rightly so, what a way to finish. He's ended up clear in profit after a sparkling day out. Strains of 'E's are good, e's are good. He's Ebeneezer Goode' can be heard soaring above a soggy Epsom as we head for the station.

Nick persuades us to take in the funfair. I swear this has been in his mind all day, and even more so now that there is money burning a hole in his pocket. Steve is reluctant. I don't think he likes these harum-scarum activities. We take in a couple of the rides, waving at Steve from our rocket ship swooping over the Downs and from the roller coaster, giving spanking views across the racecourse. Steve gives us one of those patronizing 'grow up children' smiles and looks longingly at the train station.

Next, Nick wants to investigate the contents of his stomach on that death-trap ride we saw earlier which involves being strapped to the side of a circular cage and being spun round at a million miles an hour whilst performing geometric miracles on a revolving axis. Not for me thanks. I prefer to fill my stomach rather than empty it. Think I'll have a large hot dog.

In my absence, Nick has dismounted, claiming to have enjoyed the experience and is squaring up to a punch bag. He takes a good old look, a couple of paces back and unleashes a mighty swing. Which misses the bag completely and registers a big, fat zilch. Ha. Ha. My turn. Same scenario. I'm giving the bag my best evils, focusing on the point of impact. I proceed to swing with precision and efficiency, but catch only the very outlying stitches of the bag and register but a flicker on the Richter scale. Steve, seeking to make up for his jessie-like behaviour on the rides, condemns with a scowl over the top of his spectacles and right hooks the leather ball into next week. Easy as you like. We decide it's time for bed, Florence.

But there's till time for one more diversion. We have to change trains at East Croydon. So it only makes sense to see how the town rates on the curry stakes. There's a long old hike down the main drag to find a Balti House, but we are rewarded with a fine meal, and attended to by an array of superior staff. I think we are even civil to them despite the trials of the day.

I get home late. I'm shattered. But there's a light on. Don't understand. I open the door and have to pick my way over the debris of empty wine bottles, scrapings of soft French cheese and crusts of bread. Helen is entertaining her friend Julie who is staying over. "Wasn't Danny Mills an absolute star today. Do you think we can really forgive Beckham everything? Has Sinclair got a future? Heskey's a donkey......." Julie's a Leeds fan and hadn't had anyone sensible to talk to about the game all day. She was getting no joy out of Helen. So the late night became later. I open my bag and crack open one of the five cans of lager Steve has re-distributed........

## 17. BLUE EIDERDOWN

"Follow men's eyes as they look to the skies.
The shifting shafts of shining weave the fabric of their dreams"
Rush, "Jacob's Ladder", *1980*

Rays of sunshine are slanting through my office window at a low angle. They highlight a sheen of dust covering my pc screen. Summer is exhaling easily into Autumn. I'm peering at the screen through the reflection (squinting is an easier option than moving the window blinds on this soporific Thursday) when an e-mail from Brynaldo pops up in the new messages box.

It's ten past four. This missive can only mean one thing.

"Fancy a swiftie after work boys? WW 5-10?"
Sound.

The late summer holidays have reduced our number by one: Nick is residing in a villa in Southern France with his folks. It's just me and Bryn. Steve joins us for his customary two-pint slurp. It's busy down the 'Walk and we squeeze in at the bar. It's the climax of the fantasy cricket season and there is a bit of chat on the topic, but Steve has the league all but sewn up. So there is very little wind-up mileage on that front.

Bryn is a newly expectant Father and is taking his pre-paternal duties seriously. Not least among them is finding a house for himself, Debs, and his child-to-be for the occupation thereof. Very responsible, Brynaldo. Indeed, he slips away this very evening after a couple to put the finishing touches to his property scam which involves buying a house near Nick in Worcester Park in order to force down the value, buy up the stock and become a tyrannical landlord. Only the first part of this sting is currently in place.

Mild surprise then, that come the six o'clock watershed, it's me and Steve propping up the veneered MDF. Not me and Brynaldo. Conversation inevitably turns to the approach of the jumps season. It may not represent the thoroughbred gold mine of racing, but certainly lays claim to its heart and soul. My interest in the flat season peaked with our trip to the Oaks, followed by the festival of racing at Royal Ascot. I've been on the wane since. As have my proceeds. I don't think I've had a winner since June. So we look forward and we wax lyrical about the return of Best Mate who may well stamp his champion class all the over the stayers division; about the emergence of Seebald and Moscow Flyer, the unproven credentials of Armaturk; and their ability to mix with the big boys - the prospect of the novice class of 01/02 moving up to handicap and championship company.

But it's still a shock, despite this Grade-class banter, that before we know it, the black hole is gaping before us. That strange twist of the elements that conspire to swallow time in the pub between 7.30pm and 10pm.

Where does that time go? One minute you are finishing off the last pint
ready to get your coat and be home in time for tea, and the very next
moment you are pissed, late, skint and sniffing out kebabs with the zeal of
a hunter/gatherer. It's beyond me. I glance at Steve (who's playing it
canny it has to be said.)
"Fancy one for the road then?"
"I can squeeze one in if you are sticking around", he offers.
Dangerous, loose talk is this.
"Yeah, I think I'm OK for another", and then to the barman, "two
pints of the guest ale please?"
It's slipping down well, this stuff. It's the dog's bollocks. No really it is.
Wychwood Dogs Bollocks, OG 1048, brewed in darkest Kent.
"Sorry mate, there's a £5 minimum on card purchases."
I look at my sorry piece of plastic. I've already done my real dough - the
wallet is empty. It's just like being down the bookies.
"OK, make it four pints - and £30 cashback please."
Steve throws his head back; his laugh is shot through with resignation and
inevitability. We set the controls for the heart of the black hole and settle
in for the duration.

Before the kebab rush, we have organised a day out at Exeter on 5
November. It's a good early season card whose jewel-encrusted crown is
the Haldon Gold Cup: a stiff 2-mile 1.5f around the moor's undulations.
Henrietta Knight has already declared her intention to send Best Mate for
his season's pipe opener, and Armaturk and Seebald are both likely
runners. We set the seal on our good idea with a couple of well deserved
Jameson's and head off into the (long departed) sunset.

Come the big day we are still on course. There have been a couple of
minor blips to negotiate, such as the realisation that 5 November is bonfire
night (remember, remember), with all its attendant family commitments.
Not to mention Hen Knight decides, in the end not to run stable star Best
Mate at Exeter (allegedly because of going concerns, but more likely
because an easier blow first time out at Huntingdon in a week's time is
more attractive). Edredon Bleu goes instead. No mean substitute. And we
are not deterred.

The Burger King at Paddington is just as I remember it from the heady
Cheltenham rendezvous eight long months ago. But I'm late, harassed and
slagging off the tubes. Steve, by contrast, is a panacea of calm. He has no
right to be. He's told Debs that he's bound for a meeting of the SW
England Tree Preservation Officers in Exeter. Outrageous. She won't be
pleased when she reads this!

But we have bucket loads of time and I easily recover my natural poise
and equilibrium on the journey down. Not many other obvious race goers
on view. Certainly there's an absence of drunken Irish/cockneys/upper
class twats; and a desperate dearth of leather trousers. We cab it out to
Haldon and are entertained by our cabess's charming ignorance of racing
in Exeter. I swear I recognise her - and the cab - from a conference I

attended in Exeter earlier in the Summer. She was equally charmingly ignorant about rural racism. I get all the best cabbies. And all the best conferences. The track sits in peaceful countryside on top of a hill in idyllic late Autumn glow. Probably. Low lying cloud has rolled in and veiled the vista in translucent grey.

We are in. It's busy. It's a small track and this is its biggest day. But it's not overly busy. There is room to wander and fraternise. We have planned the journey well. There is plenty of time to explore the course. Once again I move stealthily passed the owners and trainers bar and cast furtive glances inside. I'll be on the other side of that door one day.

Next is the pre-parade ring, paddock and parade ring. We linger. This is excellent. Of course the spectacle around the Paddock at Cheltenham is worth riches, but the intimacy of the ring here is marvellous. Before virtually every race we return here to see the horses warmed up and saddled, we compare the sizes of the beasts, judge their gait and demeanour (like we know what we are looking for!) and observe the trainers and connections.

Henrietta and Terry Biddlecombe have a couple of runners and they are preparing Robber Baron for the novice hurdle. They are an amazing team. Appearances belie their skill and knowledge. Henrietta exudes a deep love and innate understanding of horses, but she can't bear to watch them run and can be found in the car park on the end of a mobile phone whilst the race is in progress. She's a bit like a slightly mad Auntie Nora who always gives you jumpers three sizes too big for your Christmas present every year. But you always wear it when you are with her because you don't want to offend her. And Terry. You would never guess to look at him, but Terry was Champion jockey three times and has a Gold Cup win tucked under his enormous belt. There is quite a lot under his belt. He is the chortling Uncle Bernard who drinks in life and talks like a runaway train. He's your mate really, and he'll buy you a pint down the pub even though you are not quite 18 yet. They are the genuine odd couple, but as I say, appearances can deceive. What a team. Their genuine love for the game shines like a beacon. A bit like Terry's bonce sitting on top of his rotund frame.

Later on there is a lovely moment as Armaturk is being readied in his box for the Haldon Gold Cup. The stable lad has saddled up the chaser and the gaffer, Paul Nicholls is chatting to him. When they are satisfied, Nicholls moves off, but not before giving Armaturk an affectionate peck on the nose. This touches me. Racing often hits the headlines for all the wrong reasons - corruption and collusion and so on. Such a genuine moment as Paul Nicholls' gesture restores my faith that there is warmth underneath the hard-boiled gambling. Allegations of fixing will regularly occur and often it will be upheld. It is too much to expect the game to be totally clean. But I like to remind my sentimental side that there is another human side to racing.

Enough of that. Down to business. Let's win some wedge.

We are in the Grandstand for the first. It's packed and I'm shoe-horned next to some wide boy car dealer on an away day from Essex. His camel hair coat gets up my nose and the stench from his fat cigar gets in my eyes. The cloud is still low, but there is a very good view of the undulations that the horses must struggle round. Down the back straight there is a particularly testing pull. It's also clear from the first novice hurdle race that the
ground is riding softish. There are no surprises in the result. Robber Baron by 5 lengths. Steve and I have gone for outsiders. My Jonjo-trained e/w prospect Resistance comes in a respectable but unprofitable 4th.

No luck next time either in a very average and frankly uninteresting handicap hurdle. Soft rain is now descending from even lower cloud. Much of the course is obscured from view. Just in time for the feature of the day.  We have been scoping the contenders in the paddock. It is a fine prospect. There goes Latalomne looking frisky and nodding at Steve on each circuit. He looks game. Seebald looks in fine fettle too. AP McCoy is hobbling around after a fall in the 2nd, but as soon as he mounts up he is a different prospect, suddenly looking welded to the horse. Man and beast in seamless symphony. Ruby Walsh - probably my favourite jockey - is aboard Armaturk who is a gorgeous chestnut colour and looks well. Top weight and elder statesman Edredon Bleu glides passed us calm and aloof. It's a small field and we also get a good look at the outsiders, Castle Prince and the old rascal Ferdy Murphy's runner Ichi Beau.

Steve has an edgy and, by his own admission, sentimental punt on Latalomne. He is seeking Champion Chase retribution. I want to be on Armaturk. I think he'll win. But he's 2/1. I really don't fancy that. It's no kind of bet. Seebald is odds on which seems a bit extreme. I'm dallying. I've come all this way for the best chase of the year so far and I'm thinking about no bet. Steve remarks
      "Look at Edredon, he's out to 10s"
And he is. Everywhere. So I plunge. Steve sees my ticket and thumps me on the back and
hollers
      "Come on Edredon!"
I wish I had premonitions. I don't. But this feels like a good bet. He's just too good a horse to be isolated in the market with the long shots at double figures in such a small field.  Steve has taught me this. I can hear his words at countless venues over the last year
      "Where's the value? Where have the bookies got it wrong? Where is the market over-pricing a live chance? Find him and you've found your value."

Wise words Steve. Top advice. I'm a disciple and today it pays off. Edredon is a sensation. He takes them round for the first circuit at a cracking pace, looking very strong. They disappear into the murk and who knows what is going on. The giant screen can't pick them up. So we wait. It's like a library out there. You could hear a pin drop if course commentator Simon Holt wasn't puncturing the silence with wisecracks.

"Any body on a long shot? This is the time to imagine him in the lead. Anyone got a road map? They should be emerging from the mist....now, er.....now. Maybe not.....".
He's earning his wedge today.

But here they come for real. And it's still Edredon in full sail. Jim Culloty's claret and blue colours are carried easily and boldly in front. We've moved to the rail. No point in languishing in the Grandstand. They are not in the home straight yet but I can see Edredon's ears are pricked. Seebald is the nearest of his rivals and McCoy moves up to make his challenge just before the 3rd last. Edredon puts in a spectacular leap. An awesome leap. The crowd gasps collectively. Bloody hell that was special. I'm tingling.

He gallops away from the fence like a four year old. Seebald is left in the wake of the blue eiderdown and he never gets closer. Two lengths, four lengths. Christ, I'm filling up. Steve thumps me on the back.
"Edredon you beauty!"
But I can't let go until he clears the last. He does. He flies it. Now I'm dancing!

As Edredon flashes past the post, Steve is as delighted as me. Edredon proves to be a popular winner. It is the manner of the victory that seals the moment for us. Exuberant jumping, strong galloping and a serious value winner by 10 lovely lengths. The welcome for the old boy back in the winner's enclosure is overwhelming. At 10/1, not many of the crowd would have been on him. This is about paying respect to a worthy champion, an affectionate embrace for an old friend. Blimey, here comes that sentiment again.

This is the highlight, but the rest of the afternoon doesn't disappoint. There is a cracking novice chase featuring top prospects Montreal, Bow Strada and Farmer Jack. Next up, we somehow conspire to land a well-planned reverse exacta in a desperately strongly contested handicap chase in which Satshoon edges out Handyman by the closest of margins. Ruby Walsh picks up a 3-day whip-ban for his efforts. We see promising novice chaser Jair du Cochet post his first victory at Folkestone over the best stilton soup and pork bap combination this side of Cleeve Hill. To round things off we both back Tales of Bounty in the final handicap hurdle of the day who strolls home for a Nicholls/Walsh/Atkinson/Clark double. He's been off the track for about two years!

Memorable stuff. Top day out. The shuttle bus heads back to the station, axles groaning under the weight of our collective wedge. A couple of Stellas and whisky chasers on the train see us home nicely. Exeter is a welcome addition to the fixture list.

## 18. BOUNTIFUL TALES

*"And he's peeling off those dollar bills.
Slapping them down,
One hundred.... Two hundred...."*
U2 *"Bullet The Blue Sky"* 1987

Richard in our office has just got back from three weeks in the States. Apart from landing back home in a shocking force 9 storm and the baggage handlers refusing to unload the plane, he's had a fantastic time. Cruising round 'Frisco, Monument Valley and the Grand Canyon in a huge gas-guzzling convertible is on my wish list. In fact, Helen and I had a similar trip planned a few years back....and then kids arrived! So maybe later, when the gee-gees come in.

Richard had a laugh in Las Vegas. They toured every cheap and nasty casino they could find to play the 5c fruit machines and consume free drinks. I admire that brazenly cheapskate quality. Ruth, Richard's ostensibly sensible other half had to be dragged away from the machines! There's a turn up. Richard only persuaded her to leave after she collected a $28 win from a 5c stake! Dangerous stuff. Richard says the casinos are up front about the addictive qualities of their trade. They distribute leaflets about the risks as part of their attempt at corporate responsibility.

He's brought me one back, stowed in his lost luggage. Cheeky git! 'Responsible Gaming' it's titled, issued by the New York-New York Hotel and Casino ('The Greatest City in Las Vegas', it says here...). It's a fantastic little black, glossy fold out leaflet with wise words pointing out that "...for some, gambling is an obsession. The reasons vary, but the result can be the same  - these people develop and addiction to gambling". Hard hitting stuff. The danger signals are most alarming:

> "Gamble to escape problems and to feel better
> Return to 'get even' after experiencing losses
> Lie to cover up gambling losses
> Have problems with job, school or relationships"

Bloody hell! I think I recognise all of these! I imagine this approach is either in response to, or to head off lawsuits brought by bankrupt roulette-junkies blaming the casino for their ruination. Maybe this should be encouraged in England. Is it unreasonable to expect to see emergency 'special assistance numbers' on the boards of Barry Dennis and fearless Freddie Williams next time I pitch up at Catterick. "Do you know anyone with a gambling problem? Call the 24-hour Problem Gambling Helpline..." It would probably be a premium rate tipping service!

Not that Richard is immune to gambling. We have a lottery syndicate at work. Richard is a fully paid up syndicate member. When it comes to those oft repeated conversations about 'what I would do if I won the lottery',

Rich always plays it cool. Not sure what his on his wish list. Horse ownership, inevitably, features on my mine. Hughesy and Stu over in the corner mostly want cars. Or maybe they would buy a football team. There's enough dissection and deliberation of the premiership to keep Gabby Logan in business 24 hours a day.

We have a signed, dated and witnessed lottery agreement, complete with a set of rules and regulations. There is scope to defer to sub-committees, working parties and consultation exercises should the need to make a decision arise. (This is the Public Sector after all. Dry bureaucracy has its own comforts.)

We never win much. Any proceeds usually get re-invested. It's coming up to Christmas and Lottery Tsar Hughesy does a quick tally of the resources left in the pot. He finds £68. The decision making vehicles kick smoothly through the gears and up pops a hastily keyboarded e-mail from the boy:

> "Dear Lottery Syndicate members. If everyone is in agreement, we will spend the winnings so far (ho ho) at the Branch xmas lunch next Thursday.
>
> If anyone doesn't like this idea, TOUGH!!!!!!!!
>
> Not really, let me know and we'll try and sort it out another way
>
> FYI - we haven't won anything since the 1st two weeks!
>
> Steven Hughes
> Administration Officer"

Stu and Denise have inherited the poisoned chalice of organising the Christmas lunch this year. We are booked into a dodgy cocktail bar and then checking out the Ten Pin Bowling over in Canada Water, a God-forsaken car park in a soulless part of New Docklands.

> "...sort it out another way." I read again in Hughesy's e-mail.

You are ahead of me. But I wonder if it will actually be worth the torrent of abuse I'll get in return for the small wind up value of suggesting that we stick the winnings on the nags. The pain of the Behrajan fiasco burns like a hot poker through my brain every time I see the offending betting slip pinned up on my notice board. "Cheers Dave" it says in red ink all over Mr Hill's blue receipt proclaiming "Behrajan. £17.50 each way. Cheltenham Gold Cup." Ouch. But of course, I do suggest it. With a silly grin on my chops I reply to the group:

> "Why don't we put it all on Tales of Bounty in the 1.30pm at Taunton this afternoon at 6/1. Potential return of £408 (plus the stake back of course)?

I sit back and wait for the grief.

> Sue: "Why not?? Count me in!"

Er. Pardon. Didn't expect that. Especially from Sue who is pretty conservative. Mmm. Don't want this to be a precedent.

> Phil: "Sounds good to me but we'll need everybody to agree!"

This is starting to sound ominous.

> Richard: "Great idea - I'm with this - just think, when it loses it will buy us a good 12 months worth of flak to direct at 'tipster' Dave."

Yeah, this is what I was worried about. Rich has suffered financially more than once at the hands of a couple of tips from me.

> "Dear All
>
> We have decided to put our faith into one of Dave's tips and are going to put all £68 on Tales of Bounty at the 1.30 at Taunton.
>
> Lucky gambling!
>
> Steven Hughes
> Administration Officer."

I was genuinely not expecting this. As the e-mails have rolled in, I have become increasingly uncomfortable with my impulsive offer. I was anticipating some piss taking, as alluded to by Richard. But now all I've got is pressure. My palms are tacky and the hairs on the back of my neck are proud. I'm not sure I want to gamble with other people's money. Sure, they say 'go on, so what, it's free money' now, but wait until it loses. Behrajan will be nothing compared to this humiliation. I need some moral support. I e-mail Steve:

> "Bacchy
>
> Me & my big gob.
>
> We have an Agency lottery syndicate for which we have accumulated some winnings over the last month or so. They were to be divvied up at the Christmas lunch. I thought we could be a bit bolder and suggested a more thrilling option - Tales of Bounty this afternoon at Taunton. I think I was only joking.
>
> Anyway, they are up for it. £68 riding on the Paul Nicholls bay gelding at 1.30pm this arvo.

My balls are tightening. Nearly as much as the noose around my neck. This is another Behrajan moment. Why do I do this?"

By the time Steve's reply comes in, I'm down the bookies:

> "How can your balls be tightening, Davoski? You have balls of steel!
>
> This is his first time over fences for fuck sake, a decent field, including at least one good recruit from hurdling game (Another General).

Thought the forecast price looked interesting, though... Hope you have your 'Oh-nevermind-but-I-can-assure-you-it-was-value' argument ready if it all goes pear-shaped.

Do you have £2 on yourself, thus rounding-up the stake to a princely £70?"

So Hughesy, the keeper of the lotto loot ambles over. He's got a suspiciously battered brown envelope in his young mits. He gives me one of his side-long looks through narrowing eyes that belie his 19 years of age. I was never this brassy as a teenager!

> "Awright, here's the money, mate. I'm off for me dinner now. Seez yer laters, yeah? Be lackee"

> "No, mate, no. I need some support in that sweat shop of a bookies. You don't know what it's like in there. It will be rammed with low-life, seething with sharks. I could crack and scarper with the winnings. Don't leave me alone Hugheseeeee"

Whatever. He flashes me a full set of gleaming pearlies and leaves me to it. There's no sense of occasion with this lot. Where is the shared experience, mutual anguish and collective drama? It shouldn't be this way. Bacchy would be here if I'd given him enough notice.

I pick up the envelope. It is a genuine back-street, dodgy-deal Jiffy bag. Jangling coinage muffled by folded fivers. I slip the package into my inside pocket, check the Walther PPK on my hip, pull down my trilby, pick up my violin case, strike a match on my stubble, light up my Strand cigarette, double check the strangely deserted street and cruise out into the dank London night. You get the idea. This is other people's money I'm playing with. I think I know how Nick Leeson felt.

A local branch of William Hill's bookmaking emporia is only a few short strides down the road from the office, bang opposite the back entrance to New Scotland Yard. It's pretty busy inside. I stroll casually and confidently passed the casino-bandit and fruit machines that line one side of the wall.

Round the corner in the main part of the shop the low, nicotine stained ceiling traps the cigarette smoke in a perpetual fug. The 21$^{st}$ century manifestation of the London pea-souper. The far wall is covered with a dozen 26-inch screens, punctuated by a central Cyclops of a screen disgorging any amount of gambling information: 'early bird' prices for half a dozen afternoon races, greyhound markets, evening football, Rapido lottery lunchtime draw, and virtual racing from Steepledowns. (It's true. Bookies finally discover a foolproof way to predict race results. This is the saddest variant of mug punting I've yet encountered.) All this visual information is overlaid by a constant barrage of advice and opinion on a range of simultaneous events by the multi-tasking SIS commentary team.

One screen draws my undivided attention. Taunton. 1.30pm. First Show. Tales of Bounty is 11/2. Hmmm. I was looking for 6s. I peel away to the wall and collect a betting slip.

There are some familiar faces scanning the form over here. Joe is a balding, stubbly East End diamond wearing a weathered face and an Evening Standard anorak. His shift starts about 3 o'clock outside St James' tube station. Another guy I see in here most visits is in his usual pose, scowling at the Racing Post, roll-up, perched on his lower lip. He agitates, blasphemes and chunters under his breath, forever seeking the value from the rag in his hands. There's another regular, a big bloke with a large ruddy face and an even larger pair of glasses. He wears an expensive suit badly with a gaudy tie pulled half way down his chest.

There's a pattern to the punting in this bookies. Apart from the regulars who surely must spend their afternoons in here, there is also a steady flow of office types who congregate in front of the big screens for the big mid-week races and then slope off back to their sedentary grind. I can identify with that. How many lost causes are holed up in this part affluent SW1?

One less today. Tales of Bounty drifts to 6/1 and I strike. That sounds decisive. It isn't like that at all. The betting slip is written out three times before I'm happy that it is correct. (It was right the first time.) I count out the cash and hand it over. The cashier looks at the slip and checks the stake. She doesn't bat a mascaraed eyebrow. But I can't be cool about it. I blurt out,
"Lottery money, y'know – a syndicate. Ha ha! That's why it such an odd sum!"

"Oh, I see", she replies, a bit distractedly, and then smiles at me.

I feel patronized. She might as well have said,

"First time is it, sonny? Don't worry, it's easy. I'll look after you."

The Nick Leeson swagger has evaporated.

I take a pew in front of the big screen altar and try to settle down for the race. But it's not easy. I am riddled with contradictory impulses. The money is down, so there is no going back. But that doesn't stop me agonizing. This is Tales of Bounty's first trip over fences. He's a chasing débutant up against at least one quality opponent. Another General has decent hurdle form and he sows another seed of doubt by going odds-on as I again query my judgement. That day at cloud-shrouded Exeter, ToB was ridden with authority and composure by the supremely talented Ruby Walsh. Ruby is at Clonmel today. A long way from Taunton. Bobby McNally is the pilot here. That's bound to make a difference. ToB was also well beaten last time out. But surely, the argument runs, that's why the shrewd Paul Nicholls is stepping him in trip now and choosing a local course for his gelding's fencing bow?

Agonies of a different nature now…they are off. I can barely watch them over the first. The worst-case scenario involves an opening fence tumble and a long walk back to the office, desperately trying to justify the selection. If ignominy has a physical presence, my demeanour would betray it; if isolation has a verbal driver, the lads would voice it.

But ToB is over safely. And more so, he gives me and Bobby a confidence boosting leap. The gelding takes up a sensible mid-division place, tracking the leading group around the first circuit. Time for clichés, but I really do have a lump in my throat. The field heads off into the country for the last time. My eyes are goggling, my mouth is dry and my chest is pounding. I'd be a crap poker player.
Down the back straight, Another General and two other horses in whom I have no interest pull away from the main group. For an eternity it looks like my jock is missing the break and being caught flat-footed when a gentle turn of pace is required. I'm breathing in snatches and I can feel my temples throbbing. I urge Tales of Bounty to accelerate up to the leaders. He does so, and it's not a moment too late.

There is real confidence here now. McNally pushes him up to challenge three out. He jumps cleanly and clearly into a half a length lead and runs on strongly to increase the advantage by two or three lengths. Another General is putting in a challenge, but I'm squirming on my plastic bucket seat with excitement. If he clears the last, surely he has won. Heart stop time. ToB hasn't touched a twig all the way round, the jumping has been assured, but he could still come a cropper here. Bobby steadies his charge….. and Bounty is over easily. There is only one more slight flutter when the pack appears to close a little. But it's a trick of the perspective, merely a widening of the camera angle.

So, he's only gone and won. My heart is racing for a different reason now. I want to leap up and punch the air with a hearty "You fucking beauty". I want another Rith Dubh moment. The bookies is full, but this is a solitary celebration. I content myself with a malevolent, hissed "Yessss" through gritted teeth and start burning off the nervous energy by pacing around like an expectant father wearing the pattern off the carpet. Relief and achievement sweep over me in equal measure. I have avoided the crushing failure of another bad tip, the spectre of which I had brought on myself with an ill-judged e-mail; and proven that I know what I'm talking about – if only just this once. In my tiny slice of the world, I feel like I've pulled something off today.

I savour the best bit. I choose my moment to stroll up to the counter and single out the teller who took my bet. I hand over the ticket (checking the details again) and wait for her reaction. I'm no virgin gambler. Look at me. Roll in, strike a bet at the best price, clock the race, collect the wedge and take off. Smash and grab, mate. Smash and bleedin' grab. 'Yvonne' (it says on her name badge), counts out the 20s. I'm nodding as I count them out with her.

"Pleasure doing business with you."
I allow myself a note of smugness. I may never get the opportunity again. £476 goes back in the padded envelope (don't be iffy, collect in a jiffy) and I leave the losers to their lunchtime trifectas. I'll be back with them tomorrow.

Most of the gang has returned from lunch by the time I saunter into the office. They've tracked the race on the Internet and my attempts at a deadpan expression and an enigmatic smile are as pointless as they are transparent. Now I can indulge myself. I must resemble a whirling dervish as I wave the wonga and illustrate the race with flamboyant gestures.

"FUCK ME IT'S WON!!!!"

I reply to Bacchy's e-mail missive. He rejoins:

"REDEMPTION!!!!!!!!!!!!!!

Think of the kudos, Davoski. You won't hear the last of this until you move jobs.

Would it be bollocks if I suggested that life is made up of moments such as these?

Thought he got fatally outpaced down the back, but then within a furlong he was back on the leader's heels doing handsprings.

Doesn't even get a mention in the Paul Nicholls stable tour.

Scribbled out an exacta and then couldn't be arsed on account of Another General's skinny price!

Top bombing, by the way. Enjoy."

Richard is quick with his congratulations too. He's incredulous. Ultimately he's also a sensitive soul and I think he worries about me. I take it as a compliment. He sent me a poem the other day. Don't know who wrote it. But the message is not subtle...

**The Gamble Account**

*When I opened a new gamble account*
*To supplement my current account,*
*The bank sent me a different kind of card*
*To the usual plastic one.*
*It was the Four of Clubs*

*At the nearest cashpoint machine*
*I inserted the card,*
*And keying in my personal number,*
*The Queen of Hearts*
*And Two of Spades*
*Came up upon the screen.*
*Sixteen*

*I took the print out*
*And went straight to the cashier's desk.*
*I placed my bet.*
*Sixty pounds to withdraw.*
*She dealt the cards:*
*The Jack of Diamonds,*
*Two of Clubs*
*And Six of Hearts*
*Damn! Eighteen.*

*"Better luck next time!"*
*flashed the message on the computer screen,*
*as I paid in sixty pounds*
*to the non-withdrawable gamble account.*

## 19. LAY HEDGING

*"The feeling you get is similar to some sort of drowning
When you are out of your mind, out of your depth,
You should have taken soundings."*
Marillion *"The Last Straw"* 1987

I just love it. The build up to our third visit to Cheltenham is well under way. The ante-post markets for the Festival are fizzing away in shops, on-line and over the phone. And I'm looking to get stuck in.

But we have a few logistical issues to address. A few small spanners have appeared in the accommodation works. John, our genial host last year in the strategically significant Tewkesbury, has done a moonlight flit and moved in with his girlfriend Fiona in Putney. Now Putney is lovely for sure. But it's no use to us when we are bearing down on the finest three days' jump racing in the year. Steve and I have conveyed to John, via Bryn, our bitterest regrets at his untimely relocation. To be fair, John's not unsympathetic to our plight, though he stops short of hoofing into the street the four students to whom he has let the flat. I bet the bastard students have sub-let anyway, coining it in by sub-letting to desperate sods like Steve and I.

But Bryn has plenty on his plate already. March is going to be a busy old time for new-Dad Reynolds. Not only will his son Aaron be a nappy-rich, punting-poor 4 months old, but Bryn is also pursuing a separate agenda. He's lining up a 10-day blind-cricket tour to the Caribbean. Staggeringly, he thinks this demands his top line negotiation stance with his partner, Debs rather than the rival Cheltenham Festival a few days earlier. Even stern advice from Clarkey, whose words alone have been known to alter the very course of Fantasy Cricket rules, fails to do the trick. Bryn thinks he can take in the cricket tour and turn up with the rest of the boys on Gold Cup day. Ambitious.

So it's a bit of a double blow. Three intrepid heroes become two homeless waifs. I've been phoning round guest houses, inns and hotels like a lunatic. I'm sitting amidst a snowstorm of bus timetables, train schedules and B&B lists. There are no vacancies in the Tewksbury area, our number one choice. But the pubs and hotels are offering an outrageous scam known as the Festival Package which involves booking four nights' accommodation at premium rates. The smaller establishments are more understanding, but equally unrewarding. Most have already taken provisional bookings for the festival period from last season's customers. It sounds like a rolling year on year thing. I'd heard about this somewhere before, but to experience it first hand gives me pause for thought.

I cast the net a bit wider and check out other places with public transport connections to Cheltenham: landlords in Stroud, Cirencester and even out towards Bristol gave me the same story. One bloke said the outskirts of Birmingham might be a possibility. Surely not! My head is filled with visions of jollied-up Irish gamblers having cleaned up on home grown Like-a-butterfly and Moscow Flyer glory leaving their digs on the Friday morning. Pockets bulging like Linford's lunchbox, chest pumped up like a barrel organ,

"Ah, sure Mrs Bristow, we'll see you this toime next year. Now you won't ferget to keep our rooms for us lads now will ye? Sure we've had a beltin' stay this year. Ye've spoilt us rotten so ye have."

It's Helen that solves the problem.

"Why don't you stay with Aunty Mona. She's got loads of space."

It was true. Helen's legendary Irish Aunty (one of the many) lives in Gloucester. Near the railway station. Her children are all grown up and left home, as far as I know. Fantastic! Why didn't I think of it! I mention it to Steve.

"Nice one! Job done! Aunty Mona, that luscious Irish lovely!"

He's never met her. He won't be saying that in March. I give her a call.

"We'd be deloited to have us stay. There'll be no problem at arl. Now is it the December meeting you'll be coming for or the January fixture?"

Blimey she knows the dates!

Steve is still on a punting roll. He's coming up with new stuff, cranking up the temperature all the time, playing havoc with my fledgling knowledge. He explains his latest initiative.

"I've been exploring value each-way doubles, Davoski. I think I'll have couple of little bets set up for maybe two or three of the championship races. It should pay to have some potentially big odds winners to lay off."

We are in the Buckingham Arms, chewing the Thames out of a pint of Young's Ordinary. You see I don't really get this laying-off business and I don't really want any more information. I'm a mug, me and like my betting simple. I've worked out the value of value punting and I'm comfortable with it: small bets on decent chances at big prices equals lovely pay outs....eventually. Uncomplicated, simple and sometimes effective. Just like Emile Heskey. Indeed I've had some lovely results: Exeter and the sublime Edredon Bleu gave me momentum; Cyfor Malta at a sweet 25/1 in the Thomas Pink Gold Cup kept me rolling; and a novice called Lucky Bay at a juicer-still 26/1 in a Newbury event lifted me into unknown territory. That smashing Tales of Bounty moment which still sends tingles up and down my over-sensitive spine has seen me through to early December in sparkling condition.

But these devilish words of Bacchy's are invasive. They seep through my porous strategies, tainting them a greedy purple and washing out my opaque logic. My mind races with images of even bigger returns on speculative and yet skilfully placed small stakes. My self-discipline bobs helplessly against the rising tide of madness. Before the lifeboat of sanity is sighted, I have blown a shocking amount of hard-won big-price profit chasing unsustainable Cheltenham each-way 'value'. Ha! Wake up and smell the seaweed!

The next time I see Steve, we are again in the BA and I give full vent to my spleen.

"You owe me 40 notes! These joke each-way ante-post doubles are a travesty! I haven't got one of my first legs in the frame yet. What am I doing? I can barely grasp the concept of value punting, let alone some even more audacious long-shot plan."

Predictably, Steve laughs. As do Nick and Bryn. I'm spinning off-course like a sycamore tree helicopter in a Spring breeze. And they think it's funny.

"What have you been backing, Dave? All value I hope. Harharhar."

I haven't of course. Odds on certainties have gone down too - Tees Components is one that particularly hurts. But so have no-chance outsiders. I've been trying to set up doubles with one horse in particular: Sir Rembrandt in the 3-mile Novice Chase. Before I can get my first leg up, he's injured in training and pulled out of Cheltenham.

This has been a shambolic little episode. I decide to draw a veil over the experiment when Steve tells me that he's already got a couple of juicy first legs up and riding on Cheltenham prospects. Nice to have this in the kit-bag to pull out at the Championships. In particular, he's got a huge bet riding on Keen Leader in the SunAlliance Novice Chase which he intends to lay off and make a profit of at least £100 as long as he runs. I've got a lot to learn.

So I turn my ante-post attention back to the fields of the main championship races in search of big price contenders. Each way doubles are now officially off my radar. The new plan is really the old plan: get my cash down on a horse with a decent chance before he shortens up. The ideal, I consider (drawing on all my vast experience), is to back such a horse before he runs in a preparation race for the main event. If he runs well, the price collapses and I'm sitting pretty on a big price for a real live candidate. The trick, of course, is picking the nag with the prospects.

I think I've found one. Willie Mullins, the canny old bugger, has already stated that his charge Holy Orders is to be campaigned with a tilt at the Champion Hurdle in mind. The horse is a decent stayer on the flat and is a quality horse, if maybe a bit of a monkey. I've seen him run a couple of times on the telly, and, yeah, I reckon I fancy a punt on this fella for the Champion Hurdle. I feel all puffed up like I've landed some inside information. I swagger up to the computer and seek some ridiculous price, 40-1 or so, on Betfair for Holy Orders in the Blue Riband Cheltenham hurdle and settle own to watch him take the opposition to the cleaners in the Lanzarote Hurdle.

Only he doesn't. Holy Orders is nowhere, not even competitive. This is one of the showpiece 2m handicap hurdles of the season. My horse simply doesn't feature. It's won by Non So, whose price shortens up for Cheltenham immediately. No such luck for me. But then I realise that my web bet has been left open. I scramble upstairs in the vain hope that I can cancel the bet before someone matches it. Too Late, too late (as Motorhead are fond of saying). My stake has been matched, but not only that, the price has drifted out so far that inshore rescue would struggle to save it. There's a three-figure price available on Holy Orders now. The market's assessment of his chances after this showing is as bleak as Haldon Hill in the fog. I've basically chucked my stake away through complete negligence. There is no excuse for leaving that unmatched bet live once the tape had gone up. Juvenile, schoolboy error. I can almost hear Alan Hanson's scathing judgement on a defensive lapse of concentration.

I dwell on this for a couple of days. I haven't wagered a huge stake by any means. But my pride is hurt. I thought I had found an edge. But I'm left feeling that I've made a cock up. I've been playing my remote control while Rome has burned. I blame the system and I determine to get my own back. I've never laid a horse to lose before, but this is the right time to do it. Make the Betfair system work for me. If I back a horse to lose the Champion Hurdle I can get my stake back on Holy Orders. This will leave me all square in the race. Or even secure a small profit. Then I can in effect start again. I think I'm up to Plan C by now.

I'm starting to see the strengths of the Betfair business plan. Quite simply, the power is back in the hands of the punter. The exchange means that the weight of money for or against a horse really does set the market. It is a much truer reflection of the extent to which the punters value a horse's chances. This isn't the place to go into the potential for market distortions, or the role that owners and others in the know can play when they conspire to lay their own horses to lose. Suffice to say that the betting exchange market presents a full range of opportunities.

Rhinestone Cowboy features prominently in the ante post market. But he's a novice. Sure, the racing pages are full of wonderment and mystery about what the horse might achieve. He wins a couple of bloodless novice events without coming off the bridle. All the time the price is shortening. Norman Williamson, the Cowboy's regular pilot keeps nodding and winking about what the horse might achieve if he's ever really asked to turn on the power. But Jonjo O'Neill, the training world's fastest rising star, says the horse will take the novice route. He doesn't want to pitch the horse into the big stuff whilst he's so green.

"Plenty of time for that", he says. "Ah, he'll be taking the novice route."
Jonjo is another canny old bugger. He has a million ways of saying nothing that might mean everything. The beguiling twinkle in his eye and disarming smile on his lips belie a shrewd and hard-nosed player. But his

utterances make sense to me. On this occasion, to my regret, I believe him.

So I lay him off at a 8-1 for the Champion Hurdle. The shortest I can get matched. I fleece some other unlucky loser who has matched my bet in this virtual bookies. If he loses (which he will of course as Jonjo's just told me that he'll line up in the hell-for-leather Supreme Novice hurdle an hour earlier) I will get back a little more than I staked on Holy Orders. Revenge. Ha. A little tortuous maybe. Some running to stand still, certainly. But now I can focus in on picking a good outsider for the Champion Hurdle, having eliminated two contenders. In fact, with a little positive thinking, I can even convince myself that I am, indeed, better off!

This mirage of a punting panacea in a desert of skinny High Street bookies' odds does not last long. My shimmering illusion of betting easy street is shattered on the windswept steppes of the Somerset Levels. Rhinestone Cowboy is entered in one of the season's key dress-rehearsals for the Champion Hurdle, the Kingwell Axminster Hurdle at Wincanton. That he is declared for the race at all is worry enough. If Jonjo wants to take the novice route, this race is not the logical step. Whilst novices are also entered in the race, so are some genuine Championship contenders. Like Hors La Loi III, last year's winner for starters.

My flawed thinking is exposed by Jonjo's comments before the race. He says that the owners haven't ruled out a tilt at the Champion Hurdle. It all starts to dawn on me now. Whilst the trainer might sanction the more cautious progression through the novice ranks, Rhinestone's owners might have grander aspirations. It makes sense. His owners are no benign dowagers or malleable syndicates. The Cowboy has the awesome power of Europe's premier bloodstock broker and stud magnet driving him forward. John Magnier, proprietor of Tipperary's Coolmore operation and owner or part owner of last season's Aiden O'Brien trained all-conquering classic generation, knows a thing or two about placing horses. Yeah, my laying days are numbered. I can't see the Magnier machine being satisfied with novice events when the big prize could be on offer.

My fears are confirmed. The Cowboy doesn't just win the race, he cruises home in 2$^{nd}$ gear. He toys with the opposition and crushes them in the final furlongs. Norman Williamson stops on his way passed fellow jock Ruby Walsh on Thisthatandtother to have a chat. Ruby is going hammer and tongs on his mount - a very decent novice prospect in his own right - before seeing Stormin' Norman slip the cowboy off the bridle for no more than a couple of yards and cruise to victory. I send a text to Steve. He's well aware of my lay on Rhinestone and has been watching my rising anxiety about the bet with detached interest. My text reads: "Wincanton, Axminster Hurdle, 2:45. Oh Fuck." The Cowboy's participation in the Champion Hurdle is now a formality. On that showing, could any other hurdler in the country live with him over two miles?

I feel a bit foolish, a bit shame-faced. The way you do when you have been caught out by a cheap practical joke, or when you allow yourself an indulgent boast about some conquest or other only to find that it was all a set up. With resignation, I trudge the stairs of shame to the spare bedroom, take the ceremonial samurai sword from the wall and take my own life.... No, no, I mean get on the Betfair site *toute-suite*. After that performance I don't have the balls to stand by my lay. But even now, I'm too late to back him at any kind of value. The price has already crashed. Best on offer is just under 2-1. This is a joke. I hang on a few minutes and eventually get just over 2-1. I have to stick on loads of dosh down to offset my potential losses of 16pts and secure some profit. I need the calculator, I need an odds-converter. Christ, I need a life!

In the meantime I've selected Ilnamar at a tidy 35-1 as my value Champion Hurdle punt. He's a versatile horse and Pipe has sent him out at a range of distances over timber and fences. Ilnamar is declared for one of the Champion Hurdle trials and I fancy him as a long shot. But this particular bet is over almost as soon as it is struck. The horse lollops over the line very ragged and unimpressive 3rd behind Flame Creek and October Mist (both of whom Brynaldo has collected on previously) in a muddling sort of race at Haydock. He won't be aimed at Cheltenham at all. It goes from bad to worse!

This is a farce. An absolute disgrace. I don't know if I'm coming or going. To get anything out of the race, I need the Cowboy to win. I've backed him at much shorter odds than I would ever, ever have contemplated under any other circumstances. This is the new me as well, the recently baptised disciple of value betting undone by my Holy Orders.

My Dad thinks it's hilarious. I'm recounting the story in our dining room whilst poring over the Racing Post. He thinks that Betfair is a bit of a new-fangled thing and not really what proper betting is about. Sadly, I have to agree that laying is a dodgy business. I'm painting this picture of ever more desperate efforts to play the system. I sound like I'm lashing out aimlessly, striking random bets in any direction. I kid myself that I know what I'm doing, that I'm taming the beast. But Dad and our lad laugh more explosively at every twist of my pathetic tale. Dad shakes his head and says,

"Hang on, I'm still lost, Dave. Do you want Rhinestone Cowboy to win or to lose?!"

In despair, I move on to Plan D, which is really Plan B revisited: each way ante-post doubles. The other horse, apart from Sir Rembrandt, that I've been looking at for the SunAlliance Chase is One Knight. After a couple of attempts I manage to set a double up by backing him in an Exeter novice chase at something like 1-2, doubled up for the Cheltenham race. He trots up at Exeter, and so my 2nd leg is live. I also squeeze in the place part of an each-way double when Frosty Canyon finishes 4th in the Welsh National, doubled with Lilium De Cotte in the Triumph Hurdle. After all this I think I have two ante-post doubles limping into Cheltenham weighed down by a ballast of wasted Champion hurdle stakes. Bloody hell, this is hard work!

## 20. CHELTENHAM THE THIRD - DAY 1: ROOSTED

*"Well here we are in a special place
What are you gonna do here?"*
The Waterboys, *Don't Bang The Drum*, 1985

The feeling isn't quite the same at Paddington this year. Brynaldo is back from his outrageous "no, it's a professional cricket tour, mate!" jolly to Barbados. But as anticipated, wangling a three day pass to the Jump Racing Olympics was a piss-take too far. He's still turning out on Thursday for the Gold Cup though. That's dedication.

His trip to Barbados sounds pretty special. Officially a promotional tour by the British Blind Cricket Association, it involved exhibition games against local blind teams and also against some fully-sighted celebrity teams. Bryn sent me a .pdf of a photo he had taken with Joel 'Big Bird' Garner at one of the games. The computers at work aren't top spec any more and it took ages for the file to download line by line from the top of the photo. Joel Garner's head appeared early in the down load but it was fully another five minutes and three feet before Bryn, replete with the England ODI strip and cheesy grin starts to appear, tucked under the wing of the mighty West Indian fast bowler. An excellent memento.

Bryn's highlight of the tour was a close run thing between bowling Gordon Greenidge in one of the exhibition games and a night out at the Island's infamous Harbour Lights venue. He has a cutting from the Barbados Daily News who ran a piece on the game to mark the occasion. The Harbour Lights evening goes unrecorded.

Steve's not here yet. It gives me time to spot other Cheltenham-bound punters on the concourse. As usual there's a right old mixture. Some advertise themselves easily: a Racing Post or Sun Racing pages rolled up and stuck handily in a back pocket; or a group's welcome for a late arrival with hearty thumps on the back and a chorus of disapproval, "Johnny, you old bastard. Thought you'd gone to the dogs instead Harharharrrrr". There's plenty of the hunting, shooting, fishing country brigade too - Barbours, tweeds, mustard waistcoats and shooting sticks, but I'm surprised by how many have turned out in the full Ascot gear - big hats, spotty dresses, skimpy shoes. The women are even worse..... Ho ho.

I spot Steve emerging from the tube. Even he's made an effort and puts me to shame. He's wearing a familiar big overcoat with the secret extra-deep Racing Post pocket in the lining, but it can't hide a dapper dark suit peeping out from underneath. I reckon he's on the pull after last year's success with the leather-trousered temptress.

The train is packed, but fairly subdued. The pissed blarney will come later, no doubt. We pass Newbury race course and we make appropriate and knowledgeable noises about What's Up Boys, Be My Royal and Gingembre, for whom Steve has a soft spot (I can almost picture Nick rolling his eyes).

We are warming up with some expectant discourse about the day's racing. Top notch fare on offer of course, every race is dripping with class. There's so much quality oozing out of the Racing Post that the paper is sodden. It almost slips through my fingers. The fields aren't quite as impenetrable as last year's maximum turn-outs, but remain massive puzzles. Fantasy Festival is up for grabs of course. We have a smaller, but more select entry this year. Paul and Sharon are sitting out the competition which means that, shamefully, the reigning champion is not defending her trophy.

Steve is encountering a spot of technical breakdown. He's got one these smart-arse phones that send pictures, connect to the internet, plan the day and give back massages. Only it really belongs to his son, Dom. Steve is not in full control of this revolutionary piece of communication wizardry and has managed to turn the ringer off. It's off for good, though. Steve can't get the thing back on. So no surprise that he hasn't registered any Fantasy Festival entries. There's some urgent calling and texting to Nick from our moving base in the Gloucestershire countryside and an interim service is resumed. I think Nick's acting as a filter at the London end of the operation, but there's some doubt about the whereabouts and indeed the participation of Vaughany and Ben.

The entrance to the Courage End, our venue today, takes us past the new building works in Tattersalls. It's a much more extensive development than I'd envisaged. Should be open for next year. We are loitering by the entrance. Steve pauses.
"Got some business to attend to, something I should've sorted out yesterday, won't take a tick."
This 'bit of business' involves chasing up some cowboy suppliers who have delivered the wrong parts for a new washing machine over successive months. About four phone calls later, after being shunted to different parts of the organisation who have no record of any of the previous complaints, Steve is still labouring to get his point across. On one hand, I'm quite content to marvel at the incompetence of British industry and express sympathy with Steve's plight. Nevertheless, on the other, I am equally struck by the surreality of the circumstance. Here we are, only moments away from the start of the World's greatest test of jump racing and within touching distance of the hallowed turf. But we can't get in because Steve is tearing lumps out of some poor sod on the other end of the phone about a missing sump extractor duct. Or something. Steve's trying hard to sound tetchy and difficult, but he wants to get inside the course too, only he's told Debs he'd sort this out. And he's a man of his word. But last night was a bit busy, what with the ebb and flow of the ante-post markets to ride. So he promised Debs he would "sort it" today. And here we are. Loitering.
"No. Don't bother ringing me back!" barks Steve, eventually.
No point. His ringer isn't working.

Finally, finally, we are in. And with ample time to spare. Steve is very apologetic about his washing machine fiasco. No need. Top entertainment.

It's all change over here in the Courage Enclosure too. The old betting hall has been knocked down and there are numerous portacabins masquerading as toilets, Totes and tea-rooms pending the building of a new permanent structure. One side effect of this is that there are no left luggage facilities. I have to confess that I'm not feeling in A1 top fettle this morning. There's a bit of activity going on with my insides. I'm a bit achy and I could do to get the weight of my back. No matter, a minor irritant.

The fantasy festival entries are finally in too. We survey the scene from atop the temporary stand. Steve is placepotting over a pint. Bankers and combinations are the theme this year. Somehow I can't face it just now. Low on energy. I need to steel myself for the day. I take a nip of whisky from the hip flask and immediately feel energized.

The Supreme Novice Hurdle is first up. A strong Irish Challenge here, as ever. I'm no expert on the Irish form. I'm no expert. But a couple of the raiders make it on to my shortlist - Kicking King, Mutakkarrim and Rosaker, for starters. Edward O'Grady's Back In Front is a warm favourite. But in the end I plump for Henrietta Knight's Inca Trail. It could be a big three days for her Wantage stable and I'm happy to get stuck in early on. Steve does likewise.

It isn't easy getting a decent bet on though. Even over here in the cheap seats where there is more room to move, there is very little variation in the prices. The days of the tic-tac talk are almost over. These days bookies runners are wired for sound. Headphones and discrete microphones have replaced boxes, binoculars and long arms. Information about the prices of rival bookies is communicated back to the pitches in double-quick time and the adjustments are made. There is precious little value on offer here. Indeed it's really hard work to even get the current best price as advertised on the electronic display. Graduating to the ranks of Betfair has opened my eyes both to the skinny prices offered by the on-course bookies and to the hard labour required to get a decent bet down for the small time gambler at these big meetings. I struck a place bet on Jaboune for this race last night. It's all there. This is the future.

Eventually I'm on Inca Trail at 14s. Steve and I settle by the rail where there is a good view of the giant screen. The tape springs up and the curtain-raising cavalry charge begins, accompanied by a familiar send off from the Cheltenham choir. We're off.

Can't pick out my colours in the morass of horse flesh as they swing away from the stands and into the country. As the race develops, Inca Trail - after early headway - has already lost his chance. And I haven't spotted Jaboune at all. Coming round the home turn, Back In Front simply skips into the lead and scampers away from his rivals to win staggeringly easily, by a full 10 lengths. It's a very strong performance. One up for the Irish already. And it's the favourite. Blimey, just like last year. Rhinestone Cowboy, well-touted as the best novice hurdler in training, would have struggled to match him today. We'll see what he's made of in an hour's time.

Anticipation for the Festival builds and broods over about nine months. Once the first crescendo is scaled at 2pm, the races come in a torrent, like a damn breaking. The Arkle is a mouth-watering prospect. Possibly the strongest race on paper all festival. Favourite Azertyuiop looks a class act and has not put a foot wrong all season. But there are some seriously decent animals with rock-solid form who have been targeted at this event all season. Impek, Isio, Le Roi Miguel, Hand Inn Hand and Adamant Approach all have first class credentials. I find a mean old bookie who offers me 10-1 on Isio and I bite his hand off. Steve already has a decent ante post bet on Impek, another Henrietta hopeful.

If this was strong on paper then Azertyuiop has turned it to confetti. The Nicholls gelding absolutely screams home. The crowd gives him a tremendous welcome when he flashes past the post a full 11 lengths clear of Impek and Isio. Our selections looked sound until Ruby Walsh up top pressed the button and Azertyuiop simply flew up the hill. There's a lot of money riding on him today. He was backed off the boards. Short priced animals have taken the opening two spectacles and the bookies are taking a right hammering.

It's the showpiece of the day. There's very little I can do to redeem my position on the Champion Hurdle. My catastrophic back-back-lay-back-back hedge strategy has left me fully exposed. I think I need Rhinestone Cowboy to win in order to make any money. But, I think I also need Holy Orders to win. Or is it lose? Bollocks.

Rhinestone Cowboy is the most hyped horse of the season. But he's a novice and the field for the Champion Hurdle boasts some strong contenders. Intersky Falcon, a very classy animal, has done nothing wrong all season and has a storming chance. Steve's mate, Andy, whom he knows through the Betfair forum is part of the Intersky Racing syndicate that owns the Falcon. He is very, very confident about the horse's chances, to the extent that he's had some serious bets at a range of prices and in a series of permutations stacked up for this race. Then there is Rooster Booster who has shown spectacular improvement from eight years to nine years old has beaten all comers this season on any ground. He has earned respect by doing it the hard way, battling through the handicap route to become a Grade 1 contender.

Some are not ruling out last year's Champion, Hors La Loi III, either. There's an argument that he may have the good ground he needs today. I don't fancy him much though. Last year's renewal was a weak affair after the demise of both Valiramix and Istabraq. The speedy, classy Landing Light is also thrown in, last year's runner up. The three principles in the market are the Falcon, the Cowboy and the Rooster. Blimey, it's like a corny script from High Chapparal. Who will be Champion the Wonder

Horse, Kimosabe? (And other bad jokes from Saturday morning TV, circa 1974.)

Steve is a huge fan of the Rooster and has followed him from his handicap days. No one was more pleased than Steve when Rooster won the County Hurdle in the dying moments of last year's festival. But he's wavering today. He decides not to take a piece and lines up Self Defense instead. I can see no sensible way out of my predicament. So I do the decent thing and take a wild Tote bet on last year's Triumph hero for Nick, the Irish raider Scolardy. Both are massive on the Tote forecasts. No reason to think either of these can really take on these performers after an indifferent season, but the deed is done.

There's a farcical start to the race involving the horses lining up at least three times amongst ridiculous jostling. When the tape finally goes up Hors La Loi plants his feet and refuses to move. Almost as tame a defence of his Champion Hurdle crown as Sharon's of the Fantasy Festival Trophy!

More incident as Intersky Falcon appears to take a firm hold and leads them past us and down the hill. He looks a bit keen. He fails to take the sting out of the other contenders and, approaching the top bend, at the business end of the race, it looks wide open. Rhinestone comes under pressure. He's in a real race today. Then Richard Johnson who has cruised through the field on Rooster Booster asks for some more as they straighten up for the last and the grey gelding takes off in devastating fashion. Rhinestone tries to follow him, but it's men and boys. There's is no nitro-glycerin in his tank once off the bit after all. Rooster wins the race by miles, absolutely slamming a quality field. Johnson punches the air well before the line. Jockey and horse a grey and yellow blur, 11lengths clear of Westender who stays on well for 2nd. We are left in no doubt about who is this year's top hurdler. Rhinestone stays on for third and Self Defense - the other novice in the race - relegates Intersky to fifth, well out of the place money.

Holy Orders, the root of my rhinestone problem, runs a decent race, finishing 8th - out of the frame but perfectly respectable. I vow to back him next time out. Will I ever learn? I'm down 26 points on the race.

These have been three fascinating races. This breakneck start to the festival leaves me breathless. Tossed uncontrollably from race to race like a crisp packet in a wind tunnel. We've seen two favourites and a heavily backed 2nd favourite murder the opposition to win by an aggregate of 32 lengths in three consecutive and competitive Grade 1 races. It's hard to take in all the significance. There are some big hits being taking down in the ring. I might feel a bit pasty, but one look at the bookies' white faces and black-ringed eyes and I start to perk up. I attempt to refuel with a pork bap, but I can only give a half-hearted effort. It doesn't escape Steve attention and he raises his eyebrows as I drop the uneaten remains in the bin.

"Alright Dave?"

"Bit fatty" I mutter.
We turn our attention to the National Hunt Handicap Chase. Though dejected at our punting performance, we aim to hang in there. Knowing that favourite backers are hosing it in spurs me on.

This turns out to be a good race and the previously unconvincing Youllneverwalkalone finishes strongly up the hill to win from Haut Cercy. Still no luck for me and Steve. Wellneverwinagain. Southern Star runs no sort of race for me - another Henrietta underperformer - and Historg rolls in 6$^{th}$ for Steve. There is one grain of comfort, however. It turns out that we have both backed Barrie Gerraghty to be top festival jockey at about 12-1. This is his first win of the day.

The indifferent performances of my selections continue. I get no sort of run out of Spinofski in the Fulke Walwyn Chase either. I'm doubly cheesed off because he wasn't even particularly good value. Royal Predica springs a massive surprise at 33-1 to give the bookies a bit of a breather and Pipe his first festival winner this year. That's two races today where I've backed horses I've been following all year, convinced that there's a win just around the corner. More fool me. There's no reward for loyalty here. Nowhere to hide on these testing green acres.

Last race of the day then, and the marathon Pertemps Hurdle provides no relief for either of us. We've moved up to the top of the temporary stand again. This affords wonderful views of the track and we enjoy the closest finish of the day. The runners sweep down from Cleeve Hill as if pushed along by the screaming wind. The same wind that rips right into us in our exposed situation. It's cold up here, and my hip flask is empty. No matter, Inching Closer manages to short head the game Royal Emperor in a tenacious head to head up the hill. He is favourite, almost inevitably, just to rub the bookies noses in the brown stuff, but is also piloted by Barrie Gerraghty. Barrie is becoming our only hope.

Time to head off to Mona's. This is a fantastic arrangement. We start to shrug off the day's disappointments and pick up the declarations on the short journey to Gloucester. I'm learning from Bryn and Steve last year: onwards and upwards; no time for recriminations.

We turn the corner into Archibald Street and I'm looking forward to seeing Mona again. She greets us warmly and gives Steve - a complete stranger - a big smacker on the cheek.
"Aah Dave, it's great to see you, really great. And Steve. Is it Steve? Make yourselves at home. Sit down. Now did you have any winners today any of you?"
Steve starts to answer but she's already gone into the kitchen to put the kettle on.
"I've never been to the races there, but they all tell me about it you know. Did you say you had some winners? Aaah that's nice."
Neither of us has uttered a word yet.

"I'll have a cup of tea for you in a minute boys. Paul will be home in a minute, probably. Unless he's gone to the pub of course. Ha ha"

Before we have drawn breath two cups of piping hot tea and a plate of bourbons have arrived. Steve doesn't drink the stuff. But he hasn't managed to communicate this to Mona. Not easy getting a word in to be honest. He does his best with a few polite sips. Big mistake. Being polite is all well and good, but saying no would have been better. He'll be drowning in tea come Thursday morning.

The only time I've seen Paul, Mona's son, was at his Sister Rita's wedding reception about 8 years ago when he was ripping up the floor with a frighteningly realistic Gary Glitter impression. Not surprising then that I hardly recognise him when he comes in tonight. The four of us have had a bit of a catch up and it isn't long before Paul is escorting us to his local boozer to check out the Champions League action. It's a decent enough local with a big screen for the footie and there's also a full size skittle alley running down the side of the back room. Skittles is a big game in these parts even if it's little known elsewhere. A sort of fore runner to 10-pin bowling without the junk food and video games.

For the second Cheltenham on the trot, I'm not feeling too great and I labour over a couple of pints, whilst Steve is knocking back the Guinness with gusto. We leave Paul entertaining the crowd at the bar, though I don't think he's got as far as Gary Glitter yet. Probably not wise these days.

We are off in search of kebabs and Internet cafes. Steve has hatched a masterful plan to beat the bookies in the ring. He's been researching the location of Internet cafes in the Gloucester area so that we can access the exchanges before pitching up at the track. This is inspirational stuff! Particularly after today's struggle to find even the SP in the ring. Steve's research is spot on. We're only a five minute stroll from Mona's gaff and here we find not one but two such establishments. Who would have thought that Barton Street is at the very hub of the communication revolution? We are in business.

Even better, there are at least two decent looking kebab houses. We venture into the most welcoming. I'm still not 100% and I take the safe small-doner option. But Steve's got a Devil-may-care, bollocks-I'm-on-holiday air that sees him searching the menu. His mischievous eye settles on the house special: the Gloucester Mix.
"The what?" I exclaim.
Our host describes the contents. It seems to involve a contribution from every tray in the display chiller all stuffed into one giant pocket of pitta.
"Hoo-hoo that's the jobby for me" grins Steve, rubbing his hands together.

I can't wait to see this. I'm half way through my feeble snack by the time Steve's spectacular offering is served up, such is the preparation required. The pitta is splitting at the seams with lashings of chicken, doner, shami and shish meat topped up with the meagrest salad filler and a healthy dollop of chilli sauce. All this would add up to a world class kebab on its own, but the *piece de resistance*, the final touch of greatness comes off the searing charcoal griddle last of all. The grinning vendor places a juicy, tender lamb cutlet the size and shape of a tuba on top of Steve's precarious pile. This is awesome. This is a legend in the making. This is an uber-kebab. Steve cackles like the witch in the Wizard of Oz just before she meets her doom. He totters out of the shop unsure how to tackle this creation. You know that scene in The Flintstones when Fred and family arrive at the Drive-in and the waitress lodges a massive dino-rib on the side of their car that tips it over? That's Steve that is, meandering his way up the road with this towering inferno wobbling in his grasp. I bin the remains of my kebab, unable to finish it. I'm shamed by the audacity of Clarkey.

Steve's barely a quarter of the way through his monster by the time we are back at Mona's and he quickly dashes upstairs to stow it away for later as if hoarding rations during The Blitz. By the time he's back down stairs, Mona has a mug of tea and a digestive ready for him. She's also pouring out a nice measure of brandy to warm the cockles.

"Here you go now lads, it's a bottle I have already open. I like a tot of the decent brandy. Will you help me out here?"

Why do I think she's got it in specially for us? Paul is back from the pub by now and in good form.

"Where's this come from Mammy?"

He seizes on the Courvoisier with both hands and he's down on his knees like it's the Holy Grail.

"You've been hiding the good stuff away from me again haven't you?"

Mona grins,

"Ah, away with you, Paul."

By the time we've had a bit more blarney and wend our way to bed, the remnants of Steve's kebab must be stone cold. Much like the tea he's poured into Mona's rubber-tree plant.

I don't have a good night's kip at all. A couple of hours after retiring I wake up with an all too familiar clammy sweat down my back and a tightening stomach. I stir myself into action, fumbling for a t-shirt, and then the door and then the light switch. This is going to be close.

I can feel a retch rising as I shimmy down the stairs. Nightmare, Mona has us in the spare rooms at the top of the house. I round the landing and realise there is another flight stretching out before me.

I'm into the lounge now but everything is churning. I'm going as fast as I can under the circumstances, but the bathroom is beyond the kitchen through the utility room. There are at least two more doors to negotiate in the pitch black.

Time is starting to go backwards and I swear the bog is getting further away. I make it as far as the automatic washing machine before I convulse the day's nourishment over the floor. One more bound and I'm head down over the pan.

It's over as quick as it started really.

I feel much better now that's out and spend the next ten minutes cleaning up, checking the conditioner drawer on the washer just to be sure. Feels like I've been here before. It isn't as bad as I feared. A few spots here and there and it's soon sorted.

I weave my way back upstairs, double-checking for any tell-tale marks. My guts are still dodgy, but I can't face that descent again. So I spread a few pages of the RP out next to my bed and keep one of Mona's fluffy white towels handy. Just in case.

I can't believe this has happened here as well. Last year's incident was odd enough, but today has been bizarre. I was fine yesterday. Absolutely. What's this all about? Eventually I drift of to sleep and there are no more mishaps.

## 21. CHELTENHAM THE THIRD: AT THE DOUBLE

*"A little bit of daylight shine on your pillow*
*Come through your window pane*
*Speak of the morning, hope is eternal*
*Better look at it this way."*
Chris Rea, *Lucky Day*, 1986

Suddenly the room is filled by piercing brightness. I shade my eyes and squint at the door and make out a dark figure filling the frame surrounded by a halo of light.

"Mornin' Davoski. Here's your RP. And they've been giving away free ribenas down at Safeways, so I picked you up a brace. Top result eh? Big day today." He sees the sorry looking RP pages scattered around the floor.

"Fantastic stuff. Been doing some late night revision. That's proper dedication is that."

I can't believe it's morning so soon. Didn't I just clamber back into bed a minute ago? I feel rough. Thick head, churning guts, stale mouth. It feels like a hangover. But I'm relieved to see I haven't chundered again. I can't tell Steve. He and the rest of the lads will never let me live it down. He was already suspicious yesterday when I left the pork bap and the doner kebab. Got to play this one straight. Best foot forward.

On my feet I don't feel too bad. Downstairs, Mona's tea starts to sort me out. Steve blatantly leaves his tea undrunk on the table next to the plate that recently held slices of toast. She is blissfully unaware about his tea dilemma and is already offering top ups and fried eggs.

"I like a nice egg with a nice yellow yolk. Free-range they call them these days. Can I get you boys a nice free-range egg each? They're good, you know. You used to be able to get eggs like this all the time, but you don't see them much now. Not with a tasty proper yellow yolk. You can always tell the good ones from the bad ones. Just one look is enough……"

I don't know how this happens, but in the same sentence Mona has us reliving a family trip back to Ireland involving a train journey to Glasgow and a long wait for the ferry to Belfast. I think the wait at the dockside where they met a man on the scrounge is significant, although I'm not sure why. But they appear to have had breakfast in a café in the docks

"...and this funny peculiar man - d'ye know what I mean Dave, Steve - didn't take to his sort much at all - managed to get his breakfast for free after all that. There's no need fer arl that. But those eggs. They were good free-range eggs"

Now I have a spinning head as well as somersaulting guts. I look at Steve, but he's playing a blinder, nodding encouragement and smiling and laughing at all the right bits. Top performance.

Time to make a move and put the Internet Café plan into action. I'm feeling sort of OK, despite Steve's vivid description of his demolition of the uber-kebab last night in bed. Mona offers us her best brandy for the hip flasks, which is a very welcome and generous gesture. So we are off. Tonight, my Mother-in-Law, Mona's sister will be staying as well. The two of them together fills me with dread. Need some winners today.

If this is the road to recovery, then I'm struggling on the hard shoulder. I can do no more than nibble at my full English and sip at my coffee, whilst trying to absorb contradictory form figures spinning up at me from the dense pages of the RP.

Steve must be suspicious.
    "Can't finish yer breakfast? This is a turn up."
But I can't let on. I need to retain any semblance of credibility that I can.

We stroll into the nearest internet café. A quid buys a full hour of web-time. Nice one, looks like we've unearthed the value already. The Betfair site is humming. They expect to crash through the million pound mark during the Festival for bets matched on a single race. I set up bets at generous odds in 5 of the seven races. This leaves me a bit of scope to plunder the on-course bookies for a couple of interest bets when everything else has crashed and burned. Steve's busy. He's doing the Betfair thing, but he's also on the Spread Betting sites, setting up head to heads, match bets and other curiosities that I can't fathom. I'm ready to pack up when I check my live bets. Horror of horrors, I discover that my 12-1 on Barry Geraghty for top jock has not been matched! More exchange incompetence. That one hurts. Why didn't I just take the best price and at least make sure the money was down? Pure bloody greed, that's why. Holding out for an extra half point or something. He's available at 4s now. I'm not interested in that though. This will teach me. Except it won't.

Meanwhile Steve is exploiting the freedom that Betfair can really deliver when you know what you are doing. He has a place double riding on Keen Leader in the novice chase today. But it's a small field and KL is trading at almost evens for the place. So he lays the place against his potential return to build in a profit of a straight £100. This is how it should be done. Quids in before the off. Guaranteed profit.

Time to hit the rails. There is a fantasy festival update on the cards. Looks like Brynaldo takes an early lead thanks to a punt on the Rooster. Elsewhere its much of a muchness. I pick my selections on the train.

I'm feeling perkier. I sort out a placepot and we pick our way through the buzzing Grandstand to find a perch with a good view of the track. Tattersalls today. We are going upmarket. Nice having these bets down on Betfair already. See that bloke there with a hint of desperation in his eyes, scrabbling around at the bookies feet, searching for morsels of value? That was me yesterday. I'm on Lord Sam for the SunAlliance Novice Hurdle at about 10s.

Big Irish challenge again for this one, headed by favourite Pizarro, with Hardy Eustace and Nil Desperandum all well fancied. It's a close race and nice to be in the middle of the atmosphere. Heading for home three or four are in with a shout, including Lord Sam, and there is a gasp as Coolnagorna lurches left in front of Pizarro just before the 2nd last.

But it's Hardy Eustace who wins quite comfortably on ground that some thought might not be soft enough. "He likes to get his toe in" apparently. One more for Ireland. Coolnagorna, placed 2nd is disqualified for interference. I think Lord Sam may have been hampered in the incident, but he was never close enough to have won, having jumped a bit novicey here and there.

SunAlliance Chase now. My bets have been safely tucked away for some time. A hard-earned each-way double on One Knight - struck in those dark days when my fingers were being burnt on Betfair lay cock-ups - is my biggest potential win of the Festival. I also have a speculative punt on Henrietta Knight's Stars Out Tonight at 100-1. I'm delighted to see that SOT is now trading at 14-1! Henrietta says he needs it like a road. But at these prices I feel like I've won already! I haven't bothered laying any of this off as I've only had a tiny stake. And anyway, I'd only balls it up.

Steve is sitting on his Keen Leader lay and it looks like it's reverse exacta time for him as he heads off to the Tote. I'm starting to criticise my betting strategy. My best hope here is a place. KL and Jair Du Cochet are dominating the market. Rightly so as they have cleaned up on nearly all the best novice chases all season. But It Takes Time is also a short price. Can't understand that. I just don't see his form as being that strong.

The field is a little depleted, injuries having taken their toll on one or two novices who might expect to make this line up, and only nine horses head out when the tape snaps up. One Knight is immediately prominent, but already making mistakes. Can't pick out the errors from here as they are down the back straight, but the course announcer is in no doubt

"...and One Knight got in close to that one......another mistake by One Knight........One Knight nodded on landing...."

But he's still there, Johnson on board, at the head of affairs. Looks to me like the chasing pack are ready to swallow him up out on the back straight for the 2nd time. He's still niggling at fences too, but galloping on strongly all the same. Keen Leader and Jair Du Cochet have not yet got to him and are leaving it late. Indeed Keen Leader looks out of it. Stars Out Tonight has not been sighted and is pulled up before the home turn.

But now I am getting a few flutters. One Knight keeps grinding on and Johnson is working hard up top. At the last fence he has maybe three lengths in hand of the fast closing Jair Du Cochet. Here we go. I brace myself for that familiar sinking feeling when my horse is mugged on the run-in.

Not this time though. Jair Du Cochet may be eating up the advantage with every stride but Johnson is flailing away on the leader like a carpet beater, harnessing every muscle in his body to drive One Knight onwards. Jacques Riqou on the French raider can't get there in time. Surely he's left it too late! The Hobbs gelding holds on!

Oh, this is a big one. My best ever win, I reckon. And not a minute too soon. This is going to change round my festival. But I've also got a bit of disbelief going on here too. I don't feel the raw excitement of the Tales of Bounty or Rith Dubh moments and I think its because I was so sure that Cochet - surely Ricou threw it away by holding up his horse too long - or Keen Leader would come out of the clouds to win. Maybe this will sink in later. KL finished out of the frame. First class call by Steve to lay the place on the exchange. Wonderful piece of cool headed punting.

Moscow Flyer is marvellous in the Champion Chase. He wins very assuredly and gives a wonderful display, piloted expertly by Barry Geraghty who is now nip and tuck with Richard Johnson for the festival top jock spot. I love this race partly because of where it comes in the programme. We've just seen two hell for leather long distance novice events with oodles of rip roaring action. The follow up could not be a greater contrast. Here we see the Rolls Royces of chasers purring round the minimum trip at a high cruising speed and showing pinpoint accuracy at the fences. Edredon Bleu, almost inevitably is leading them round these gorgeous green acres at a good clip. These boys are the finished article.

The group rises and falls with the undulations of the course like children on a merry-go-round. Steve and I have both had sentimental wagers on Edredon at good prices. Steve also has a semi-mental bet on Latalomne. Despite his fall last year and having a quiet season so far, Steve's logic is that Latalomne loves it round Cheltenham and has been laid out for the race.

I've had a proper bet on Kadarran who could be a bit over priced. But he isn't. The Nicholls 2$^{nd}$ string is out of contention quite early after making a mistake. Latalomne isn't though! I'm in danger of eating my words. At the business end of the race he's looming up against the leaders full of intent. They approach the 2$^{nd}$ last. Everyone is thinking the same thing. Will he fall like last year. Steve's impassive, but he must be urging Vinnie Keane to climb over the fence with every fibre of his being. But even this is insufficient.

Unbelievably, Latalomne falls again. There's a little dip before the fence and quite a drop on the other side. The horses are all running with the throttle wide open by this point and Latalomne tries to put in a little extra stride. His legs are all over the place on the landing side and it leaves horse and jockey with no where to go. They tumble to earth. Steve sees it a fraction before me and his face tells a story. No longer impassive, he's as sick as a dog. He's not sure whether he feels better or worse than last year. It's almost identical. Seebald also pitches up when going well, though not as strongly as Latalomne. Moscow Flyer runs out a comfortable winner.

What else is there to say? Another awful piece of luck for Steve at the 2nd last on the Old Course. So many of his best hopes have come to grief here.

We decide to change scenery. It's been fantastic to catch the three Grade 1s from in the Grandstand without having to move a muscle. But now the Tattersalls hordes are a bit more mobile and there's more room to manoeuvre. We stand by the rail for the Coral Cup where Tony Martin's Xenophon cooks up a significant handicap scam. He cruises up at 4-1 having been backed in from long odds, overhauling Samon in the run-in. I'm on Yeomans Point who I don't lay eyes on for the entire race. He rolls up last of the 25 to finish. By the time he crosses the line, Mick FitzGerald is walking Xenophon past the stands into the winners enclosure. We are leaning over the rail and get a fine look at the beast. Fitz is slapping the winner's mud spattered neck. We applaud politely, in accordance with tradition. Bastard.

Steve's arranged to see Intersky Andy by the parade ring for a quick natter. He's putting a brave face on the Falcon's performance yesterday and is reasonably upbeat about festival, but it's apparent that he's lost a packet on the Champion Hurdle. Particularly because the horse failed to make the frame. All Andy's ante-post accumulators went down in a pile. He feels that the blame lays with the tactics used in the race: running too freely in the early stages may have cost him at least a place. Sounds like a laugh over in the corporate box though, despite the overcrowding and distance from the finishing post.

I leave them to chew the fat for a while longer and move over to the Guinness enclosure for the four-miler. The lucky Guinness End. The lucky four-miler. My Rith Dubh this year is to be Lucky Bay. Well, that's what the script says.

It's a fair old race and Lucky Bay runs respectably in mid-division, but no more than that. Jonjo O'Neill plots up a huge win as Sudden Shock at 25-1 catches Stormez up the hill. I don't know where Steve is, but if he's caught the race he will be screaming at the track. The burden of his wedge has fallen on Hedgehunter who has made a major blunder at - where else - the 2nd last whilst gunning for the lead and going like a dream. The mistake puts paid to his chances and he struggles home in 12th. I hook up with Steve as I'm tucking in to a delicious steak bap. I think I'm on the comeback trail. He's shaking his head. I sympathise with him. That was harsh. He saw the race on the Tote screen with Andy and his reaction is unprintable.

The Milmay of Flete is won by Young Spartacus, trained to perfection by Henry Daly after being off the track for over a year. I'm on Silence Reigns who never gets a run.

Back to the rails for the Champion Bumper. This is the race we missed last year. Getting to grips with the form is a nightmare. There is a field of 20 plus and they all have 1s against their name in H graded bumpers. I just don't follow these races at all. The talking horse is Pipe's Liberman, with Henderson's Back To Ben Alder. So we avoid those. There's also a whisper for Be Fair off the flat. Michael Hills is riding and the price is crashing in. The bookies are running scared. It's slaughter down in the ring. Every camel-hair coat for himself! Steve and I have taken a similar approach, minimum stakes on a couple of outsiders and we lump together on a reverse exacta! Come on, last race of the day!

To my mild surprise, it's a belter of a bumper. There is plenty of grunting and grinding in mid division and some allegations of obstruction coming up the home straight. One of my Betfair hopes, Widemouth Bay is screaming over the hill fast and late. Looks to me like he suffered a bit of interference, but for a moment I think he's going to nod it on the line. The angle is deceptive though and Liberman takes the race with Widemouth Bay a 'fast finishing' 3$^{rd}$. McCoy's first winner of the Festival. Be Fair is a huge disappointment, rolling in 21$^{st}$. We see them all come past the stands and Be Fair is massive. Head and mane above the others. "Chaser in the making" we knowingly mutter to each other.

Back at Mona's Chris, my Mother-in-Law has arrived. She can't let me go anywhere. Or maybe she's checking out the company I keep! Mona and Chris together are a dangerous prospect. The tea is already brewing in the pot as we let ourselves in (Mona's given us a key and everything). They are both 'deloited' to hear that we've had a good day. We took into chocolate digestives as the two of them detail plans for their Skittles Club trip to Blackpool. Does Blackpool know what it's in for? (I later hear that Mona had an argument with a barman in the Tower because he put ice in her brandy! He really should have known better.) There are about a dozen of them going and it sounds like a right laugh. Paul's arrived from work and he's in fine form.

With a couple of beers inside him and an audience to work with Paul switches to his showman persona. He's having a bit of chat with us all, taking the mick out of Mona and Chris's never ending conversations - the way they speak at the same time as each other, changing subject by osmosis without losing the plot, and never seeming to breathe except maybe through their ears. Chris is nearly in hysterics.

Paul's on form. His eyes are bulging and his frame is wired. He pulls out a chair from under the table and straddles it American TV cop-style. He flicks his full head of hair back in an extravagant manner and focuses on the middle distance.

" 'Now, Paddy. What's your specialist subject?' " He delivers a compelling and hilarious rendition of the Irish Mastermind contestant joke in dialect-perfect County Cork accent. I'd last seen this in Pete McCarthy's book 'McCarthy's Bar'. Paul's name checks of the landmark Irish terrorist events are flawless.

" 'Ireland: The Easter Rising and the War of Independence 1916 to 1921' says Paddy."

"Oh, I've heard this before, Paul it's a bit rude" chimes Chris, but she's grinning from ear to ear and can't wait for the punch line. Paul continues.

"So Magnus fixes Paddy with a beady eye. 'First question: name one of the leaders of the 1916 Easter Rising' 'Pass' says Paddy. 'Name the leader of the IRA who later agreed to partition.' 'Pass' replies Paddy again. 'Name the first leader of the Irish Free State.' Again Paddy is impassive. 'Pass' he responds without a flicker. Then someone at the back of the audience pipes up...." Paul dwells on the cusp of the punch line and looks at each of us.

"...'Good man, Paddy. Tell the bastards fuck all!' Harharharhar."

This man should be on the stage. He's wasted in the Post Office.

Steve and I plan to venture further into Gloucester for a beer tonight, but Mona's on the tea run again before they head off to the Irish Club.

"Could I have a coffee Mona?" Bold move from Steve.

"Eh? Oh. Coffee you say? Oh well, yes we have coffee round here somewhere. Paul is really good at making a nice coffee. You know in the café thing. Don't go for it much myself. Paul? Paul? Steve wants a nice coffee. Can you make the boy one?"

"No, no, an instant coffee is fine. Don't go to the trouble of filter", pleads Steve.

Too late. Paul makes a great show of putting down his dinner, trudging into the kitchen, knocking the crockery around and finally producing a cafetiere for Steve.

"Lovely" he comments. Way past the embarrassing stage now. I'm enjoying the show.

We stumble upon a fine old coaching inn not far from the Cathedral where we indulge in a couple of excellent ales. Steve spots Looks Like Trouble on the pump clip of one of the local beers. What better advert could there be? Liverpool are on the telly in the Champions League and the beers slip down easily as we mull over the days highlights. This is how it's meant to be.

On the way home, Steve takes on the formidable Gloucester Mix again. Its an inspiring performance. This time he feels no need to sneak upstairs polish off the colossal feast. Mona and Chris are back from the Club and we fall into meaningless banter until bedtime.

## 22. CHELTENHAM THE THIRD: BOOKIE MASSACRE

*"Blood in the street. Blood on the rocks. Blood in the gutter.*
*Every last drop. If you want blood, you got it."*
AC/DC *"If You Want Blood"* 1980

Steve is all furrowed brow over the fantasy festival update.
"You're back in with a shout, Davoski!"
One Knight has put me in the frame, but Brynaldo is still flying high after producing Moscow Flyer. I notice Steve is sipping a mug of coffee.
"Made it myself!" he grins.

There's time to nip out and buy Mona some flowers and a bottle of brandy before we depart. She's been an absolute star and a fantastic host. Mona and Chris leave us to lock up as they head off shopping "for a few bits and pieces". It will take them all day. But not before they have given us bets to put down in today's big races. All Irish selections, of course.

I'm busy getting stuck into the day's fields on Betfair, still cursing the Barry Geraghty cock-up, when Helen texts me. "Raj saw you on telly yesterday at the races". Hey hey! Fame at last. Raj owns my local newsagents and we often swap hard luck stories about the nags. I told him a month or so back that I was sweet on Spirit Leader for the Tote Gold Trophy at a massive price. Come the day I talked myself out of it and of course she duly trotted up. Never change your mind. Raj backed her though. And thanked me for the tip! He must have caught us when the cameras were filming Xenophon yesterday on the horse walk in front of the stands.

We meet the boys by the entrance. I think they've only just arrived. There is a symphony of greetings. But something is wrong. Where is that dapper, well-spoken chap with the polite manner and conservative staking plan? Oh no! Vaughany is missing! Nick and Bryn have been trying to get hold of him all morning without success. They rightly decided to head off without him. Pressures back at the office are to blame, we conclude. That's the price you pay for such naked ambition.

We spill out on to the steps in front of the bar. Jesus it's cold. I'm stood next to Ben and for the first time I notice that he looks a bit grey.
"Oh Dave, it was a bad one. Launch event for the White Paper. Don't know what time I got in." Paul is here too.
"He slept nearly all the way on the train."
Ben cups a cigarette against the wind and tries to open his eyes wide enough to fix me with a pitiful look. He's got two days' worth of stubble to keep his face warm but he's still shivering.
"This is the start of a week's leave. Think I'll just sleep through that as well!"
He does look rough.

Selections are coming in for the fantasy festival. I'm on Spectroscope for the Triumph hurdle at a big price on Betfair and in the fantasy competition. He likes good ground, but he doesn't seem to be fancied at all. Nick has had no tips on the journey down and so is playing safe. Select and protect. He's on the Pipe horse, Well Chief. Bryn's on the favourite, Golden Cross. He's trying to consolidate. Bloody favourite backers. He sidles up to Steve seeking to consolidate his position at the head of the competition.

"Yeah, I'll have a little tenner each way on Golden Cross"

At this point I think he even gives a little furtive look around in case one of us is trying to overhear his selections. But maybe I'm just making this up.

"….and while you're at it, I can give you my horse for the Stayers too"

A rare note of smugness from Brynaldo

"Tenner each way on Limestone That should do it."

"Awright, Brynaldo, consider it done."

Steve notes the transaction in his little black book.

Five of us move down to the apex of the triangle between the course proper and the run in. Sharon and Gunner look after the bags (no left luggage of course). This is a great place to see the 20 or so juveniles skitter past the stands and away into the country. Not much between them at this stage. Come the home turn the sight lines are not so good and I'm relying on the big screen for info. Over the last Well Chief seems to have the lead. Nick is looking edgy. Is he going to land a $1^{st}$ race jackpot again? But Spectroscope, with that lovely Barry Geraghty aloft is flying up the track. I can feel the ground move under their hooves but I can't see a bloody thing. I think the course commentator has called Spectroscope the winner.

"Woo-hoo!" I declare as Nick spits out the result.

He gives me a filthy look and he stamps out his butt with mock aggression on the concrete. I think it's mock!   Jonjo O'Neill. You little darling. This is a top result. Spectroscope nets me a nice little wedge and Lilium De Cotte has snuck into $4^{th}$ place to land my place double set up by Frosty Canyon at Chepstow in December. Ecstasy! I have a wobble when Steve says the bookies are only paying out on the first three, but I check the slip and I definitely have the four places for an ante-post. I can scarcely believe this Cheltenham. This and the Sun Alliance Chase have easily given me my best ever festival haul. I feel like I'm walking on air.

Back at the bar, Steve reports that after the race Bryn once again sidled up to him and whispered

"Er, you know that fantasy wedge on Limestone? Well, I think I need to scrap that. That'll be OK won't it?" My turn to be smug. Move over Bryn. I'm planning to clean up on the fantasy festival too!

The Stayers should be a good race. Baracouda looks at the top of his form once again and I'm looking forward to seeing the legendary Limestone Lad, relieved of Bryn's wedge,  take him on for the first time. With the novice Iris's Gift lobbed in by Jonjo O'Neill and luminaries such as Classified, Deanos Beano and Galileo out to show their mettle it should be a fascinating contest. The front-running Limestone will ensure a true pace from where Baracouda will love to pounce, although he has been caught out by giving away a soft lead before.

I leave the lads so that I can strike a reverse exacta plot involving Baracouda and Brother Joe who must come good again sometime soon. But the ladies in red are messing me around.

"Ah'm sorry sonny. Ah divn't nar wot's up with the masheens, like, but ah cannut get ya bet doon. Can ya come back lyater, like?"
No I can't go back later. As I'm translating this irritating news from Geordie into English, the tape goes up. I end up watching the race from outside the Tote booth beyond the bar. It's not a bad pitch as it happens. I can hear the commentary and can see the group led by Limestone Lad at a merry clip all the way round the circuit. I'm getting a different perspective. It's clear the Brother Joe will not be in the mix. He seems unable to get himself into contention and looks fatally outpaced down the back. Good. I'm not on.

With two to go the winner could come from any of the three principals. Iris's is running the race of his life. The Lad refuses to give up, but Baracouda looks imperious. Thierry Doumen glides the French raider past the game Bowes beast and into the lead before the last. But it's still not over as Geraghty on the Gift rouses his mount for one last assault. He's closing but Baracouda shows unexpected resolution in front to hang on by ¾ length. Another thriller to set the crowd alight before the Gold Cup and another favourite ships more water into the bookies sinking vessel. If Best Mate trots up in the big one there will be carnage.

I catch up with the gang. A couple of us were on Baracouda but not much has been staked or won. Such a short priced winner does nothing to change the fantasy festival standings either.

Five of us watch the Gold Cup from close to the winning post: Me, Nick, Steve, Bryn and Ben. I've got a live ante-post bet on Valley Henry and Steve's got a massive price at small stakes on Truckers Tavern. But none of us can really see much beating Best Mate. I'm not sure why I haven't backed anything each way in this. It pans out exactly that way. Best Mate is glorious. Valley Henry and Chives give him a serious race from the top of the hill. Chives quickly falls away, but Valley Henry is still up by the side of Best Mate with three fences to go. For a brief moment I catch myself wondering if VH is about to run the biggest race of his life. But it is only for a moment. No sooner have they cleared the fence then Jim Culloty on the Champ squeezes the accelerator a little. That's all it needs.

The Grandstand thunders its approval. I swear the whole enclosure does a little shimmy. Matey is soon clear. The pack can't live with him. This is his manor. He doesn't touch a twig over the last and is roared all the way home by an ecstatic crowd to win by a cool 10 lengths. Everyone's Best Mate. This is a majestic, mighty performance.

Valley Henry finishes very tired and is pushed into 4th on the run-in. At least he was out to race today. Truckers Tavern and Harbour Pilot fill the frame, but were probably only running for place money anyway.

Best Mate rightly gets a hero's welcome. He destroyed that field. I feel genuinely privileged to witness to a legend in the making. We exchange knowing looks, whistle through our teeth and pass comments of a general awestruck nature. Five go ga-ga in the Courage End.

Best Mate has given the bookies another kick in the teeth, returning at 13-8. I read later that despite his being ante-post favourite for virtually the whole year, over £500,000 was taken out of the ring on the day. This includes one bet of £100,000 to win £150,000. It wasn't me. Coral's said that nationwide, Best Mate cost the firm a payout of over a million pounds. I don't think my One Knight swoop caused too much of a ripple then!

I'm having a fairly serious conversation with Nick about the quality of the last race, when I tackle him:
"You're having a poor day, mate. Getting anxious yet?" I probe. He looks at me like he knows something I don't.
"How's your placepot doing? Mine's still up!"
What?
"What?" I say. It's true. He's backed favourites in every race so far and they've made the frame each time.
"It's only short price stuff, and there's still three races to go anyway." I scoff. He's got Kingscliff in the next, the Foxhunter Chase. This one may be the Gold Cup for Amateurs, but it still leaves me a bit cold after the big one. Kingscliff goes off favourite and returns 1st past the post exactly 6 mins and 49.5 secs later. I join Nick back at the bar and he's still grinning. Four up.

He's on Vol Solitaire in The Grand Annual next. So am I. It's a decent race and Vol Solitaire has every chance until two out where he seems to be just a bit outpaced. Palarshan wins in fine style and Vol Solitaire finishes a game 4th. I have a quick look at the card and there are more than 20 runners in the handicap. 4th is good enough for Nick. He's still alive with his first non-favourite. No good for me though, I've backed the Nicholls beast to win.

We have the final scene of Fantasy Festival to act out. The Cathcart is the last race in the comp. The other boys are still playing catch up since well-fancied horses have won both the Stayers and the Gold Cup. They are forced to back outsiders to reel me in. I'm tempted to resort to Bryn's erstwhile cautious tactics and have £10 each way on short-priced favourite La Landiere. I really do think about it. But decide I don't want to sink to his levels and prefer to out him as a wuss! 20 quid on Poliantas then, my original selection. I'm with Ben at the top of the temporary stand, surveying the battlefield under steely skies. It is starting to feel like the Festival is winding down. The end of another epic journey.

This Cathcart isn't a classic renewal on paper. La Landiere has put together a string of very impressive wins this season and held entries for the SunAlliance Novice Chase and the Gold Cup. She receives a healthy mares allowance and is well-weighted here. It seems to have frightened off some of the other competitors. It's a good race though. Poliantas runs well without really getting amongst them. La Landiere clears the last in the lead to a huge roar from the crowd and comes home to fill the boots of the punters again. This is the first Cheltenham winner for Richard Phillips and he is ecstatic. Later he says

"This is my first Festival winner and it is what I've dreamed of since I was a child"

He's quite emotional. And rightly so. He goes on to say of his star mare,

"Put it this way. If Best Mate had bollocks, they'd make wonderful children!"

Excellent stuff. A bit of real enthusiasm. A bit of real Cheltenham spirit.

Paul is looking in vain for some real Cheltenham spirit of his own. We are back at the bar and a shocking story is emerging. Paul's backed La Landiere down in the ring, cheered her home like everyone else and the unscrupulous bookie has scarpered without settling any of his bets! I can't believe that this sort of shady behaviour still goes on, particularly at the showpiece meeting of the year.

This does the games' image no favours at all. Some joke bookie has been happy to take everyone's wedge on the Phillips mare, but has closed his fat satchel and bolted for the exit before the race has finished. It stinks. I bet he's not the only arsehole to have taken money in good faith and made a swift exit either. Steve takes Paul to the harassed Betting Ring Manager. After a bit of arguing the toss, he honours Paul's bet and promises to take the matter up directly with the offending bookie. This is the right result in this case, but the manager won't be in a position settle all the bets. What about the big punters? And another thing. Steve knows his way around the racecourse. How many people with winning La Landiere tickets would know that such a manager existed? Or would be able to find the office in the scrum of the Courage Enclosure? How many who leave without cashing in their winning vouchers won't bother following up the issue after the races? I bet plenty went home with unsettled bets and a bitter taste in their mouths. Maybe it was their first visit to a racecourse. Maybe it was their last, too. Yours faithfully, disillusioned of Cheltenham.

Nevertheless, the punting stats for this festival are frightening. Ten out 20 races are won by favourites. The bookies have taken an absolute hammering.

"It was an unmitigated disaster for bookmakers on- and off the course," says Channel 4s John McCririck.

A respected layer describes it as "an absolute bloodbath" It is later estimated that the meeting as a whole cost the industry about £20 million. It is claimed that even the stock market was later affected as the value of some bookies plunged.

Fair enough, but this all sticks in my craw a bit. Ultimately, bookies still come out on top and a bad festival doesn't excuse the disgraceful behaviour of those that take the punters money and run. What would happen if I should refuse to pay for a bet one day on the basis that I'm taking a bit of a beating? I'd be laughed out of the shop. It doesn't work like that. Taking the rough with the smooth is how it works. That said, there's plenty argue that punters have never had it so good. I read in the RP that with no betting tax, new opportunities on betting exchanges and increased competition between bookies, anyone who can't make money on the horses should take up basket weaving. This tongue in cheek view probably says more about the industry view of horse race gambling than it means to. Evidence of increased competition in the ring is thin on the ground from where I stand. And even with betting turnover running at record levels, the industry is still moaning about the competition of exchanges rather than developing opportunities; and shrouding its commentaries in negative spin and permanent pessimism. I'm not paranoid it's just that they are all out to get us. Yours faithfully, disgruntled of Cheltenham.

Thank the Lord that there is another race or I might end up a right miserable bastard. It's County Hurdle time. A good test of stamina this one. Not the horses. Mine and Steve's. I think I've peaked already. But Steve is still waiting to scale his zenith. He leaves it late. He's on Spirit Leader at a lovely price. She leaves it even later, picking off Balapour in a true rip-snorter up the hill to win by a neck. She defied a big weight to land this and it's an impressive performance. She's had a great season, landing three quality handicaps and I haven't backed her once. I find out later that my newsagent Raj has. Again. That horse owes him nothing!

But this is Steve's moment. He's waited all day for this one. A genuine festival saver. Quality call. I think he's also got Balapour to beat something trailing his wake in a match bet too. And it gets better. Who's on board? Barry Geraghty. Steve lands his bet for top festival jockey, too. Geraghty has ridden 5 to victory, pipping Richard Johnson by one.

No, I'm wrong. It's also Nick's moment. He was also on La Landiere in the Cathcart earlier and his placepot has come up! I'm taking the piss about the number of favourites that have gone in I tell him he won't even get his money back. He's now on his way back from the Tote, picking his way through race-goers heading homewards. Six of us are gathered expectantly on the steps of the bar, trying to read his body language. We can see his face as he clambers over fast food rubbish and discarded plastic glasses. He's grinning. The ladies in red have done him proud. He waves a fistful of dollars.
    "Oh ye of little faith!" he bellows triumphantly. "£45!"
We all roar approval.
    "Hey hey! Murdered 'em today!"
What a way to finish.

We take the bus back to Festival Central rather than the circuitous route via the boozers in Montpellier. The station is heaving by the time we arrive and we huddle at the end of the platform hoping to sneak onto the end of the train and secure ourselves some decent seats. The train stops with a carriage door right in front of us.

"Ye-e-e-e-e-es!" we chorus.
But it's the guards van and we can't open the door.

"No-o-o-o-o-o!" we scream and charge to the other end of the carriage.
High farce on Platform 1. We end up sitting two-by-two airline style. But Ben is oblivious, he's asleep virtually before the train leaves the station. He has to be woken up to drink his Champagne. Yes. We've finally beaten the bookie in Fantasy Festival. Our combined winnings are more than we started off with. We've waited four years for this. Steve honourably and magnanimously buys a bottle of bubbly from the opportunistically well-stocked trolley that passes down the carriage. I annoy Nick for the rest of the journey by totting up my winnings on the schedule of shame and asking him who's won the Fantasy Festival trophy the most times.

## 23. VODKATINI

*"You know you're gonna lose, and gambling's for fools.
But that's the way I like it baby, I don't want to live forever"*
Motorhead *"Ace of Spades"* 1980

The late 80's found me scratching around in London's private rented sector, moving from Charlton to Peckham and back again, trying to squeeze a small foot on to the overcrowded lower rungs of the property ladder. During this period I spent much time with my Bookie mate, Simon. We enjoyed some excellent trips to Kempton, Sandown and Ascot for some ace racing. Simon was a relief shop manager for William Hill. I shared a flat with him in Charlton briefly.

Charlton was a strange old place. It didn't feel like London. It didn't really feel like anywhere in particular, but it definitely wasn't London. Greenwich back up the road certainly was - all sophisticated shops and maritime history. So was Woolwich the other way - cosmopolitan bustle and purpose. Charlton felt flat.

I lived opposite The Valley at first. The Addicks ground was derelict then. A very sorry sight indeed. Not much glory was left about the fine old stadium. The roofs had been removed and well-established weeds invaded every nook and cranny of powdering concrete walls. The walls in turn were ringed by rusting security fences keeping out prying eyes. The steeply banked stands had been reduced to nothing much more than rubble. The patch of wasteland in the middle where the pitch used to be was host to half-filled skips, chunks of concrete and assorted debris. My mate Mike told me he saw The Who here in 1972. It was almost impossible to visualise this place as a shrine to the mod generation and venue for the loudest rock n roll band of the time.

The stadium's dereliction contributed to the overall vacuous atmosphere of Charlton. My flat did little to elevate the emotions. I had a claustrophobic room at the back of the house above a kitchen secreting multicultural culinary odours right to the foot of my bed. The room had the oddest wallpaper which illustrated power boats of various shapes, sizes and knottage. I always assumed the room had been occupied by a child, but you never know. They were a strange bunch round there and my flatmates fitted the profile alright. John: "I'm a kick boxer. Because you can't always run away, right?"; and Ahmed: "From the north, yeah? Mushy peas, right, I work at Sainsbury's. I can get you some". Irritable neighbours completed the picture: "Hello I'm Nora. Your music was too loud last night."

I probably got off likely, come to think of it. My first experience of renting anywhere in the private sector was at college in Stoke-on Trent. Me and two mates moved out of a condemned college-owned tower block into a flat share in a part of town called Cobridge, very close to the dog track. I'm struck once again how my life is studded with gambling landmarks. The rent was £10 week for a room in a festering pit of a mutilated terraced house. It was filthy top to bottom. Only one room had heating, a gas fire in the living room that pumped out more carbon monoxide that heat. The flimsy bathroom extension was particularly Arctic having been attached to the end of the kitchen with Pritt Stick.

The best bit was the front bedroom though. This was occupied by Vicky. Mr Majed, our landlord described her as a 'working girl' when we moved in. Sure enough she clocked on at 8ish each night and entertained a number of guests in her room till the early hours. Even the landlord collected the rent in kind. She used a legendary light of *'Roxanne'* fame in the hall to signal her availability, although it was blue, not red.

Vicky was a sad case. She could be perfectly OK in the early evening, but she had a real problem with glue sniffing and she could undergo a complete character transformation in a few short hours. You would look at her and she'd be staring right through you with a chilling sneer on her face and gabbling all sorts of rubbish.
   "You boys. Boys. You are spoiling my trade. I was alright here before you moved in, boys!"
I'm not sure she would ever have been dangerous or violent, but there were plenty of nights when I wasn't sure.

It was a stinking, scary house and we lasted there about 6 weeks. Even that included three weeks at home for Easter.
   "How's your new house, Dave?" inquired my Mum. "Me and your Dad thought we'd come down and see it." Er. Don't think so…….

The landlord, anxious to hang on to his reliable, gullible young tenants, found us somewhere nearer the college that was almost habitable. He asked if we wanted to take Vicky with us. We politely declined and said we would find someone else to fill the fourth bedroom! The house and dog track in Cobridge are both long gone. Demolished as part of a Potteries regeneration project. God knows it needed one.

So Charlton was obviously a step up the property ladder, powerboat wallpaper and all. Woolwich Road was the main artery following the river linking Greenwich with the rest of South East London. This is where my bookie mate Simon rented a flat above the junk shop next to the Chinese take-away.

Whilst a few notches above Cobridge on the tally stick, it still left a bit to be desired. The living room had a nice feel. But it sloped down to the river on a shockingly steep gradient and had wallpaper straight out of the Trotters' *Only Fools and Horses* Nelson Mandela House pad. I don't particularly have a hang up about wallpaper. I just happen to have had some bad encounters with the stuff in this corner of London. The flat was freezing too. Perishing. When it rained water cascaded down the light flex in the hallway. Rather disturbing.

Just down the road was an odd, recently built and featureless pub called The Watermans. There was hardly ever anyone in there. We went in pretty regularly though. As my first London local it left a lot to be desired. Thin, flat Courage best bitter turned sourer still by the po- faced landlady. Goose as she was known. Never acknowledged us in all the months we drank there.

There was a decent enough looking pub across the road called the Antigalican. It was a striking boozer - the exterior was a maze of ornate white plaster-work on red brick. It was also a brew pub. I could probably have had a decent pint there, surrounded by character full south London charm. But Si refused to drink in there. "Crap pub" was all I could ever get out of them. I was never man enough to go in by myself (I was a simple northern boy in those days and always acquiesced to my betters and wisers).

This idiosyncratic flat, the welcoming Watermans Arms and the Antigalican with all its unfulfilled promise are no longer there. Gone. There's a theme developing here. And it's not just the wallpaper. I discovered whilst running the London Marathon in 1997 that this delightful corner of south east metropolitan charm had been lost to the Woolwich Road improvement scheme. Part of my life buried under a bus lane.

But knocking around with Simon the Bookie didn't teach me anything about winning on the horses. Si was the first person I had met who was serious about gambling. Perhaps not in the amount he spent (we are not talking silly money), but more by the fact that he kept a record of all his bets, knew the form well and was prepared to lay off his potential losses. Stunning. I have still not got my head around this basic requirement of successful gambling. Even now.

Once at Kempton there was a very close finish - needless to say, not involving my horse. Simon's selection was in the frame though and this was the first time I had seen anyone back against their horse on the photo to get something out of the result. My synapses do not fire that quickly!

I was turning up to meetings (I'd only just stopped calling them 'meets'. "That's what fox hunts are called", rasped Simon) with no real purpose and no prospect of winning. I never arrived at a track full of confidence. The biggest kick I ever got from the bookies was trailing up and down the pitches and taking a moral victory when I struck my £2 bet at 7-2 rather than 3-1.

But I did enjoy the spectacle. I knew good horses when I saw them. We were privileged to see some cracking fixtures, and some of the jump game's best chasers, particularly at Sandown for meetings like the Tingle Creek Chase and the Whitbread Gold Cup.

I was lucky enough to see Desert Orchid at the peak of his powers. Dessie, the housewives favourite, has had as many eulogies dedicated to him as any horse since Arkle. Nothing I have to say can add to the legend. But I know how he made me feel when I saw him jump. There was something genuinely exciting about the way he stood a country mile off his fences and cleared them like a flamboyant showjumper, barely brushing the top and gaining two lengths on the opposition. That's how I remember it every time. Even now when I see a good jumper like Edredon Bleu on his day, I catch myself saying "...just like Desert Orchid". He was the first beast that I saw in the flesh that took away my breath when he took on a fence. You never forget the first time. He brought clichés like "made the hairs stand up on the back of your neck" to life.

It's all been said before, so there is no point in talking about how striking he looked. Particularly from a distance where his near-white colouring made him stand out, exaggerating his leaps.

Seen close up it was a very different experience. One meeting at Sandown, Simon and I headed across the course to watch the race from the far side. We had no betting interest in the 3 mile chase. Desert Orchid was a short price and I don't think I would have contemplated opposing him in those days. We stood by the famous Railway fences – three stiff obstacles in a line adjacent to the main London-South Coast route. We were able to get in close to the middle fence. Two things struck me about seeing the race from the track side. The first was that the field seemed to be tearing along at a right old clip. Much faster than it appeared from the stands. These horses were amongst the best staying chasers of their day and it was quite something to get a feel for their deceptively speedy cruising speed. The other revelation was the noise. The thud of hooves in the soft turf and snorting of battling horses is so often lost in the roar of the crowd. Out there in the country the race seemed very detached from the commotion of the grandstand. Dessie didn't disappoint at the fence. He was up to it and over with all his customary panache. His rivals rustled the birch with foreleg and hind leg - almost deafening out here. But not Dessie. I swear I never saw him so much as caress a stick in his whole career. Honest.

I'm not going to mention his oft-referred to tenacity and courage, either. And there's no point repeating the plaudits he earned for that inspirational performance of guts and determination in the legendary Gold Cup of 1989 when going the 'wrong way' (he favoured right-handed tracks) and in bottomless ground (there was still snow on Cleeve Hill), he chased Yahoo up the home straight and passed him to bring the Gold Cup back for David Elsworth. Not a dry eye in the house. A story to bare repetition alongside those other courageous performances like Dawn Run catching Wayward Lad in front of the stands.

I remember backing a horse called Vodkatini a lot in those days. We saw him campaigned over 2 and 3 mile chases with some success around Ascot, Kempton and Sandown. I even won on him a couple of times. He was entered in the Tingle Creek Chase in 1988 when Si and I were there. I backed him of course. Kiss of death. The bloody horse planted his feet and refused to start. Richard Rowe was his jockey most of the time and I remember his hapless urging on top of the truculent sod. Vodkatini was 2-1 favourite as well. He had had a fantastic year that included a win at the Cheltenham Festival. 2-1 sounds like the sort of price I was looking for in those days. I was not amused. My love affair with him ended right then! Desert Orchid went on to win at a canter. My new hero. Vodkatini turned out at Cheltenham the week after and won at 5-2! That was the last race he ever landed. 1988 was his golden year.

My last visit with Simon to Sandown Park for years was in 1990 for the Whitbread Gold Cup. This was always a showpiece fixture. A marathon event over 3½ miles held at the end of April. It was always seen as bringing the curtain down on the domestic jumps season. Simon had had a weekend in Paris visiting his sister and had come back in a stinking depression because he'd met someone out there and couldn't bear to leave her behind. He was hardly interested in the racing and I struggled to maintain my enthusiasm in the face of such defiant misery.

We talked over at length what had happened, but there was no thaw in the mood. Looking back on that day, I suspect that the result of the showpiece event of the day was more significant than Simon's grief. Sorry Si! It was a shame that I couldn't pay events on the track their due respect. The Kim Bailey trained Mr Frisk won the race easily by 8 lengths. He was sent off as the 9-2 favourite, which was mildly surprising as he had won the Grand National only two weeks earlier. To win both these stamina-sapping slogs in the same season was the remarkable achievement I failed to notice. Empathy for my friend obscured from me the fact that this was the first time such a feat had been accomplished. Marcus Armytage was the jockey on both occasions. It was a good year for stamina-rich chasers - Durham Edition chased home Mr Frisk for 2nd spot in both those races! The National was a thriller, Mr Frisk only prevailed by ¾ of a length.

I was on Seagram at an adventurously long 5-1. Another top day's racing ended profitless. That was my last visit to Sandown for 12 years.

## 24. SUNRISE AT SANDOWN

*"There must be some kind of way out of here*
*Said the joker to the thief*
*There's too much confusion*
*I can't get no relief"*
Jimi Hendrix *"All Along The Watchtower"*, 1968

It's surprising how many of these tales involve train journeys. Maybe I should be seeking sponsorship from Network Rail….. Today I'm enjoying a very pleasant jaunt to Dorchester and just now I'm getting the edited highlights of South West London flashing by the window. My old haunts of Clapham Junction, Earlsfield, and Wimbledon appear and disappear with disrespectful haste. No time for a proper nostalgic moment on this plush South West Trains express.

Still early. I'm bleary eyed and caffeine deficient. The scalding plastic beaker of coffee in front of me will address both these issues when I can pick it up. In no time at all, the view outside my window has moved from tightly packed terracing of youthful Inner London to semi-detached suburban mid-life spread. The day promises to be a fine Autumnal glory. The skies are clearing and the mist is lifting from the patch of open land away to my left. I catch my breath as I see the roof of a Grandstand emerge, and then notice the fences almost within touching distance of the train. This isn't any old common ground. This is Sandown Park. Those are the railway fences. Is that the ghost of Dessie? No, I'm getting carried away.

The vista has gone in a moment, but I hold this romantic, mist-shrouded, sunrise scene in my head. I will have my nostalgia trip. In fact the memories are quite fresh. I've had a fantastic Summer of racing and punting. And a real highlight was an evening meeting at Sandown.

I finished the jumps season in a very healthy position. My tiny stakes on what I had hoped were value horses left me clearly in profit by over £300 once Aintree and the Punchestown festivals were over. The great five-day Irish Festival was particularly sweet as I finally hooked that most slippery of fish, a Holy Orders win! That felt better. The score was levelled.

So I was quite happy, luxuriating in my success. A little profit over the season from small stakes was all I was looking for. I had long since acknowledged that the principles of value betting were sound. But now I had the evidence of my own betting records that I could make a bit of money from this approach on a season-long basis.

But what next? Much as I enjoyed the flat - at least after a fashion - I couldn't see me making it pay. I didn't fully understand how it works. Nor could I see an angle for me. A long summer was stretching out before me, with nothing but flat racing to fill the gaping chasm left by the end of those blockbuster national hunt Saturdays. I even dabbled in the Summer jumps programme - but quickly abandoned that as a bad job. Shocking races, small fields, no value (though I did have a bet on my old mate Tales of Bounty at somewhere like Plumpton one evening. He was brought down!).

I was back to buying the Racing Post sporadically rather than every day, scoffing at Tony Morris's World of Breeding column. I spent 15 minutes on the train a couple of times a week trying to work up some enthusiasm for minor cards at places like Hamilton, Nottingham and Yarmouth. It was May before I got my first break. It was the Derby trial at Chester and the first time the season's mile and a quarter classic generation were making their seasonal re-appearances. The Dee Stakes was a four runner race and caught my attention because three horse were priced up at short odds and the fourth was a big price. The horse was Kris Kin and I'd stumbled upon the name when casually flicking through Mark Howard's fantastic little book *Ahead on the Flat*. His winter equivalent *One Jump Ahead* was already my bible for unexposed hurdlers and chasers at the start of each season. He paid out a massive 26-1 on Betfair after he cruised to victory at 20-1, along the way beating Big Bad Bob, the odds-on favourite and erstwhile Derby prospect. Suddenly Kris Kin was being touted as a possible entrant. Mark Howard, I owe you one!

I wasn't laughing a few days later. Pride before a fall and all that. Incompetence reigns. The return of mug punting. The following Saturday I fancied a Mark Johnston outsider called The Bonus King in a sprint at Lingfield. He seemed to have some form going back a bit and obscured by some more recent poor results. He was available at 46-1 on Betfair. A fair price I thought. So I had my regulation minimum stakes bet and the deal was done and I clicked OK on the bet. As the screen disappeared a cold realisation trickled into my dull brain. I could still see the bet confirmation box on the inside of my eye-lids: *Your Stake - £46 Your Odds - 3.0. Bet Matched*. Oh my God. I had struck the transaction the wrong way round! I had asked for a bet of 46 quid at 2-1 instead of £2 at 46-1. The horse's chances only warranted a £2 punt.

Without the Kris Kin win earlier in the week I wouldn't even have had that much money in my account. The way Betfair works is that it matches the stake to the best possible price available. So, although I had mistakenly asked for odds of 2-1, the bet was struck at 44-1 because that was the level at which the horse was currently trading. So someone had staked at least 46 quid on The Bonus King losing at odds of 44-1.

I felt sick. I knew that in theory I could win £2,024 on the race now. But that didn't help. I had no confidence in the horse winning at all. This was a tragic error to rival the Rhinestone Cowboy debacle of only 4 months previously. I told Helen of course. She laughed. Predictably.
"Oh well. Easy come, easy go!" she chuckled heartily.
"What? Easy come? I sweated blood for that win, scouring the Racing Post for days to find a suitable race, weighing up the form and all sorts of other complicated things you wouldn't understand."

I was clearly grasping at straws, embellishing the truth and doing myself no favours.

"Yeah, yeah", she's such a cynic, my wife.

"So has the race been run yet?" she inquired.

I shook my head.

"So there's still a chance then?"

"No chance", nausea sweeping over me again.

"Why did you put the bet on in the first place then?"

Good question.

"Well the horse is value for £2 at 46-1 but not for £46."

I could see that this flimsy reasoning would not sneak under Helen's bullshit radar.

"There you go again. Value, value. If you think it's going to win then that's all you need to know surely? Anyway, let's watch the race."

So we did. Helen made herself comfortable in order to watch my demise.

"Which colour is it? Which number is it?"

The Bonus King went off at 20-1. He broke well from stall 7 and went into an early lead. Despite my resignation at striking an incomprehensible bet, I did feel the odd flutter at this point. Maybe……

"That's yours in the lead isn't it? Do you think it might win?"

It was only a fleeting moment of excitement playing callously with my emotions before being extinguished like a match flame in a gale. The gale came in the form of the chasing pack who quickly swallowed up The Bonus King and a horse called Bonus (I kid you not) breezed up the finishing straight. A moment of sympathy flickered across Helen's face,

"Oh dear. That's that then."

I was inconsolable. The Racing Post analysis was clinical. 'led first two furlongs. Stayed chasing leaders until weakened two furlongs out'. The Bonus King is owned by the bookmaker Fred Done. The strap line outside his shops emphasises the point. *'Fred Done Bookmakers. The Bonus Kings.'* Done. I have been.

Steve and I went to the Oaks meeting a few short weeks later. There was no World Cup to absorb and less of us to absorb it anyway. Nick was not available, so last year's cast was depleted by one, and neither Bryn, Vaughany or Ben were available. Bryn still claims he doesn't do the flat.

What a meeting, though. Me and Steve both cleared up. Steve was off to a flyer in the second race when Passing Glance hosed up in the 1m handicap at a cool 16-1. My selection Highland Shot ran on for second, but was a 2 ½ lengths adrift and well beaten. It got better. Steve then landed a belter when Warrsan came from well off the pace to land the Coronation Stakes. It was a high quality field too. But Warrsan left luminaries such as Bandari - my tip - in his wake. The Clive Brittain-handled winner is an endorsement of the much maligned flat handicap route to success. Warrsan has come through the ranks. Top win and a decent price too, 9-2. Steve was flying.

I managed to exorcise The Bonus King demons when Casual Look got luck in running to steal The Oaks with a late pounce. I backed her ante-post at

12-1 and enjoyed one of the biggest rushes of my punting career when Martin Dwyer came with a rattle and hum down that golden highway off the inside rail. Aiden O'Brien's top filly Yesterday was desperately unlucky if I'm honest. Mick Kinane was aboard. He had held up Yesterday for a late run, but found no daylight between the horses in front. He switched to the inside rail, only to find that route blocked too. Mick brought her out wide and finished with a blistering burst, but it was still not enough to rein back Casual Look. We were up in the Gods at the top of the Grandstand and I wasn't certain that the Balding beast had held on. What a moment when that was confirmed.

The telly in the grandstand showed Clare Balding falling apart as Casual Look trained by her brother Andrew flashed past the post. This was Andrew's first season as a permit holder, having taken over the yard from his father, Ian. Classic success at the first time of asking was a sensational achievement. Clare was bursting with pride for her brother and this was a rare display of unbridled emotion at the BBC.

Steve had been telling me all week that he was going to get stuck into Tarjman in the 7 furlong event at the end of the day. He was appalled though by the forecast price at no better than 2s. We'd both had such a belter that he decided to get stuck in anyway. I was berating him mercilessly for his scandalous abandonment of value principles down by the rail at the very moment that Frankie Dettori lit a fuse under Tarjman and exploded off the last bend. Tarjman came from last to first like a guided missile to squeeze home by a short head from Court Masterpiece. The latter had only hit the front with 75 yards to go and his jockey must have thought that the race was in the bag. The snarling Tarjman appearing at his elbow with the post in sight must have felt like a bolt from the blue. I had rarely seen such coruscating acceleration.

There was only modest repetition of the previous year's beer-liberating. Though I think we were entitled to enjoy some welcome refreshment after a stunning day's punting. I was emptying my pockets of dead betting slips when something made me double-check my placepot token. Who knows what rumbled in the darkened crevices of my brain, but closer analysis revealed that this had come in too! I'd managed to put the wrong horse down for one of the legs and he's gone on to finish in the frame. To much whooping of delight and cries of euphoria, we jollied off to the Tote booths, cackling things like "woo-hoo! The bookies see us coming and run a mile….turned over the boys in the pit again……they'll be putting our faces on wanted posters…Coome oooon!" It was all a bit presumptuous really. The ladies handed over about £4.50, barely covering my stake on the bet!

It was a top day though. There was no Nick to cajole us onto the funfair, so at Tattenham Corner I sloped away to buy a bottle of brandy to fuel a celebratory drink on the train home. Steve looked a bit anxious by the time I returned. No doubt he was wondering if I had found the excitement too much and gone to puke my guts up. In fact the brandy buoyed our spirits to the extent that we decided to carry on at a mate's graduation party in the West End. A few of the fantasy cricket league lads were there. I was bladdered by the time I got home.

There's a bit of a footnote to the train journey back from Epsom. In the heat of banter, Steve scribbled in big bold red biro all over the racing page of the Evening Standard. Brimful of confidence and Courvoisier he nonchalantly rattled off his selections for the Derby meeting the day after. "Atlantic Viking. Can't lose. Been made ready for this sprint tomorrow. Good draw. Favourable ground. Get on at around 10s." I did get on and it didn't lose. Steve found the annotated Evening Standard a few days after and realised that at least three of the audacious selections had gone in …..And he hadn't backed any of them! I also backed Kris Kin in the Derby. Rude not to after the Chester trial, and of course The Bonus Bridge King incident was all ancient history by now. Kris Kin was still a good price when I put my little bit of wedge down. Keiron Fallon's now famous charge turned the weekend into one of my most memorable. I can't rival Bryn's spectacular Triple Crown performance at Cheltenham last year, but this little Oaks-Derby classic double is up there with my personal highlights.

High Summer at a packed Sandown Park evening meeting couldn't provide a more stark contrast with the sight of the track now as I rattle through Surrey on the train. It's a bit of a desolate, empty scene: mist obscuring the stands and hanging over the trees; early-falling leaves strewn across the chase course. A few bone-jarring howls and a sprig of heather or two and it could be a scene from The Hound of the Baskervilles. Maybe I exaggerate. Anyway, Sandown in July was a roaring success, hounds or no. Quite by chance we had settled on a meeting billed as Ladies Night. This worked out well. Steve's and Nick's wives had both been persuaded to come to the races and so had Helen. They got in free. Steve, me, Nick and Vaughany had to pay our way.

This was my first experience of evening racing. It seemed to be popular judging by the number of people who edged their way with sharp elbows onto our already rammed slam-door stopping service. The train stubbornly refused to depart Platform 16 at Victoria. I distinctly remember being very uncomfortable trying to maintain some fantastic contortion as the carriage got busier still: standing on tip-toe so that my heel didn't crush the toes of the lady who had squeezed in behind me; leaning forwards to grab an overhead rail; and twisting my head through 90 degrees to avoid the worst of a sweaty armpit lodged before me at nose height. Helen was no better off and Vaughany claimed he was worse because the vibrations from my phone receiving messages rattled distinctly closer to his sensitive areas than he would prefer. I reckoned he enjoyed it. He reckoned I was sending myself messages.

So, predictably, the course was packed as well. The turnstiles couldn't cope with the number of race-goers who heaved off the bulging trains. The ladies were ushered through separately, which helped the crowd control a little.

"This way ladies", invited the stewards which in turn invited a predictable retort from somwhere within our number: "That's no lay-dee!"

Juvenile.

Vaughany, Helen and I found Nick and Denise just outside the course. Steve and Debs arrived later. Steve was phoning through his selection for the first race as they were walking across from the railway fences. We could almost pick them out.

This was not a serious punting evening. Much more about having a night out, a bit of a laugh and a few beers. Just as well. As a betting experience it was an unmitigated disaster.

We saw the first race whilst doing a few introductions. Not all the partners knew everyone else. After drawing a blank (the Fallon powered favourite prevailed) we went inside for a beer. The main betting hall had changed considerably since I came here in Desert Orchid and Vodkatini days. Unrecognisable. Very plush it was now. Light and airy with loads of bars and food outlets. Nick and I were on the beer, red wine, white wine spritzer and Pimms run. Easy to tell the girls were in town. The bars were understaffed though. The impressive line up of lager and bitter pumps running the length of the bar top was undermined by the fact that only about two of them were hooked up to any beer. What use is a beer pump without any beer? It was close to race time and Steve battled his way to join us at the bar.

"Do you know what you want in the next? I'll get your bets down" It was a 7f maiden. I was looking at the Tregonning/Sheik Mohammed beast Manyana for no other reason than Mohammed seemed to do well in these sorts of events, like Wessex at York earlier that Summer.

Steve went off to do the deed. By the time we fought our way back to the gang the race was over. We caught the replay on the screens. It was a very close finish but Manyana had just got up on the line from Capped For Victory. Before I could think about celebrating, Steve shook his head and handed back my fiver.

"Sorry mate, couldn't get the wedge on. The bookie was just shouting 'no more bets' as I tried to get on the Tregonning horse. What can I say?"

Bastard.

"How about 'Here's your 20 notes mate'? That would be a start" I offered.

He simply laughed. Den had got her bet down though and she was delighted.

"Ooh I've won, I've won! Nick, can you go and collect my winnings? What's the matter David, didn't you back that one?"

Ho ho.

This was to prove the only winner of the night for any of us. Den's winner and mine that got away. Den didn't let me forget it either. She taunted me in fine style through the next few races.

"Any winners yet David? I thought you were the big shot gambler. Where's the evidence of all these winners you claim to have? I reckon you and Steve make it up! Not having much luck are you? Want any tips?"

She was merciless and I was powerless to fight back. Helen was loving it - I get no respect. All my nags had gone down. At one point I was chatting to Debs about the next race when I looked up to see Den fixing me with a mischievous stare and making an 'L' shape with her forefinger and thumb on her forehead.

"Loser! Loser!" she was chanting.

I was being hounded. We had got the bar run a bit better organised by this time and the drinks were flowing more steadily. This probably explains why Den's 'L' for loser was the wrong way round. Not that it made me feel any better.

There were, at best, a couple of near misses, and that was all we had to show for our endeavours. But the crack was good. As good as I can remember it. Vaughany was on fine form, I've rarely seen him so relaxed. Den was clearly letting her hair down. She and Helen spent much of the night taking the piss out of me and Nick. Debs was obviously sceptical about the whole business of betting.

"Steve tells me he's had a big winner and says he's only had a fiver on. Why didn't he put more on if he thought it was going to win? That's logical isn't it?"

I've heard this somewhere before. She must be in league with Helen. Debs, nevertheless, is disconcertingly impressed by Andrew's rarefied manners and dignified charm. He really should be moving in different circles. The rest of us can't compete.

The card wound up to a sprint finale. Hardly incandescent in terms of quality, but still the brightest race of the fixture. We all looked to Steve for a bit of guidance. He had been bearing down on these events this Summer. He had developed an expertise in the genre. Track bias, draw advantage, ground preference and relevant form were all given an appropriate measure in a potent cocktail of analysis that left the ill-fated Cheltenham Matrix cowering in the weighing room. Surely this race would play into Steve's hands? Debs who had been single-minded in her selections all evening looked to her husband for advice.

"Whistler" says Steve. "Matched a huge price on Betfair before I left the office."

The sprint track at Sandown runs slap bang down the centre of the course. We walked over it to get to the grandstand. I wish I'd tested the ground a bit more thoroughly. Unfortunately I'd left my penetrometer at home. (They've recently been relaunched as Going Sticks - can't see that moniker impressing anyone.) So we are very reliant on the track-side screen.

These 5f races are over in a flash. There's supposed to be a massive draw advantage at Sandown, but none emerges tonight because the outside rail has been moved in 4 or 5 yards, which gave enough room for all the horses to run on fresh ground. The race is a screamer with the closest of finishes. Everything happened in the last few strides. Whistler came late to claim the race and barely a moment later Turibus was breathing down his neck. Both Brighton specialists these two, which explains their long odds. It was impossible to tell from where we stood who had won. Tiberus was announced the winner by a fag paper. Steve was not happy.

The racing was over by ten to nine. It was still light and still early. This is where evening racing has a marketable edge. There was no gentle ushering of punters out of the gates by fluorescent-jacketed security guards. On the contrary, all the bars and food outlets stayed open and in the betting hall a covers band was starting to crank out some good-time rhythm 'n' blues.

We felt no compulsion to leave. We settled down on the steps by the bookies pitches with a few drinks and pass an hour or so rediscovering the lost art of conversation and good humour. The subtle aroma of fried onions and roasting pork inevitably tempted me over to Hog Roast caravan and I returned with a selection of baps and chips. They didn't last long and I looked at the empty food wrappers in dismay. I hardly got a bight. Me. The self-appointed junk food connoisseur. There's no justice.

Top night. We resolved to do it all again soon. Debs changed her mind almost immediately, though. The trains from Esher were sporadic that evening. Debs and Steve ended up missing the last train to Basildon and a rendezvous with their car. Public transport deficiencies put a spanner in the works once again. Think Steve may have caught a bit of flak as well.

................................................................................

I snap back to the present. The train is taking an odd route. I appear to be on a circum-navigation of Poole Harbour. Every time I look out of the window I'm surrounded by water. It's expensive water though, judging by the number and of size of motor cruisers floating in it. That will be me one day. *'This time next year, Rodney......',* etc. So I finished a good few quid up on the flat season after all, which had followed a decent performance over the jumps. I'm allowing myself a fanciful flight of dreams. The staking policy on the flat was exactly the same as over the jumps - tiny stakes on big odds. I had finished the season about £200 in profit. Kris Kin and Casual Look were the highlights and I managed to pick up a few other tasty returns here and there. This flight of dreams thing is amusing me. I'm using this train journey to do some stats.

Supposing. Just supposing there is half a chance of turning punting into a serious income. There is a seductive idea. Walking away from the dull daily grind of the rat race appeals. Leaving behind the crushing repetitive boredom and pointless paperchase of the office is the only motivation I need. I'm not qualified to do a proper job. I have no transferable skills. I have no trade. But what if I could deliver an income through the nags? The bald stats are encouraging if interpreted in a slightly ambiguous way. For instance, I extrapolate from my average profit on turnover of 70% since the previous October that I would need a capital injection of £16,500 to build in a £13,500 profit and an annual income of £30,000. Current strike rate 11.7%. How about that for a business case to take to the bank manager?

The illusion doesn't last long. I'm travelling back up the line to London from my uneventful but sobering meeting in Dorchester, flicking me back to the stark reality of earning a crust from the job I've already got. The holes in the fanciful business case are as wide as Poole Harbour. The sample of bets is too small, the time frame too narrow, assumptions about future profit on turnover too optimistic. Just for starters.

Ultimately, this train of thought is just another example of escapism. I know that I would never have the balls to turn a hobby in to a living. Just imagine the stress of needing to find a winner from an all-weather card at Wolverhampton on a wet Tuesday afternoon in November because the mortgage repayments were under pressure. Or having the determination to stick to principles and put down £150 on a value bet in a claimer at Market Rasen on the back of 20 to 25 similar losing bets. The thought sends shivers up my spine. I'm only in this for an affordable thrill. Only risking the few quid I can bear to lose. Full stop.

But Steve might not be. We are in the Wetherspoons at Victoria. Nick is here too. Steve is still pushing ahead with his accelerating staking plan. He's still making money and is still acquiring and displaying knowledge at an alarming rate. I'm getting washed along in the wake, interested but not dedicated. Thrill seeking, not studious. I show Nick and Steve my calculations on the train and we have a laugh about it.

"Nah. It was an interesting little experiment, just to see what it would take to turn punting into serious money. Course it's all based on my performance over the last year. What is it they said on endowment mortgages? 'Investments may go down as well as up'! I reckon I'm going to use the £500 I've made over the last year and buy a Summerhouse for the kids in the back garden. And I'm going to get a little metal plaque engraved to put up inside. It will say 'Bought with the proceeds of value betting: Jumps 2002-03; Flat 2003'."

We are outside at the Wetherspoons watching the ebb and flow of commuter trains shuttling in and out of the station. It's a busy Friday night. Steve says

"Ha ha! I reckon you're right Davoski. Mark the occasion."
Nick looks at me over his pint, leaning on the rail above platform 9.

"Do you know what? In all the mad discussions you two have had about gambling over the last God knows how many years, that is the most sensible thing you have ever said!"

But back to Steve. I seriously wonder whether he could make it. This year he has had a string of excellent pay days through solid research backed up with a touch of inspiration. Steve specialises on the sprints in Summer and restricting his selections to 5f and 6f events has come up trumps. But the bets are getting increasingly sophisticated. For instance, he is landing the odds with spectacularly big-priced winners like Vanderlin at a huge price and Irma La Duce at Carlisle at 21-1 for a tenner a time. He also sends me an e-mail about scoring on an outrageous match bet with an old war horse called Roses of Spring which beat a 'fragile' 3 year old called Caught In The Dark. Then there are his spread bet escapades. Ela Figura netted him a £60-odd payout in a place spread market where she finished 3rd in a make-up of 50:30:20:10. Apparently. No, I can barely keep up either.

I tell him that I want to write a book about all our gambling adventures and that he is the ending of the story, but only if he jacks the job in and becomes a professional punter. I tell him that I write slowly and that he has a year to strike out solo so that I have enough material to make a book worthwhile. I want to know what the plan is. What is the betting strategy? What are the stakes? What are the benchmarks and milestones? How does he measure success? Questions, questions. He tells me to "write more slowly!", and that:

"doubling the dough on an annual basis is still the fundamental idea. To achieve this I need to forget the sophistication, get back to basics and have the balls to occasionally put the money down. The long term aim is to have raised enough wedge to give it a go full-time, via a career break, by Oct 2007. Retirement on 50th birthday Nov 2013!"

I resolve to increase my stakes to a minimum £5 per bet and have more bets. I think I can live with that!

## 25. TOASTER

*"Your name it is heard in high places*
*You know the Agha Khan.*
*He sent you a race horse for Christmas*
*and you keep it just for fun,*
*for a laugh, a-ha a-ha.*
Peter Sarstedt, "Where Do you go to my lovely", 1969

Somehow I feel we should be tucking into breakfast in a pub near Billingsgate Fish Market. What other reason could there be for sitting in a boozer this early. It's hardly light yet. To my addled brain, this is early.

But here we are in a former coaching inn on the High Street of forgotten Towcester tucking into pints of Bombardier like they are eggs and bacon. The blokes on the table next to us polish off Guinness for black pudding. The atmosphere is jovial, friendly and relaxed. Everyone inside the boozer is talking and reading, eating and drinking the races.

It's Boxing Day. I've never been to the races on Boxing Day. This is another of those rites of passage. Boxing Days past keep repeating on me like this ale. Listening to Uncle Terry and his Mick and Peter Easterby stories, and the faithful repetition of racing talk from countless Northern tracks. Now I'm doing it for myself. It is fitting that Dad and brother Paul are here too.

The pub has opened early because of the race crowd who want some refreshment in comfort before heading up the hill for an early start at the races in these dark December days. We are early because Helen, who has dropped us off, needs to get back home so that she can organise the sortie over to Chesham. The girls (five of them - two Grannies, a Mother and two daughters) are going to the Pantomime. We've had a genuine family Christmas. Picking up on the cross-party holiday theme of Cork a couple of years ago, my lot and Helen's Mum are down to do the big Festive thing at our house for a change. It's working out well.

"Has he been?" said Elizabeth at about 7am yesterday morning. She was blinking at the two plump stockings hanging on the little fireplace in the room she shares with her Sister, Catherine. 7am is not bad actually. It could have been considerably earlier. The present opening follows swiftly afterwards, aided by a few glasses of Bucks Fizz for the grown ups. I'm not sure who enjoyed the present opening more - the grin on the Grandparent's face was easily as wide as the children.

My eldest picked out a tidily wrapped A4 sized present from under the tree, read the label and marched over to where I was sitting on the arm of the settee surveying the scene with a Fatherly air.

"This is for you Daddy. 'From Mummy with love. Don't get carried away!' it says. Look."

I took the present with a hearty thank you. Hmm. Intriguing. It was too thin for a book and too big for a CD. I ripped open the attractively wrapped gift with gusto. Father Christmas ho-ho-ho-ing on his sleigh gave way to a folder embossed with 'Alternative Gift Company' in black and gold inch-high lettering. Oh no, I thought. Please not skydiving lessons….. I flipped open the cover.

"Oh Yes!"

'Welcome to City Racing Club' screamed the front page of the owners pack.

This was sensational! Finally. A share in my own race horse! No details about the horse or training plans and the like. Not yet anyway. I had to send away to the club to register my share and I would be sent the info. Helen knows I've been gradually seduced by the idea of owning a racehorse for some while. Now I'll get to wear an access all areas badge, hob-nob in the owners bar, discuss race entries with the trainer, talk tactics with the jockey, give Nick the finger from inside the parade ring….the works! Well almost - this package is designed as a taster - there's a one-off payment for the share and a few other perks. But it's just about perfect. This is exactly the sort of introduction I wanted.

Helen said she thought about wrapping up a horse shoe, but thought that was probably more than I actually owned of the horse! The first thing I did was text Steve and Nick:

"Guess what I got for Christmas? A race-horse!"

Got to talk these things up.

"Bloody hell, Dave. All I got was a sodding book!" replies Steve.

"Fantastic! Is it in the King George at Kempton tomorrow?" replies Nick.

Ha ha. This is the stuff.

It is a really grim old day in Towcester. Biting wind and rain in the air. Chilly with it. We still have a few minutes to kill, so we have a look in the bookies at the early-bird prices. Paul wants a bet on Edredon Bleu in the King George because it's a lovely horse. I scoff.

"Yeah, yeah. Lovely horse. Doesn't owe me a penny. But this is a different thing. He was woeful the last time he tried 3 miles and he's 12 now. Kempton is a fast track and he will never stay."

Dad is scathing too. He chuckles and shakes his head.

"What?" says Paul. "25-1 is a great price for a horse like him. Just a quid each way, Dave. I'm saving my money for later today."

He nods up the hill towards the track. I put the bet down for him and never once consider putting a couple of quid of my own down, just to top it up. I will regret this.

Boxing Day is such a massive day for the industry. There are so many fixtures that the bookie doesn't have enough wall space for all the form. There is layer upon layer of pages from the RP blue-tacked in every nook and cranny. I don't visit the bog, but I can guess what will be plastered above the trough. The TV screens banked-up in the middle of the wall scroll regularly through myriad races already priced up at four or five different tracks. There are plenty of early bird punters in here taking advantage.

Towcester is well down the list in terms of its pecking order on today's meetings. This and Market Rasen don't even get the full colour form-guide treatment in the Racing Post. Not enough room. So we have a fair idea of the likely quality of racing.

It's a stiff walk up the hill heading out of town to the track. Most of the way we follow a wall which skirts the course. This is the boundary of Lord Hesketh's estate. He owns much of the land in these parts and resides in a stunning mansion, Easton Neston, within. The track falls entirely within the boundary of his estate. We take our place in the healthy crowd snaking up the hill.

I love going to new tracks. We turn into the entrance which is guarded by an impressive three-arch stone-built formal gateway topped with a sculpture and featuring the Hesketh coat of arms. Not a turnstile in sight. No security guard nor steward to spoil this Edwardian scene. In fact, it's free admission today. And all season. Towcester racecourse has been closed for the past year or so as stabling problems in the town gave way to stalled redevelopment plans. The building works are not yet complete and this may be the reason for running a free-admission experiment. But the facilities are fine. The newly built stand down the hill looks sufficiently dignified for a place on the estate and there are temporary stands in front of a huge marquee with two bars and a few screens. I check out the eating options, of course, and tick off the requisite attendance of Hog Roast, burger, Cajun chicken, Indian and baked potato emporia. All seems well.

The other important feature is unrestricted access to the parade ring and winners enclosure. I nudge Paul.
    "That will be me in a week or two. Stood on the other side of this fence, passing the time of day with the trainer and sticking up two fingers to poor sods like you. I'm elitist now!"
He grins.
    "Piss off!"
Brotherly love.

This track is probably a bit smaller than Exeter but offers the same friendly atmosphere and easy manner. Me and Steve made a repeat visit to the Dartmoor track in October to renew our acquaintance with the Haldon Gold Cup. With a couple of notable exceptions it was like déjà vu. All over again. The cloud descended after the first race and the course commentator was reduced to making up stories about what might be happening out in the murk; Edredon Bleu won the showpiece event in fine style; and Steve even cleaned up on some well-honed reverse exactas.

The repetition extended right through to bearing down on the stilton soup served up in the bar and downing of swifties in the Head of Steam before the train home. The notable exceptions were significant however. This year there were four of us. Ben and Bryn also came along. Both had winners, too. That was the other difference. I didn't. Not one. Not even close. Potless.

To be fair, Ben nearly didn't bag his winner. He backed the wrong horse in the 2.10 and it won. He was unexpectedly cheering Oh So Wisley after telling us he was going to back Happy Hussar. He sheepishly admitted that he'd pointed at the wrong number on the board, rather than bluff us any longer. Respect! Bryn collected on his old mate Ceannanas Mor In the handicap chase and also on Edredon at 7-2. That horse is a legend. The Haldon Gold Cup was again a strong renewal. Azertyuiop was making his seasonal debut in his build up for the Champion Chase and the field also featured other top chasers Kadarran from the Nicholls yard, Seebald and Wahiba Sands from Pipe's formidable string.

The mist was a bit of a novelty the year before, but this time it as really annoying. It was probably even more impenetrable this year. Azertyuiop fell at the first fence and nobody saw it. The fall took away a bit of the lustre away from the competition. Someone had managed to capture the fall on camera. It appeared on the front cover of the next day's RP. Quite a feat under the circumstances. The photographer must have had his nose hard up against the wing of the fence to see anything at all! Turned out that Mick FitzGerald had been unseated when the horse slipped on the greasy surface after clearing the fence. It was still a huge thrill to see Edredon bound over those fences up the home straight. Men and boys.

Just as well Bryn had taken his fair share out of the ring. The ticket collector on the Exeter - Paddington took it off him again. Rarely have I seen a more fastidious, pedantic and rigorous official. An absolute credit to SW Trains and a complete liability to the rest of society.

"This ticket is not valid", he proclaimed in clipped tones after the briefest moments' examination.
He handed back the ticket to Ben, who by now was only interested in sleeping ahead of his departure for Prague the following day.
"Oh, you'll have to speak to Bryn, my mate. He bought them".
Ben puts a well-judged bit of distance between himself and the formidable ticket collector. Bryn returned and was informed of the situation.
"We got a problem with the tickets, mate", said Ben who had already crumbled and was reaching for the debit card.
"No, hang on Ben. I'm not happy."
I could see he wasn't happy. He was wearing his belligerent face and ready to take this geezer on.
"What do you mean not valid? I bought these at my local station in Worcester Park. I asked for two return tickets to Exeter returning the same day using my disability card. That's what I've got. So how is that not valid?"

This is where the argument entered a surreal phase. Mr Inspector painted a well-rehearsed and almost believable picture of tight-fisted joy riders buying cheap tickets for a service via Reading, Honiton, Dorchester and a range of vaguely rural West Country market towns, and then scandalously using them on this Exeter Express instead. Our man with the eagle eyes spotted these scams like shoplifters in a cash-and-carry. Bryn went through confusion, incredulity, rage and despair in a protracted debate with the intransigent inspector.

Under great duress and not without a dogged fight, Bryn ended up paying the excess. He later wrote to SW trains in a 'disgusted of Worcester Park' sort of way and was refunded the difference. All in all, this was a perfect demonstration of farcical rail bureaucracy in its undiluted glory. The episode soured the day for Bryn, but did at least provide a moment of top drama as he spat out the words "silly twat" with Inspector hardly out of earshot. The rest of the carriage seemed to enjoy it too.

...............................................................................

The view from the stands at Towcester is excellent. The finishing straight is uphill rising to a peak about 2 furlongs past the post and then the track falls away dramatically to give a wonderful view of the historic town centre. The horizon is dominated by a squat, square Church tower complemented by the seemingly random arrangement of low- rise market-square shops, pubs and houses, spanning every decade from 1600 to the present.

The back straight is just visible at the bottom of the hill running along the boundary between the estate and the town, before the course takes a sharp right hander and hits the rising ground all the way up to the finishing straight. It's a punishing course, described by one disgruntled trainer as "uphill all the way round" after his charge had failed the stamina test. The ground doesn't help either. The clay-based sub-soil means the track loses more than its fair share of fixtures to water-logging. For one Towcester meeting, the going description in the paper was 'good to soft, heavy in the home straight'! Isn't water supposed to run away from the highest point? It's a unique track to say the least.

None of us have any winners in the first race, which is a lamentable Class F mares only hurdle slog over the minimum trip. This is going to be painful. Drawn by the irresistible aroma of sizzling pork, we retire to the Hog Roast van for some comfort food. I'm startled to see that a queue has formed at each of the outlets. I realise that the crowd has probably doubled in size since we arrived an hour ago. Towcester races on Boxing Day is clearly the place to be. The avenue of bookies adjacent to the marquee is seething with happy punters who need little persuasion to be parted from their Christmas spends.

Next up is a 2½ -mile novice chase. Looks like another shocker. There are barely any trainers on the racecard that I recognise, never mind the runners. The wind is still whipping in from the east and bringing with it a stinging slap of rain. The stands are extremely exposed up here on top of the hill. I look up at the big screen broadcasting races filled with the cream of the season's jumpers from Kempton and Wetherby. What are we doing here?

Dad and me fancy Con Tricks, one of Paddy Mullins' horses. It won last time out and has drifted from a forecast price of 11-10 to 5-2. We are both tempted. So we go off to do battle with the Christmas hordes in Bookies Boulevard. I manage to lose Dad and find Paul. Bet Dad's gone inside for a pint. The start of this race is down at the bottom of the track. That's as much as I see of Con Tricks. Looks like I've been the victim of one. He falls at the first fence.

Paul is doing a bit better though. There is not much quality about the event, but as the already strung out field turns up the hill and approaches the last bend, Paul's selection, Tourniquet, is very prominent making good use of the conditions. We are very reliant on the big screen to follow the race. By now the concourse in front of the stands is heaving and there is precious little chance of glimpsing the horses well away to our right. Paul is getting animated and starts yelling encouragement at the screen. The favourite Jamerosier appears to be catching Tourniquet, but they are desperately tired horses. I'm cheering on Paul's beast now too. We can't all go back potless. Tourniquet is hanging a bit to his left, but has managed to increase his advantage plugging away up that grinding home straight. Jamerosier has no more to offer and Paul's selection is actually eased down to no more than a canter as he crosses the line 1 ¼ lengths clear. These are the only two finishers.

Paul is indulging in some serious delight, and a good proportion of the crowd seem to have backed him too. The horse came in to 5-1 from 7s and 8s. That's a handy little return for me bruv. He's already starting to mutter something about getting me back for the caning I dished out at York. I do my best to ignore him and continue with my unbridled and selfless congratulations about his lovely bet.

The next race is a poor quality handicap hurdle landed by a rank outsider Camross at 25-1. Some bleedin' value and I missed it! The bloke behind me didn't. He's barking into his mobile phone.
   "Yeah, yeah, 25-1! No I'm not kidding. Didn't I tell you. Bet you wish you'd listened now!"
These lucky punters can be so insufferable.

We have a wander down the track to see if we can find AWOL Dad. It's much less busy down by the last fence and we undertake to watch one of the later races from here for a good view of the horses. No sign of Dad though.

As we are meandering back up to the main stands I realise that the big screen is showing the King George from Kempton. Looks like they are about a mile into the race. There's no commentary, but I nudge Paul.
   "Bloody Hell. That's Edredon in the lead."

I try to pick out some of the others. Looks like Valley Henry is well up there, close to the pace. This is my main bet over Christmas, I've got him in a double with Take the Stand in the Welsh National tomorrow. Can't see Jair Du Cochet up with them. He would have gone off a warm favourite after turning over a below par Best Mate at Huntingdon in the Autumn. Paul is pretty excited.

"C'mon Edredon. Ha, ha, ha.", cheers Paul.
I'm impressed too.

"Lovely horse. Doesn't owe me a penny", I rejoin. "He'll never stay the three mile though. Just watch him fall away at the business end of the race."

Finally we get a bit of commentary. Jair Du Cochet has been pulled up at the rear of the field. Fondmort and First Gold are all in contention. Valley Henry is looking very good when he makes a blunder down the back straight and falls. His jumping is a real liability round this course. I'm gutted because he looked very smooth until that point. Edredon is still there at the head of affairs though, where he likes to be.

They look to be straightening up for the judge and I'm eating my words because the game 'Blue' is still there dictating matters. First Gold comes up along sides to take the race.

"This is it Paul, he's run a top race, but he's going to get swallowed up now. Three miles is just a bit too far for him".
"Hmmm, maybe" mutters Paul, clearly disappointed.

But I'm astonished to see Edredon battle back to the lead. For all the world I expected First Gold to go on and finish the job. Edredon under a fine drive from Jim Culloty displays staggering resilience and character. Culloty coaxes another of those breath-taking leaps from his mount three fences out. They never fail to raise a gasp from the crowd. He's jumping like a stag. The French raider fades and Edredon even has the strength and depth to fight off a late challenge from Tiutchev - another 2 ½ miler - who came from out of the clouds to get within a length or so of the leader.

Paul of course is ecstatic. £1each-way goes a long way at 25-1. But I'm delighted too. I let Paul have his moments of gloating and I take it all on the chin, because in fact I'm full of awe for this horse who has provided so many highlights and today has proved even some of his hardiest supporters wrong. Just now I'm not interested in arguments about the quality of the renewal or the strength in depth of the field.

My turn to strike in the next race. Mug punting at it's finest. Helen has a CD coming out on the label she's involved with which is a new recording of the composer Elgar's choral work. In fact, some of the material has not been recorded anywhere before. There's a horse in the 2-40 handicap chase called Elgar. She wants £2 to win on it. I put my fiver on as well. What the hell. The beast jumps the rest of motley crew into the ground and hoses up the muddy straight like a spring-heeled gladiator to win by a cosy 12 lengths. I've found a winner, but lost my credibility. Again.

We find Dad during this race. He caught the King George race on the telly. Sure enough he's been hiding in the beer tent whilst it's been raining.

No luck for any of us the next which is a particularly punishing 3m 1furlong endurance test over fences. My horse, Auburn Spirit is caught on the run-in by The River Joker. Auburn Spirit had made some awful mistakes at fences down the back straight and was probably lucky to make it round.

A Bumper to finish the day! The rain has returned, but I'm determined to pick my horse out from then paddock. These horses are all unexposed 4, 5 and 6 year olds, with barely any form to speak of. Let's see if I can select a horse on the basis of breeding lines and what I can judge from the paddock.

The grass has turned to mud and the underfoot conditions are nothing short of treacherous over here. It's more like a skating rink. I give up on the analysis and plunge on a horse called Stern Leader whose sire is Supreme Leader. I've heard of him. That's good enough for me. 12-1 is pouched.

I'm still making my way back from the bogs when the tape goes up. The race is run at a much more sensible pace and the field are still well packed heading back up the hill for home. The pace suddenly picks up about 3 furlongs. Stern Leader is coasting round the outside looking good and I'm starting to get excited. He starts to make his move for the front as the leaders make the home turn.
    "Go on, go on", I urge.
He looks good to me.

And then disaster. The horse violently jinks left and loses his stride pattern as well as about four places before the jockey wrestles the horse back into the race. I'm not happy. I'm overcome with a sense of injustice and unfair play. I want to join Amnesty International and nail my honest colours to the mast. Surely my horse would have won without that, er, incident. I feel robbed. What did happen? At first I though the jockey's saddle had slipped as he accelerated through the last turn. But under those circumstances he would have pulled the horse up rather than rallying to finish 4th. The RP the next day claimed that he had made a bolt for the stables, the path for which emerge onto the track at that point. It's possible I suppose. These horses are still inexperienced.

I relay my bitter experience to Dad, only to find he has an even more galling story to trump it. He was about to put his tenner on Lazerito, a well fancied Venetia Williams horse, having watched the price drift out to a good value 4-1. But the tapes had just gone up and the bookie wouldn't take Dad's money. Inevitably Lazerito won. There is no more painful a gambling cock-up than failing to nail a winning bet. Especially in the last race of the day.

The track has surely had more punters turning up than expected. There are cars parked three deep on the grass either side of the drive back up to the ornamental entrance. This must be the overflow car-park. There was nothing here at 12.30pm. The grass is sodden after a day of rain and a host of flash four-wheel-drives are churning it into a quagmire, helplessly slithering around spluttering mud in all directions and generally struggling to climb the verge onto the drive. It's like watching a swarm of angry bees climbing over each other in a hive.

I read in the Racing Post next day that 12,000 people attended the meeting. This smashed all previous course attendance records and is an absolute vindication of the policy to allow free admission. The management must have made a stack from concessions, race-cards, bookies percentages, etc. Back in town we pop into the local bookmaker to collect Paul's wedge. I notice the stark contrast between this morning when he was too sheepish to place the derisory £1 each-way bet himself and now when he is more than happy, bold as brass even, in his approach the counter to redeem his slip. A swift pint is in order whilst we wait for Helen who has offered to come and collect us. My phone rattles. It's Bryn sending me a text. He's pleased as punch. He backed Edredon Bleu too.

I'm back at Towcester only a few short weeks later. I enjoyed the Boxing Day trip so much that I decide to go back for the next meeting. It's a Friday afternoon fixture and promises to be an excellent start to the weekend.

Nick is keen to come too, though neither Bryn nor Steve can make it. We sorted this out on the Wednesday but it's only now, sat on the train after leaving work at lunchtime that Nick texts Den with something outrageous like:
    "gone to Toaster (sic) races with Dave. Spur of the moment".
Shocking behaviour. I can't let him get away with it.
    "Spur of the moment my arse!", I text her. What a grass.
    "He's dead!" comes the reply.

The weather is iffy again. By the time we are being ripped off in a cab from Milton Keynes station the weather is horrendous. We are aqua-planing up the A5 through a downpour. The cabbie is trying to regale us with horse racing anecdotes but we're not interested. Partly because he's fleeced us for 20 notes and partly because of nervousness about the weather. I can see us taking refuge in a pub and doing our dough on some shocking regional racing meeting on the sand from Southwell.

We are both scouring the track for activity as we walk down the drive.
    "Still on then?", says Nick to the gateman.
    "For now", he replies, pulling up his collar against the stinging rain.
Hmm. Doesn't sound good.

We've missed the first race, but the next is potentially the best of an admittedly poor show. It's a mare's only chase featuring Jonjo O'Neill's highly regarded Ar Muin Na Muice. We are in time to see the horses emerge onto the track. Oh Dear. Only two have turned up. The O'Neill mare is not one of them! The race is a farce for about 1 ¾ miles. Jockeys Roddi Greene and Paul Flynn hack round the first circuit as if they are cantering up to the gallops.

I've never seen such a slowly run race. The jockeys are having a natter to each other as they pass the stands. We can just about hear them from the rail. The competitive nature is further undermined by the removal of two fences in the home straight because of the condition of the surface. This is barely raceable. Monger Lane is clearly the quality horse of the two, and is sent off at an unbackable 30-100, but she has a scare down on the bottom straight and very nearly comes a cropper after a bad mistake. Nick and I have had a little interest bet in the rank outsider of course, and we momentarily get excited. But that's all it is. Monger Lane romps away up the home straight to win by a mile. A bloke turns round to Nick with a huge grin slapped across his face.

"I've just won a grand!", he declares.

Christ knows how much he had to put on to get that back we think. Bet he wasn't grinning like The Joker when his banker dived at the fence down the back!

There's time and room to down a bap and a pint before the next. The crowd today is healthy but not mobbed like Boxing Day. The next race is a staying hurdle. The conditions are shocking. We see the horses pass the stands on the first circuit and the hooves are sloshing through slop in some parts and sticking like glue in others. This clay-pit ground would be more at home on a potters wheel than a racecourse.

The races all follow a very similar pattern where there is a steady pace on the circuit allied to cautious jumping. The business end happens very quickly half way up the home turn with about 4 furlongs to go. In this race, my horse is already dead and buried but Nick's selection Galwaybay Stan is still in front, leading the ragged field up the hill, out there to be shot at. He looks knackered, in all honesty. Combe Castle looks to have saved a bit, and steps past Stan. Down the home straight the race changes again. Combe Castle and nearest pursuer Harry Collins are finding this uphill finish too much of a grind. They've bottomed out on the bottomless ground and the relentlessly one-paced Galway Bay Stan reels them in easily. One pace is better than no-pace! In the end he wins cosily and staggers across the line well clear. One up for Nick at a very handy 5-1. The Racing Post called it "an unedifying war of attrition"! Never was a truer word written.

Back in the bar, we fall into conversation with a bloke who has been a regular at the track and has missed it whilst closed for renovation. He fancies The River Joker in the next and I think he's almost impressed when

I say I saw him beat my horse here on Boxing Day. Never mind Royal Ascot and Glorious Goodwood, I've found my level now.

The race is infact won by Dalus Park which makes me feel even more at home in due course, because I find out the next day that there is a link between this and the horse I have a part ownership in. The papers from the racing club finally arrive. My horse is called Dashing Charm trained in Lincolnshire by Chris Bealby who also trains Dalus Park. Wish I had known, I could have skipped over to the winners enclosure and introduced myself. Instead I back another loser.

I'm doing a lot of this at the moment. Winners are eluding me and in the cry of many an anguished punter before me I frequently moan "...another one beaten on the run-in.....another 2nd place..". Maybe my judgement is a bit faulty as well. Too many times I'm crossing the grey line from good bet to mug bet when mistaking a big price for value, and giving too little emphasis to the horse's real chance of winning the race. The chances of repeating my success of the previous jumps season are none and slim. "...and slim is out of town" (as Don King once famously said about the prospects of a Heavyweight World Title rematch between Lennox Lewis and Rehman).

Bryn on the other hand is having a stormer of a season. He is like the come back kid. He takes a couple of years out to tour the world with his cricket team, move house, settle down have a child and then bang! Back on the scene with gusto. Value winners at Exeter, Kempton and a host of other pay-day Saturdays. He's hot.

Nick's luke warm. Galwaybay Stan has set him up for the day. I'm officially cold. Nothing changes that in the next race, but we certainly see a horse to put in the notebook. If we had one. Tighten Your Belt, a Venetia Williams bay gelding is sent off a very warm 1-2 favourite for a 2 mile novice hurdle. The bookies don't price up any of the competitors in single figures. Nick and I both go for outsiders who fail to upset the odds. But Tighten Your Belt wins with style and with a monumental 17 lengths in hand.

Winning with style on this ground and at this track takes some doing. The way he glided past the post a distance ahead of everything else as if he was on casters was seriously impressive. I'm still not much of judge of a racehorse either in the paddock or on the track, but to my eyes this horse moved so smoothly and fluidly. Like Castrol GTX round chrome pistons.

Steve tells me that "No winner at Towcester this season has scored anywhere else" As if to prove the point, Tighten Your Belt comes out a month or so later and absolutely hammers another novice field at the same track. I back him on Betfair for Cheltenham at 55-1, knowing he'll be lucky to even make the starting line up. Sentiment again.

We are back in the covered marquee, crawling over the form in anticipation of the last race. The bookies runner is here again and he's had a winner or two today. I'm all for backing Stern Leader, the beast who bolted for the stables in the Bumper on Boxing Day. He's short though. The bookies runner points out a recruit from the flat called Monteforte who is impeccably bred from classic winning stock. But he's been off the track for well over a year.

"He'd be a nailed-on certainty but for the fact he's been in his box for so long. Jim Old doesn't have outstanding success with wins first time out".

I don't know what to do. As we arrived I told Nick to remind me not to go for broke in the Get-Out Stakes last race of the day. He does so now:
"No doubling up on the short priced favourite just because you haven't had a winner!"
"Hmm", I mutter.
We are looking at the beasts parading around the ring.
"Looks like a chaser in the making", I nod at number 7.
"Yeah, big sod isn't he?" replies Nick. Deadpan.
Both of us delivered the lines like pros. I only hope someone heard us and was impressed. Bullshit is very important. It should not be under-estimated.

In the end I do back Stern Leader at a ridiculously short 3-1. Can't believe I've done it. Monteforte shows he is a class above the rest and trundles away from the field as easily as Tighten Your Belt did earlier. He wins by 26 lengths. Nick groans. He tried to get a fiver on the beast at 7-2 just at the off, but the bookies wouldn't take his dough. More last race bumper agony at Towcester.

Once again Helen is happy to pick us up from Towcester and take us back to Berko. She's a fine woman and no mistake. But it still means we have an hour and a half to fill. There's a lovely looking boozer on the high street that takes our fancy. It is a bit like a tardis inside. A small door on the street leads to a series of ever larger rooms culminating in a barn with a pool table as centre-piece at the back of the pub, or more properly a coaching inn in a former life. The outhouse where the coaches went is now home to the outside bogs. Progress is a wonderful thing.

The pool table is irresistible and we have meandered ourselves through at least six frames of intricately executed games before it is time to go. I think Nick has squeezed ahead in the final analysis, but they are hard fought games increasingly fuelled by Charles Wells' Bombardier.

Home then, via the Mother-in-Laws to collect the kids. We have time to sample the local Tring brewery ales in my local, The Lamb, before Nick pushes off for home. Top day. Perfect aperitif for the weekend. I want to see my horse out now.

## 26. UP AND DOWN THE CITY ROAD, IN AND OUT THE EAGLE

*"I go checking out the reports – digging up the dirt.
You get to meet all sorts – in this line of work."*
Dire Straits, *"Private Investigations"*, 1983

You know how some evenings just go wrong. But you have to think very hard afterwards to pin point where the event went off the rails. There's usually some little spark or change of direction in the conversation. You might be aware of it. But by the time the full significance dawns like sunrise over the Serengetti, it's too late. You know you are already spinning out of control; powerless to alter the course of events.

I meet up with Nick, Steve and Bryn for a couple of gentle beers in the WW. Turns out it's one of those nights. It's a Tuesday night, this time. Everything normal so far. I've had a call from Rupert who is up in town and on the loose for some beers. I try to persuade him to come and join the boys in Victoria for a couple of sensible bevvies. But Roo fancies a night out in Covent Garden. So I relent. It's been a while since I've been to the Lamb and Flag, and a change of scene won't do any harm. Nick's up for it too, so we have a couple of looseners, discuss the aftermath of the Racing Post Chase and stroll over to the West End.

It takes us a while to find the pub – like I say, it's been a while. Rupert is tucked under the stairs, scowling into his bitter. I can see he's in one of his belligerent moods. We exchange hostilities.
 "Fuck's sake Rupert, why did you drag us right over here, you lazy bastard."
 "Fuck off Atkinson. This is shit beer this is."
Nick chuckles to himself. So we are off and running.

But it is horrible beer. Things have gone down hill in the West End. Nick suggests we move off and check out the footie. European action. Rupert agrees, questioning the sexual preference of the customers frequenting the establishment we are now leaving. The next boozer is a bit poky, but the ale is a passable London Pride. Nick's telling Rupert about this season's gambling.
 "Dave's doing alright. Surprised he hasn't told you. Yeah, 500-odd quid up last year".
Rupert gives me a bleary eyed squint. Easy for him with his polynesian parentage.
 "Yeah? You've never backed a winner in your life! What about all those donkeys you made us back when we were in the Commission. Losers! Every 'kin one!"
I remember them all too well. A neat side step is called for.
 "Remember Nichol's Liverpool double bet that went down. I could hear you laughing in my flat in Peckham when Michael Thomas slotted in Arsenal's winner!"

And so the reminiscing starts. It's Rupert who remembers the Lord Nelson first.
"What's that?", Nick casually enquires.
I'm starting to hear warning bells.
"Kin amazing place. Somewhere near the City Road. Strippers like you've never seen. Oh, scuse me – erotic dancers!", explains Rupert. I concur.
"Shocking place, venue of a mis-spent youth. Never seen a floor show like it. Sad, sad. All very sad. And ancient now."

It was sad. I try hard to be a sensitive soul keenly aware of the feelings of others and never wishing to cause offence. A modern thinker; liberated, tolerant and sensitive. Bollocks. I am weak. I'll admit it. On more occasion than one, in those heady days of youth, I found myself softened up by an alcohol suckerpunch, seduced by the vision of those many and varied talents at the Lord Nelson.

"Is it still there?", says Nick.
In the crystal vision of hindsight, this is where the evening starts to go pear-shaped. There's a devilish grin in Nick's eye. We're all beered up and it's obvious that we all fancy a visit to this hostelry of ill repute.
"Well", Rupert slouches forward insane grin decorating his chops, "We gotta find out, ain't we? Hahahahaha".
"Sounds like a top night out to me, where is it again?" Nick's up for it. No surprise!
And despite myself, so I am I. I can hear myself saying,
"Look, it was nearly 10 bloody years since we were last there. None of us can really remember where it is and I bet as sure as hell that it isn't there any more. Anything can have happened since then. It's probably been flattened for a Sainsbury's"

But I already know the deal is done. The arguing is over before it's started. If we don't go, the evening is lost. The beer in this pub is naff, Arsenal on the box are worse and Roo has been angling for something like this since we hooked up.
"We gotta do it Atkinson, for old times sake. Hehehehe. C'mon, sup up, man. I'll get the cab up there."
Now I know he's serious. Such casual generosity is not an oft-sighted Woods phenomenon.

Even in the cab it feels like going back 10 years. Rupert still has a juvenile grin welded to his face and is jabbering away to Nick and guffawing at the prospect of the evenings' entertainment. There is no doubt, we used to have a top-notch laugh here.
"Nick, last time we were at this pub it nearly signalled the end of Rupert's marriage. Keith was introduced to the boozer by one of his mates who works in the City. So we were in there, having a good gawp as this act doing her show, gyrating away to 'Chain Reaction'. And then, bloody hell, two of Keith's mates walked in. The one's who showed him the boozer in the first place. Keith nearly spat is beer out in surprise. Then he

recovers and goes 'oh, hi Duncan, James'. You should have seen Roo's face!"
I'm nodding at Rupert, who momentarily stops grinning.

"Yeah, 'kin nightmare. Here we are in a smoky boozer down some back street and two of Keith's mates walk in! If Dianne ever found out I'd been in a place like that, it would have been all over. She wouldn't have put up with it."
I continue,

"But do you know how close it was? Duncan was good friends with Keith's girlfriend. He's one of these enlightened sorts and he just mentioned this occurrence when he was round one night as one of those funny stories. As you do. Alison thought it was a bit sad and wasn't too upset, but Keith had to beg her not to say anything about it in front of Dianne – *your wife* - the next time we all met up. I'd say that was bloody close!"

"Too fuckin' right. Ouch that's close", observed Rupert.
Nick's pissing himself but introduces some common sense,

"But surely it's just a bit of a laugh. Yeah, sad maybe, but nobody gets hurt. I think Denise would just think it was a bit pathetic – y'know, boys will be boys."
Rupert shoots him a glance,

"Yeah, but you don't know Dianne."
It's true. I reckon it's the danger that eggs Rupert on.

We are here. I stumble out of the taxi and trip over road-work paraphernalia which is littering City Road roundabout. There are about six exits to the roundabout. I look at Rupert. This is where the memory fades.

"Which way?"

Rupert gives me some half remembered virtual tour around some local landmarks and we set off down City Road itself. Suddenly I have a recollection and as we approach a junction I think I know where I am.

"That should be it over there on the corner."

It isn't. We look more closely and decide that it was once a pub. I'm convinced that it was indeed once the Lord Nelson. Rupert's not so sure.

"No, it was a much quieter, sort of back street boozer than that."
But we must be close for me to recognise the street. I've only been there when bladdered.

We check out a bit further down the road and settle on a pint in an innocuous looking pub to talk tactics. Nick asks the barman where the Lord Nelson might be. He's a bit sheepish, but not as bad as Rupert or me would have been. But the barman gives Nick directions with a perfectly straight face. We bolt our pints and we are on our way. Oh the thrill of the chase.

Ten minutes later, we emerge from the end of a promising dark alley to round on a pub called the Lord Nelson! But it's the wrong one. We stare into the windows and wrack our memory, simply willing this to be the right pub. But it doesn't work. This is turning into a bone fide Grade 1 wild goose chase. Ill conceived and poorly executed. It's started raining and I'm getting pissed off.

At Rupert's insistence, we do another sweep of City Road, venturing a little further than on out first recce. Still to no avail. I get the hump and take unilateral action by branching off to a welcoming pub showing the death throes of the dull footie. Nick joins me and Rupert turns up a couple of minutes later. He's a tenacious bugger, but I'm wet, hungry and I've given up. I resort to calling Woods every name under the sun. He's impervious and simply shrugs off my jibes. He's on a mission.

The art of conversation seems to be stuck in a minimalist cul-de-sac tonight. We are still chewing over the pointlessness of the evening a pint or so later when a suspicious looking bloke sidles over and asks us if we are looking for the Lord Nelson pub. I spotted him and his lop-sided hair-piece earlier at the the bar. He's overheard our sad conversation, no doubt. I'm sceptical as he gives directions in broken English to Nick. We need to go back down City Road, apparently, but further than we had been earlier. Turn left at the Barclays and there you are. Bob's your uncle. Pop goes the weasel.

So we set off on one last pathetic route-march. I'm not sure what the evening is all about now. A Woods obsession maybe. A nod to nostalgia and an attempt to rekindle a spark of seedy adventure that was doused years ago.

We pass the Barclays, hang a left soon after and something clicks into place. Rupert is having an enthusiastic spasm. A revelation even.
"Yeah, yeah, this is it, there's a playground just there on the corner and the pub is at the end here." I'm with him now. I do remember. And sure enough there is the pub. Right on the corner where it always was. Bloody hell!

*Was* being the operative word. It's been closed down. But we have a good look round the outside anyway. Yep this is definitely it. Rupert is animated. Mission accomplished.
"I knew it was off the main street. Closed down though. Can you believe it!"

The three of us are stood around looking like lost souls. Think I know how Captain Scott felt at the South Pole when he found he'd been beaten to it. We are not ready to move on yet. The moment demands a little more meaningless loitering and a few more empty gestures. We peer in at the big picture windows and look at the painted plaque above the entrance, depicting Lord Nelson in full pomp. This is the place alright. Pub architecture right from the gable roof down to the polished ceramic bricks on the front. A guy walking down the street crosses to the opposite footpath, deciding to give us a wide berth. Rupert calls out to him,
"Hang on mate. Was this the Lord Nelson pub?"

The guy looks at him quizzically,
> "Oh, yeah, yeah, the strippers' pub. That's it, the Lord Nelson. Closed down about a year ago. They're turning it into flats."

My heart sinks. Another small part of me is buried under anonymous housing. Charlton, Stoke on Trent and now The City. I'm having a wee emotional wobble. But Rupert's still effusive. Guffawing now.
> "Flats! Ha! Did you hear what that bloke said... 'strippers pub' Hahahaha!"

So this is it. The venue of legends is no longer open for business. It's way past last orders anyway. Time to go home and draw a veil over this pathetic, desperate, futile and faintly emotive expedition.

I e-mail Keith a few days later and confess this sad and sordid little tale. He said he couldn't keep a straight face all day. His head was filled with images of shifty private dicks under dirty trilbies flitting about the shadows arranging seedy rendezvous and chasing rumours around rain-soaked North London. About right really.

## 27. SUNSET AT SANDOWN

*"I'm all sixes and sevens and nines
Say now baby, I'm the rank outsider*
The Rolling Stones, "*Tumblin' Dice*", 1972

Nick is a revelation. I read and re-read the e-mail blinking back at me from my computer screen.

"Noticed in the five-day decs that there are a few good horses likely to be out at Sandown this Saturday. Anyone fancy it?"

There are a number of remarkable features to this communication. I hardly know where to start. In order of prominence then, the first fact to note is that here we have cynical Nick 'luck will out' Jenkins who usually has to be dragged along to the races because everyone else is going and he doesn't want to be left out, now leading from the front and setting up the trip. Next most important is that he's noticed that there is a race meeting on Saturday. Flowing from this, we should also be aware that he has taken the trouble to look at the advance declarations. A neat wrinkle here that betrays his new found enthusiasm is his use of the term 'decs', instead of 'declarations'. He sounds like a pro. And finally, it should be recorded that here we have Nick displaying some qualitative judgement about the sport when he asserts his view that 'a few good horses' will be competing. Never mind revelation. This is revolution. Or is he taking the Michael?

I e-mail Steve and Bryn to see if they can make it.

"Can I just point out that this was Nick's idea. Bloody hell, what's going on?", I enquire.

"Christ Almighty" is all Steve can manage.

Bryn can't make it. His folks are round that day. Steve is harder to pin down. I'm all clear after having checked in with Mrs A. So I'm stuffing my face with a Cornish pasty at Clapham Junction on Saturday lunch time when I spot Nick idling outside the buffet with a copy of Raceform sticking out of his pocket.

"This is a crock of shite", he declares as he waves the rag at me.

"I know. It comes out mid-week and doesn't have the final declarations in it."

"Bloody hell", he says. "They didn't have any RPs in the newsagents so I forked out bloody £2.50 for this and it doesn't even have the runners!"

"It's for the serious punters, that is", I console. "It's probably got some decent Cheltenham pointers."

Nick's not convinced. He looks at my RP and crosses out his fancies that won't be lining up today. Nothing worse than doing your homework early only to find out afterwards that you've been doing the wrong subject.

"You couldn't persuade Steve to come then?", I enquire.

"No. I called him yesterday and he said 'Mr Woodentop had more chance of winning the Grand National than I do of getting a Saturday off!'"

We are having our own Tote Ten To Follow mini-league between the four of us this season. Nick's rank outsider, Mr Woodentop, won early season in some dodgy handicap at Wetherby. Steve then backed him for the Welsh National at astronomical odds where he barely got round the first circuit.

It's the usual scrum at the course turnstiles down by the railway fences. We are near the front of the queue, but it still takes far too long to get in. We have a scare when someone says they heard on Radio 5 Live that the first race had been brought forward by half an hour. Two crumbly life-long Sandown Park members are struggling to operate a turnstile each with no-one to help them fumble for change or issue raffle ticket entry tokens. We will never make it on to the track in time. The increasingly fractious crowd snakes back up on to Esher station and the progress into the course becomes farcically slow. Given that Sandown has had millions spent on it over the last few years I am stunned that a few quid could not have been found to spruce up and modernise the ticketing and turnstile arrangements. It shouldn't come as a shock to the stewards when for each fixture thousands of people arrive by train. These petty inefficiencies drive me scatty.

The moment of panic has passed. The races have not been brought forward and we pouch our tickets with no further alarms. Nick is digging his heel into the chase course. He looks at the muck on his shoe, sniffs the air and utters a single word:
"Unforgiving".
He's even out-pointing me on the bullshit!

At that very moment we are hit by five minutes of horizontal rain driven across the track by a violent wind. In no time at all we are soaked. Showers were forecast today, but I wasn't expecting a high velocity assault by a pressure hose. By the time we reach the stands the maelstrom has moved on to wreak havoc in other parts of suburbia. The ground remains testing, Nick confirms, as a whorl of mud slithers from his shoe.

It's the end of January and I'm definitely in pre-Cheltenham mode for this fixture. There are only six or so weeks to go to the 2004 festival and today will provide the last trial for many horses holding Cheltenham entries. This is a great card featuring a reigning Champion, Baracouda, running in a hurdle handicap for the first time; and a Champion pretender, Rhinestone Cowboy taking on some top opposition. The card also features an excellent 2 ½ mile novice chase and a cracking handicap chase. Pound for pound this is the best fixture I've been to this season.

To kick the day off we are treated to top-drawer juvenile hurdle. Nick and I have just about managed to slurp off a pint and get our bets on before the field goes to post. I'm on the unexposed Jonjo O'Neill trained juvenile

Cherub whilst Nick has plumped for the Henrietta Knight-handled Tusk. Other notables include Kjetil from the Nicholls stable and Moulin Riche, Francois Doumen's French raider. Many of these are Cheltenham bound.

The circuit around Sandown is quite narrow, which affords excellent views from the Grandstand of the field hurdling down the back straight without entirely relying on Cyclops-o-vision. I follow the green silks of my selection until we lose the pack for a short while at the turn into the home straight. It is here where the big screen shows that Moulin Riche is bizarrely carried out off the track after getting bunched in on the rail.

Before the last flight only two horses are left with a realistic chance. Inevitably it's Tusk and Cherub. Tusk has been out in front for some while now and coming to the last I'm sure Cherub is coming to take the race. This is fantastic. Nick is bellowing his lungs out for Jim Culloty on board his mount and I'm screaming for Liam Cooper on mine. This is no friendly Galwaybay Stan moment. This is no time to be magnanimous and grateful that at least one of us will win. On the contrary, this is every man for himself. Tusk v Cherub. Nick v Dave. Pride is at stake on the very first race. The two horses are eye-balling each other on the run-in. It's Cherub who gives way. He may have had his nose in the lead for a fraction, but Tusk finds more up the hill and stays on again. Nick roars him home. I'm gutted.

"Bloody hell. I thought he had that!", I despair and then "You bastard!", in response to Nick's broad, smug grin.

"Ha ha! I enjoyed that one!", he crows.

"Go and get your money and I'll get the soddin' beers."

Cracking race though. Tusk is one to consider for Cheltenham after he stayed on up the hill here.

We enjoy a pint on the balcony at the back of the grandstand. It overlooks the parade ring and just now it is catching some watery Winter sunshine. The runners for the Champion Hurdle trial are shown off to perfection in its warmth. Every taut hock and finely tuned fetlock is emphasised in the slanting rays as the beasts circumnavigate the ring. Rhinestone Cowboy attracts the most attention after his exploits in last years' Champion.

We settle back in the Grandstand and watch him win here. But hardly with commanding authority as he beats my fancy, the novice Garde Champetre into second. We fall into conversation with a couple of regulars on the terracing by the track. They are unconvinced by the Cowboy too. They clearly love their racing and have a share of a horse in training with Nicky Henderson. Nick looks at me, but this is no time to venture that I own half a hoof of a bumper horse somewhere in Lincolnshire.

Nick and I are not sure exactly what Rhinestone has beaten either. We are back in our place up over the parade ring and are dissecting the race. Neither of us would fancy him for the Champion Hurdle. We conclude (having given the matter some weighty consideration that lasts at least the time it takes to slip down half a pint), that he seems to fall apart in the serious races when the pressure is on. Ungenuine.

So, two runners-up for me. It's as near as I get all day. In the novice chase I manage to talk myself out of backing Patricksnineteenth because the price is too short. I take a crazy each way bet about One Nation. It's another mug punt because there are only seven runners and the Henrietta Knight charge needs to finish 2nd for me to collect. What kind of each way bet is that? I keep making these basic mistakes. We are down by the rail to see Patricksnineteenth win well on the soft ground that he loves and One Nation to stay on into a game 3rd. The worst possible result.

Hard to believe, but Nick manages to concoct an even worse one in the feature Agfa Chase. The 3-mile handicap slog is won in some style by Sandown specialist Kings Mistral. Nick is ecstatic. He's come up trumps again and wades into the ring to collect his returns. I'm left to contemplate where my next winner is coming from. The contrast between this season and last could not be more stark. I may be in a Cheltenham frame of mind, but I'm struggling to raise any confidence about my lumbering portfolio of ante-post bets. I text Steve to pass on the details of Nick's glorious afternoon.

But I'm a bit premature. Nick comes back potless. I can't help but howl with laughter as he tells me he's backed the wrong horse. Instead of backing horse number 4, Kings Mistral, he has mistaken the '4' chalked up next to favourite Hersov as the horse number when they are actually the odds. Same cock-up Ben made at Exeter before Christmas. Only then it worked in his favour. Nick's howler was compounded by not checking his ticket. But who does? I feel for Nick. No, I really do. What a shocking blunder. We are two complete novices, imbeciles, incompetents. We shouldn't be allowed out without name-tags on our clothes and The Green Cross Code tucked under our arms.

The highlight of the day, in purely racing terms anyway, is Baracouda. He gives a wonderful weight carrying performance to win the Sandown handicap hurdle. The champion stayer is viewed by the handicapper to be so far ahead of his rivals in this field that he concedes 19lbs to the next on the list. The minimum weight for this race is 10st, so it means that all the other runners are actually out of the handicap, ie, they are viewed so far inferior to Baracouda that their allotted weight for the race is less than the minimum weight. Crazy, for such a valuable race. One of Paul Nicholl's horses, Alexanderthegreat is a full 27 lbs 'wrong' at the weights! These discrepancies start to show on the run in when Baracouda who has opened up a big lead starts to tire. The hill takes its toll and jockey Thierry Doumen has to pull out the stops to cajole the champ over the line. My exacta is in tatters as the outsider Yogi stays on for second and Alexanderthegreat defies the handicapper's logic to come in a very respectable 3rd.

After racing (an old Exeter mate, Farmer Jack, wins the final novice chase), we decide to check out the local boozers. We emerge by the railway fences and make for the other side of the station where we imagine Esher town centre lies. But there is nothing to be seen but endless streets of semi-detached Terry and June-ness. The place is a social desert. We walk round the streets for about 20 minutes and all we can find is a nail bar and a florists, symptoms of bloated middle England. How to people live around here?

We are on a main road which looks a bit more hopeful. Nick stops a likely looking bloke and asks him where the nearest pub is.
"Hmm. Not much around here", he muses. "You could try the police sports ground up here and left at the lights. They have a public bar", he offers.
Nick replies,
"Police ground? Ha. Ha. No thanks. Not quite what we had in mind."
The bloke glares at him and walks off smartly.
"He was probably a copper", I suggest.
"Oh shit!", says Nick.

Our hopes are raised briefly by a pub-looking building on the corner. We investigate further to find that it was once the Rising Sun, but is now a Café Rouge. But this is no time for charcoaled minute-steak and spikey chips. We give up on soulless car dependent Esher and get the train back to Clapham Junction for a proper pint of real ale in the honest, unpretentious Falcon Inn. That's better.

The rest of the evening becomes a bit of a blur. We have a kebab at some point and I note that Nick has graduated to chilli sauce with his doners instead of mayonnaise. We make some deeply hurtful allegations about Steve's commitment to racing after his no-show here and at Towcester. I think Nick accuses Steve of "showboating at the big fixtures and abandoning the grass roots of the sport". Right on!

Later, there's some footy on the telly and we are in deep conversation about it with a bloke at the bar. It's all good-natured stuff, but I can tell by the nonsense I'm spouting that I am the worse for wear. Nick must be too. It all falls apart when we spot some colourful looking ready-mixed chasers behind the bar. They appear to the by-product of some failed chemical experiment. Infact they are vodka shots that mix a ghastly range of fruit extracts with alcohol to produce near fluorescent pink, lemon, blue and green drinks. Well, we can't leave these untasted. So I order a couple. The barmaid tells me that they are "two for a fiver, love". So we order four. Carnage ensues. They taste like the stuff dentists would give you to rinse your mouth out, only they've found it is more effective at cleaning toilets instead. I think we have a whisky each to take the taste away and I honestly can't remember how or in what state I got home.

## 28. CHELTENHAM 2004: HARDY PERENNIALS

*"When I get to the bottom*
*I go back to the top of the slide*
*Where I stop and I turn and I go for a ride*
*And I get to the bottom and I see you again"*
The Beatles, *Helter Skelter*, 1969

We have been here before. I feel like an old pro. This is a well-worked routine. No accommodation or logistical turmoil this time. Everything is slipping together cosily like sheepskin cheekpieces on a recalcitrant gelding (!). We even have reserved seats on the Festival Flyer with a proper table at which to scoff the traditional Burger breakfast. The couple sat opposite Steve and I serve to emphasise the old hand feeling.
    "Yeah, we've been every day since 2000."
Bullish words fall easily from chapped lips, particularly considering the 2001 festival was cancelled! These two are regulars as well, but mostly only for the Tuesday, though this year, they are returning on Thursday.

We drop into easy banter all the way to Cheltenham. We swap bankers and bismarks and tales of past glories. It's soon clear that she is the brains of the outfit and supplies the expertise for the adventure. Her nap today is a Philip Hobbs novice in the opener called Lacdoudal. The more I look at this the more I think she's right! I'm desperate to kick off the festival with a winner. I've never done it at any festival yet.

We pick up another tip to be tucked away in the kit bag a few minutes later: they go regularly to the Arc de Triomphe meeting at Longchamps every year. Only a fiver to get in apparently. A fiver! What value. The day is a seamless parade of Group 1 races, but is largely populated by English punters making a Parisian weekend of it. Now there's a thought.

The train disgorges hungry punters onto Cheltenham Spa platform 1 on time. We head straight for the track. Stepping off the shuttle bus I brace myself for the first rips of slicing wind raging over Cleave Hill. It doesn't materialise. In fact the weather is positively clement. Warm even. Batting away swarms of ticket touts hanging around like irritating flies adds to the Summer-like illusion.

Watching the weather and, more pertinently, the watering plans of Clerk of the Course Simon Claisse are always pre-festival sports guaranteed to cause consternation. This year there has been sufficient rain to make Claisse turn off the taps reasonably early. But the suspicion remains that he wants good-to-soft ground on the opening day so that it will dry out to give good ground on Gold Cup day. Cheltenham has a contract with Met Office man John Kettley to provide weather forecast advice. This isn't enough for one trainer though. In an RP the previous week, the Middleham-based trainer Ferdy Murphy says,
    "I have an owner in the pig business and he has a ten-day forecast for the Cheltenham area that predicts showers for Friday,

Saturday, Sunday and Monday, with rain on Tuesday. If that's right I would be happy. If it isn't I wouldn't be."

Never mind satellite imaging and radar technology. Pig farming is the future of weather forecasting!

Building works are now complete at Prestbury Park and we know that there are even left luggage facilities this year. Steve e-mailed Cheltenham managing director Edward Gillespie to congratulate him on the improvements brought by the renovation and to enquire about the availability of left luggage. Mr Gillespie replied in the affirmative. In fact he was so impressed with Steve's tone that he replied twice. The second e-mail said something like "we seem to have had a lot of enquiries about this particular facility this year". Dozy twonk.

"Your Managing Director says you've got left luggage facilities. We'd like to leave our Bags please", asserts Steve at the Information Desk.

"Er, yeah, think that's here mate. Yeah, just need to do a search and I'll give you a ticket."

He rifles the bags, gives us a raffle ticket each and chucks the bags on the floor behind him. This guy is ensconced in a tiny cubicle. I have visions of him cowering under a leaning tower of luggage come the Pertemps final.

The new stand is fantastic, though. We make for the Desert Orchid bar on the top deck, line up some Guinesses and take in the sun-bathed track laid out like a carpet before us. There is a constant stream of helicopters flying in owners, jockeys and wealthy members.

"It's like Apocalypse Now", I remark to Steve.

"Ha ha. 'I love the smell of napalm in the morning' ...", he quotes, without breaking his stare at the choppers.

This is a splendid vantage point and for the first time affords a proper high-level view of the courses from the Courage End. There are three of them interweaving across the venue - Old (first two days), New (Gold Cup day) and the cross-country course. There used to be a fourth, the Park Course, now abandoned. I get a proper look at some of the notorious obstacles that cause mayhem in the heat of battle. The water jump on the New Course which accounted for Beef or Salmon last year and the infamous second last on the Old Course which left Vinnie Keane punching the ground in unforgettable despair two years on the trot after Latalomne came crashing down.

Cheltenham offers conferencing facilities in the main grandstand complex when there is no racing. I attended an event held there the previous November and can vouch first hand for the excellence of the facilities, even if the conference was long and dull. Lunch was held in the spankingly good panoramic restaurant at the top of the Grandstand. I spent the time it took to demolish roast chicken breast, ratatouille and boilies followed by lemon syllabub boring fellow delegates to distraction with lyrical observations and remembrances about the festival; spraying them in my enthusiasm with morsels of the table d'hote. These events are all about networking in my view.

The corporate boxes were used for seminar rooms and I had one of those 'this will be me one day' moments as I took in the well-apointed balcony seats, TV screens, mini bar and fridge (wouldn't want the champagne too warm...). I even got chance in a quiet moment to amble round the national hunt horse-racing museum.

The atmosphere in the bar is building nicely. It's easy to tell Steve and I sense the anticipation keenly. The beer is going down a bit too easily, the bitty conversations are punctuated by frequent and unsolicited hand-clapping and "C'mon"s. Infact we are both now gabbling like excited kids on Christmas Eve:

"Got your placepot down, Davoski? Yeah, yeah. Me too. Playing it straight this year. No fancy systems this time which crash and burn at the first. What a farce that was last year, eh?"

"Seen this on the telly, Bacchy? It's Dessie in all his pomp clearing the last. Fine beast. What a horse."

"Hey, what about that trip to the Arc that those two on the train mentioned. I fancy that."

"Yeah, blindin' that. We should get the girls organised. Tell 'em we're taking 'em to Paris for the weekend. Ha ha."

"Where are we standing for the first? I want a good perch. Down by the rail maybe"

There's still a good hour to go before the off, but we both feel compelled to check out the best pitch as soon as possible. I need a leak first and have a strange Fawlty Towers-esque moment. I follow the signs for the loos at the top deck of the stand, go round the corner, down the stairs and push the door marked 'to the toilets' to find myself blinking into sunshine dappling the main food concourse at the back of the grandstand. "Jokers", I spit whilst joining the long queue for the bogs in the usual place. Not such a well-appointed new stand, then.

Another complaint. Unless you are flush against the running rail there is no chance of seeing the big screen on the course side of the Courage End. There's another big screen overlooking the food court, and tellies in all the bars, but you can't see the course from there. So in a tactic straight out of the Tony McCoy coaching manual, we tuck ourselves tight up against the rail.

I really want to get off to a good start. Have I already mentioned this? In the Supreme I've replaced my non-running Lingo bet with an each way double starting with Albuhera. I'm also on Cardenas each way and now decide to have a little saver on the beast recommended to us on the train.

My ante-post book is a shambles this year. I've had many more bets than last year but because of defections, injuries and basic mug punting I am almost £50 down before the tape goes up for the opener. Steve has a much healthier looking portfolio, starting with Perle de Puce and Brave Inca in this. He is not disappointed.

The customary roar sweeps over from the packed Tatts enclosure to mark the start of the 2004 festival. Here we go. Helter skelter. By the time I come up for air it will be 3.30 with three Grade 1s already over.

Brave Inca is just that. Incredibly brave. In a quickly run, competitive and characteristically choppy Supreme, the Willie Mullins trained gelding gets the better of a shoot-out up the hill with an outsider. Neither of us recognises the outsider.
"What the bloody hell is that?"

It's War of Attrition. Another Irish raider. The result is difficult to call until the final half furlong or so. Steve is hoarse from urging on the Inca, but is ultimately rewarded by a fine late thrust from Barry Cash. Inca wins by a neck. This is what Steve needed. 200 notes in the bag and the pressure's off. The Supreme is turning into a gimme for the Irish. This is three years on the bounce that a short-priced raider has bagged the opener. Albuhera doesn't get close, and it looks like the hard season is catching up with him. All my other bets are down. Cardenas shows best of all, staying on strongly to finish 4th,

Turns out that Stormin' Norman Williamson had tipped War of Attrition as an each way steal. Not a bad result at 33-1 for the former jockey-turned-pundit.

Steve has targeted the Arkle. It's just about his favourite festival race and this year has some very tasty ante-post bets that have shortened up nicely allowing him to lay them off for free bets. He's mob handed with Caracciola as his trump card, but with Central House, Kicking King and a couple of other interests to complete a nap hand.
"Don't get the Henderson beast mixed up with Central House, Steve. They both sport natty blue dots", I chirrup.

I'm only on Richard Guest's Our Armageddon now after the first leg of the double went down with Albuhera. I can see Steve's fascination with the race. This is a real test for novices with pretensions to join the big Champion Chase boys. A fast pace is nearly always guaranteed and there is such a premium on good accurate jumping. Last year's performance by Azertyuiop and Moscow Flyer before him have elevated the credentials of the race. Can't see a Moscow Flyer in the field today, but it proves to be a very competitive affair.

Well backed Thisthatandtother, Steve's main fear for his treble chance makes a howler at the very first fence and must be unsettled because he crashes out at the next. There is a cry of anguish from the thousands of festival favourite backers. Caracciola also appears to be a faller in the middle of the race and Steve is mortified, screaming expletives at the jockey Mick FitzGerald. Central House goes well. Our Armaggedon seems to have missed the break and is pulled up quite early.

But when push comes to shove at the top of the hill it is Kicking King kicking on from 2 fences out. But who's this sneaking up on the rail?... bloody hell, McCoy on Well Chief. He's only had one outing over fences. A muddling victory at Taunton. Didn't convince me. But McCoy has him in a peach of a position. He fluffs the last to gasps all around. Goes right through the top of it. KK has a chance to close up and does so, but Well Chief finds his rhythm again well. He idles a bit in front, but the champ is having none of that he drives him home with the irresistible purpose of a JCB to record a length victory. It was close, but the Pipe horse was in fairness a good winner. He had the best hurdles form of any of these and was still allowed to go off at 9-1 in places.

Next day, reading the results in the RP we find that Central House had fallen and Caracciola ran a blinder. Steve had been cheering on the wrong horse!

They come thick and fast. The Champion Hurdle is one of the most keenly anticipated and open renewals for ages. There are doubts about the form of all the principals. Defending Champion Rooster Booster has not hit the heights of last year's scintillating performances; Rigmarole is unproven at the highest level, Intersky Falcon may be unsuited by the track. Other contenders like Rhinestone Cowboy and Spirit Leader have been re-routed or pulled in recent days.

An Irish bloke next to us has been lively all afternoon and we are having a bit of a laugh. Just before the start he rips off his jumper to reveal a blue T-Shirt emblazoned with 'RHINESTONE COWBOY' in two-inch high letters.
      "Wehey", we go.
He turns round and on the back it says "CHAMPION HURDLE WINNER, CHELTENHAM 2004". At least he's keeping his sense of humour. Better luck next year, mate!

There has been some debate in the press about how the race will be run. Rooster and others are better coming off a strong pace, whilst Rigmarole's connections feel that a slowly run race will suit their horse. In the event, the debate is settled by Hardy Eustace who takes off in front. Hardy was my ante-post choice for the Stayers until re-routed to this minimum trip. I couldn't believe it. His trainer Edward O'Grady also had him in the Coral Cup tomorrow, a 2 ½ mile trip.

As the race unfolds it becomes clear the Hardy Eustace is not stopping. From out of the chasing group comes Rooster Booster. Johnson has had enough of holding up his mount and is coming to win the race. A monumental cheer rolls its way down the enclosures like thunder. At the last flight both put in good jumps - Hardy with a neat compact style, Rooster with his trademark splayed front legs and low clearance. Rooster looks to have edged the lead for a few strides and for all the world I would have called him the winner. But Hardy has more left. He comes again, pulls away and wins well under an emotional ride from Conor O'Dwyer. Hardy Eustace was ridden last year by Keiron Kelly to win the SunAlliance Hurdle. Kelly died after a horrific fall in Ireland earlier this year and in a touching moment, this win was dedicated by all associated with the horse to that rider.

No blame attached to Rooster either, who gave all in glorious defeat. Johnson who has attracted criticism in some circles (me included) for pushing for home too early, rode a blinder today. Intersky Falcon stayed on for third and so Steve's mate Andy would be delighted. Good. We are hooking up with him tomorrow. Might get a beer out of him.

Steve notices that Bryn has tipped up Hardy Eustace in the Fantasy Festival competition. I'm supposed to be making an honourable defence, but Bryn at £10 e-w on the O'Grady beast is already home and hosed in the competition. Barring further massive price winners or big stake elusive doubles, I'm kissing goodbye to the trophy I never even saw. Then my phone jangles. Bryn's texting me:
    "Had £2.50 EW on Hardy Eustace at 25-1. Just collected £80 thank you very much."

Fantastic punting. Where did he get that bet from? I'm gobsmascked. I'm desperate for him to tell me that he worked it out and saw something in the form of his last run. I couldn't bear it if he said it was just a lucky hunch.

OK time to draw breath. My assault on the first three races with anteposts, each ways, doubles and singles has spectacularly failed. I'm a good few quid down now. The closeness of the races is in stark contrast to last year, but that is scant compensation. I take a few consolation nips of the Irish whiskey sloshing around in my hip flask. Steve makes a good call.
    "Let's catch this from the top of the new stand."
Yeah, a change of scenery is required. My spirits lift with every step up the banking.

The field for the National Hunt Handicap Chase had looked very strong only a week before the festival, but had been savaged by late defections. Only 11 are now gathered at the post. I'm already on Fork Lightning, a novice from Alan King's yard. Fork Lightning was an old mate of mine from novice days. We were about even, me and the Lightning. Great jumper and game as hell on his day, but the form is not rock solid. Steve is on his old mate Marlborough.

It is a good race. Fork Lightning doesn't let me down. Robert Thornton (who I've also backed for Festival top jockey) runs a very smart race, tracking early leader Kelami, picking him off and holding well the challenge of Shardam. Marlborough seemed to hate humping top weight and short priced favourite Haut Cercy doesn't run much of a race.

This win is not going to turn my loss into a profit in one fell swoop, but it is deeply satisfying. This is a horse I've always liked and he's won in great style. It's my first winner at the festival this year. I'm on the map. I feel more relieved than elated.

It's the Mickey Mouse Fulke Walwyn amateur riders 3-miler next. I don't much like this race. I have a bet. Obviously. Flushed with success it would be rude not to. I back Ferdy Murphy's Dominikus and Steve's on Toto Toscato whom he is convinced is the subject of a Pipe plot.

There are pundits that tell you that even the best jockeys rarely make significant differences to the outcome of races because of outstanding rides. That may be true as a whole. But bad jockeys can certainly lose races much more regularly. There are a lot of jockeys losing this race right now. It's carnage after a mile with most of the field already strung out like washing on a blustery Monday.

There are three good races at the festival for amateur riders. This seems a bit excessive. For a meeting that prides itself on the undiluted quality of the horses that take their chances, why is there a race every day for make-weight pilots? It adds a certain lottery-like quality to events. Today's spin of the roulette wheel does indeed throw up a Pipe plot. But it's not Toto Toscato. It's 40-1 shot Maximise that catches long time leader Merchant's Friend on the line.

Steve has been plotting up the Pertemps Final for months. In January he was e-mailing Andy Intersky who, of course, has top connections to the Jonjo O'Niell yard. Steve wanted any inside info on any scams that were afoot. Steve was right to target Jonjo. He has a tremendous record in this event. And as the early declarations approached, we see him pitching in both Iris's Gift and Rhinestone Cowboy. I bet his Irish eyes were twinkling as that went to press. Needless to say, neither of these luminaries makes the starting line up. Steve has watched all the qualifiers. I think I was only dimly aware that there were any. I sort of recollect that Stormez ran well in one that was won by another O'Neill horse, Tardar. But I back Derivative, a Venetia Williams outsider. Steve has a very good price on GVA Ireland who, apparently, ran very well in the Punchestown qualifier and has been laid out for the event.

We are back on the rail to watch this thriller. It's a cosy little spot - handy for the big screen, but by no means buttock to buttock, nose to armpit like in Tatts. The bars are crowded and the rave-tent off the food court is completely rammed. There must be thousands here who don't see a horse in the flesh at all. Steve is just squeezing the last drops of juice out of his hip flask when bloke in his late twenties, sporting a crew cut, enough blingage to sink a cruiser and a grin as wide as the Severn Estuary, rushes up to his mates stood next to us and screams,

"Ye-hey, you fuckin' beauty! Ha. Who needs fuckin' Cheltenham when you can land 4-1 at Southwell!"

Steve and I roar with laughter.

"He's at the world's greatest steeple-chase meeting and he's chucking his wedge at the sand donkeys on the telly!"

Steve is merciless in his condemnation. I can't decide whether this is better or worse than the lager lads in the tent.

The Pertemps is run at a serious gallop with plenty swapping the lead in the early exchanges. As so often, things start to happen at the top of the hill. GVA Ireland has been prominent for some time at the head of a group of about 10 who have kicked away. Can't see Derivative amongst them. Steve is glued to the big screen, but he's not so animated. The pursuing pack look ready to swallow up the Irish raider at any point coming down the hill. But as he hurls into the business end of the race, GVA Ireland is still leading, tenaciously refusing to be passed. This horse has spirit.

"Go on GVA", urges Steve as the horse maintains the lead at the last fence.

He is pushed out for home as Alexanderthegreat and His Nibs make bold moves in his wake. GVA is starting to look a bit weary though and is vulnerable to a flash of green and gold weaving in and out of the pursuers. Creon in JP McManus stripes is leaving it late, but eating up GVA's lead. Another Jonjo O'Neill plot is unfolding. GVA Ireland is tired and his jockey can get no more out of the horse to resist this late surge. Amid screams of anguish, notably from Steve, but from most of the other Irish contingent, Creon catches GVA 100 yards before the post to win by half a length. He's returned at 50-1.

Steve is crest-fallen. He's had horses involved in three close finishes and has only bagged one of them. Brave Inca set the standard. This has been a very good day for him, but it could easily have been so much better.

The bookies are laughing. They must have got back every penny in one day that they claim to have lost over three last year. Fearless Freddie Williams asserts in the next day's RP that he got stung for a huge amount by laying Brave Inca. I'm not sure I buy it.

Mona has laid on a great spread for us. I had told her earlier in the week that we weren't sure what time we would arrive with her, so she shouldn't bother getting anything ready. But she has and it is very welcome. She is typically understated.

"Ah well, Dave, Steve, it's only bits and pieces that I had in the fridge. You know, it's just a bit of cold stuff that wouldn't waste if you'd already eaten."

A bit like Freddie Williams, I'm not sure if I buy it. There is a massive cartwheel of a quiche (none of your Iceland nonsense either); two sorts of ham; three brands of cheese; bread rolls, bread buns and sliced white; enough salad to shame a small market garden and more tea than Steve drinks in a year.

"Now Steve, you don't like tea do you? I'll get Paul to make you that filter coffee when he gets in. I can't get on with it."

I can't believe she's remembered. But Steve's ready.

"No that's fine Mona. I like the instant stuff. I'll sort it out."

And he's up in a flash.

I'm taking the lid off a brand new jar of mango chutney to go with a slab of Wensleydale the size of a house, when Paul comes in. There are two other unopened pots of exotic chutney on the table that betray (if nothing else does) the effort Mona has gone to. She's an absolute gem and this spread is a life-saver. Paul has just come back from the boozer and is in good form as ever. He clocks the table groaning with the weight of food.

"Ah, see you've got the best stuff out for the guests, Ma?", he grins.

"Ah away with you Paul", retorts Mona.

Paul's looking devilish. He tucks into some quiche.

"We haven't seen these cups since your silver wedding anniversary, Ma".

He winks.

"Were there spiders in them? Hargh hargh haaaaarrrrggghhhh".

I'd forgotten about the most infectious belly laugh in Gloucestershire.

Later, when the meal has subsided, we slope off for a couple of quiet ones in Paul's local. But it is precisely that. After two pints of lager (yes, lager), Steve pulls up a stool and leans over the bar like he's ready for 40 winks. I'm checking out the jukebox, but there's more chance of chomping my way through a legendary Gloucester mix than finding a Motorhead track in this r'n'b, boy band collection. Paul is a huge Beatles fan, but there is not much here for him either. The landlord lets him loose on the karaoke now and again, we hear, but he's limited to one number! He plans to go to the races tomorrow and we check out the decs.

But the day has wasted me and Steve and we are back at Mona's in very sensible order. The rigours of the day seem to have left no indelible mark on me and unlike last year I retire to the top room confident that I will remain there until Steve breaks down my door to deliver a Ribena and the Racing Post next morning. Service with a smile.

## 29. CHELTENHAM 2004: PADDY'S DAY

*"Ragz to richez or so they say*
*Ya gotta-keep pushin'*
*For the fortune and fame*
*It's all a gamble*
*When it's just a game"*
Guns n Roses, *"Paradise City"*, 1987

It's St Patrick's Day today. This is the first time Paddy's Day has coincided with the festival since I've been coming here. The races, the Irish and something to celebrate seems like a potentially explosive combination to me. Mona has already got her evening sorted out. She has a gig at the Irish Club round the corner. She's not impressed though.

"They're not much of a band though. Too much swearing for me. I don't mind a bit of bad language, Dave, you know what I'm saying. But, sure, it's every other word with these lot."

I bet she's the first one up and dancing.

We slip into last year's successful routine and take in a fry-up on the way to the Internet café. We use the same place as last year, but now there are many more customers. A lot of them have today's Racing Post nudging against the keyboard and Betfair data blinking back from the screen. The revolution is gathering speed.

The bloke next to me tells me that this is his first Cheltenham and he can't wait.

"Yeah, my girlfriend bought me and two of my mates the tickets for a birthday present. Fantastic. She didn't want to come herself, though."

Top present, top girlfriend, I think. Then I remind myself that my wife bought me a racehorse for Christmas (well a bit of one anyway)! Ha! Beat that!

As usual Steve needs the full hour and more to nail his selections. Today he has a few each-way doubles he wants to lay off and he has to wait a while before they are matched out there in Betfair land. Maybe he's trading with someone in this room. Who knows what happens in this ethereal electronic bookies.

My portfolio is a little threadbare after all yesterday's ant-post bets fell. So I take singles in a couple of the races, but I leave a little scope for some activity on course. Particularly for the joke amateur race and the impenetrable Mildmay of Flete.

On the train to Cheltenham I tell Steve about Lambourne trainer Charlie Mann coming acropper in the corporate hospitality stakes. He reckons he has been stitched up by company he engaged to sort out the hospitality for his principal owners. Turns out that the marquee they pitched up for the group is not even on the course! It's across the road on some spare ground and they can't access the track or the parade ring. They can see the racing on the box of course, just the same as anyone else. Charlie's in the Racing Post chuntering away.

"I didn't pay two-grand a head for my owners to sit in a tent in the car park. I'll be having words with the organisers."
The hospitality specialists are unrepentant.

"We offer a first class package including a four course luncheon and silver service. Mr Mann was made fully aware of the location and facilities at the time of booking."

There's a green and white striped gazebo - the sort of thing you might pick up in a B&Q sale - just outside the entrance to the Courage End. We both look in as we pass, but there's no sign of Charlie inside.

I'm getting into the guinness. We are in good time again and have a couple at the top of the Dawn Run bar whilst mulling over placepot selections. Steve is also collecting fantasy festival entries for the day. It's going to take some punting to overtake Bryn though.

The card today is again chock-full of quality races. We are drooling at the chops. I've got beer down my shirt and it's not even 2pm. The first event is as mouth-watering a prospect as any. Steve has been looking forward to the Royal and SunAlliance Hurdle for many a long month.

I'm looking for Fundamentalist to win as my main bet, struck on Betfair at 19-1. I also have my crazy bet on the Towcester mud-loving revelation, Tighten Your Belt. Steve has Sadlers Wings and Fundamentalist in a double with Rosaker in the Coral Cup later.

I had tried to set Fundamentalist up in a double for this race, but the first leg went down. He's the one I fancy. But I also have the Howard Johnson hotpot Inglis Drever in this, doubled up with Our Vic in the big novice chase later. Some of the doubles I've struck are fanciful. This one in particular is the product of muddled thinking. I've been so seduced by the talk about both Inglis Drever and Our Vic that I've felt obliged to smash in to whatever value I think remains.

Mark Howard, whose guides I buy and whose race analyses I like, is really gushing about Our Vic. Indeed he recommends biting bookies' hands off now for prices for the Pipe novice in next year's Gold Cup. Howard is one of considered opinion. For him to nail his colours to the mast so decisively is a surprise. There's no doubt that I have been influenced by this a little.

All that will be settled in about 40 minutes. We have this monumental hurdle race to live through first. Down on the rail we are awash in good humour. Not just our own expectancy. There are more people in this little corner of Prestbury Park than yesterday. Plenty of Scots and Irish around us and they are all serious about their racing. Anticipation so keen it's palpable.

We are not disappointed. This looked like a quality field and right from the tape they go a good lick. The race starts to shape up on the final circuit and the big hitters move through. A group of five or six are positioning themselves at the top of the hill to play their cards. I don't know who to cheer on. This is the problem with multi-bets. I see Tighten Your Belt move off the back of the leading group and pull wide.

"Go on the Belt"

"Fuckin' Tighten Your Belt!" snorts Steve. "Who is this animal? I'll eat my hat if he wins"

But he can't quite sustain his effort and he's outpaced from three out. There will be no hat-eating today. But my picks are all still in the mix. Who is next? A mighty bellow, laced with thick Irish vowels rings in my lugholes,

"Goooo ooooon fuckin' Fundamentalist. Let him gooooo"

Indeed Fundamentalist is moving menacingly behind the leaders. But Steve and I saw his last race at Haydock and we know he needs to come late. He almost caught Royal Rosa, a very respected hurdler, that day. He's best as a hold up horse on all available evidence.

"Hang on to him, Carl", urges Steve. "Don't let him go yet."

Llewellyn rides a perfectly judged, well paced finish. We are going wild on the rail. How can he be so calm in this white-hot tussle? He must have ice in his veins. Fundamentalist pushes into the lead from two out. Inglis Drever unleashes his final burst and half of me expects him to assert his authority when it matters. But Fundamentalist is like a terrier and won't be beaten. But he hits the last. And he's idling. This would be thrilling stuff if it wasn't my wedge he's pulling through that timber. Llewellyn coaxes more rhythm from the horse in the final strides and he does enough to repel the game Drever. The winning margin is only half a length, but it could have been more without that last hurdle blunder.

Fantastic race. This is the real thing. I've just seen a special event. Me, Steve and the loud Irish man are leaping around screaming for joy and thumping each other on the back. Mutual respect. Plenty of others are cheering too. The Twiston-Davies gelding is a popular winner.

This feels like the right result. It feels like one of those lovely wins that I've worked out and plotted up. But it's an illusion. If Tighten Your Belt had won I would be calling Nick and myself geniuses for picking the form from the middle of a Towcester bog. If Inglis Drever had prevailed I would be congratulating myself on an astute win-double saver. But that cold analysis comes later. There is no doubt that I'm savouring this moment.

When we've calmed down a bit, Steve goes flat. He enjoyed that win as much as anybody on the course, but he is having a reality check.

"I've cocked this up big time, Davoski. That was a stunning win, but what have I got to show for it? A big fat nothing. I've got Fundamentalist in doubles and silly combinations, but I haven't collected anything from that. I've fancied this horse for months. I can't believe I didn't have a straight win bet on him. Shambolic."

He's being hard on himself.
> "Yeah, but think of the prospect of cheering on Rosaker in the Coral Cup. This could be the bet of you life, Bacchy!"

But I know how he feels. It's all or nothing in the Coral Cup now.

The Royal and Sun Alliance Chase is a messy race. The field is already depleted because of injuries and defections to some of the season's best novice chasers like Strong Flow, Therealbandit, Lord Transcend and Nil Desperandum.

Our Vic is all the rage, of course, but I have no punting interest in him now. I've also been burned in the ante-posts twice already - a double that crashed on the first leg and a defection to the four-miler. I took a price about Pizarro this morning and I have a place double remaining on Royal Emperor. Steve has Nicky Henderson's Calling Brave.

The race is ultimately disappointing. Steve cries with anguish a moment before Calling Brave hits the deck,
> "Steady Fitz. Don't boot him into that fence".

The jockey does exactly that and the horse stumbles on landing. He can't pick up. Steve has been watching his progress like a hawk and has a theory that FitzGerald always looks for a big leap at that fence on the top of the hill to kick start his drive for home. Steve has called it to perfection. Small comfort.

There are other casualties. Pizarro is brought down by Mossy Green when both looked to be going well. Rule Supreme is blundering every fence but seems to be galloping relentlessly. Our Vic looks to be travelling well and Royal Emperor is in the mix too. Tony McCoy asks Our Vic for a final effort and finds nothing. Rule Supreme gallops on when I swear that everyone at the track expects the Pipe horse to overwhelm him. The Irish raider stays on to win by over a length from Royal Emperor. I collect a bit of place money on the Sue Smith horse. Game as the day is long. Owes me nothing.

Our Vic comes home a bitterly disappointing 3rd. The crowd have swallowed a cheer as if strangling an lbw appeal at Lord's. The winner is received in near silence. Not that the jockey and connections give a hoot. But this is surreal. There have been bigger priced and less well-fancied winners of big races, but rarely has collective expectation has been crushed so quickly. Our Vic never made a real fight of it. Mark Howard can get any price he wants about the beast for next year's Gold Cup!

I'm looking forward to the Champion Chase, my favourite race of the festival. Strong pace; elite field; fast fencing; purring chasers. Poetry.

This year it promises to be a showdown between two of the very finest two-milers. Moscow Flyer, reigning champion versus Azertyuiop, young pretender. The race has been set up for this shoot-out since the two met at Sandown in December. The Champ held sway that day, but subsequent runs by both – notably when Azertyuiop gave everything and lost nothing in a stunning weight-carrying defeat at Ascot; and by Moscow in imperious style at Leopardstown over Christmas – have franked their class.

It's not much of a betting heat though. The two are short in the market and it's pretty much any price you like on the other contenders. All I have is a bit to collect on a Venn Ottery lay. I backed him for a place at ridiculous odds after he started to hose up low-grade chases for Paul Nicholls. His idiosyncratic owner, Oliver Carter was convinced he would make the line up for the Champion Chase and so I backed him and laid it off when the horse kept winning. I think this is the first time I've ever done that properly.

Steve has a plot. He keeps going on about a reverse exacta plan. He's been telling me over the course of the last few weeks that he's going to take Azertyuiop and combine him with every other horse in an exacta. Basically betting against Moscow who will probably go off odds-on. I listen with mild interest, but this sounds like big staking for possibly small returns. Not my scene.

Anyway, it's close to the off and I still haven't got a bet. So I pursue this exacta nonsense a little bit. Yeah, I fancy opposing Moscow. But I'm not going to take him on with the field. I settle on a minimum stakes exacta with Azertyuiop and the old trooper himself, Flagship Uberalles. I'm not sure what Steve does....

I always catch my breath during this race. Every year there is a little moment to make my heart beat a touch faster. I crane over the rail and look back down the hill so that I can watch the glistening chasers cruise round the bend. The group is tightly packed and making smooth progress. In a moment they are gone. I realise that I am the only punter looking that way. Everyone else's face is turned as if looking at me, but really squinting at the giant screen behind me.

Ultimately we are deprived of the grandstand finish between the two principles. In the heat of battle and under a strong pace, Moscow, or maybe pilot Barry Gerraghty, makes a mistake. Whatever, Gerraghty is jettisoned. Azertyuiop is absolutely faultless all the way round. He's bristling up the hill. Perfection. Hard to say what would have happened if Moscow and jockey had stayed together. We'll never know, but this was a quality display from the new kid on the block.

In his wake it is Flagship who stays on for 2nd, repelling a late thrust from Tiutchev.
    "That's my exacta up then", I grin.
Steve is visibly stricken. In pain. Knitted eyebrows and curling mouth.
    "You stole my fucking bet! I've been plotting up that one for weeks. 'Reverse exacta, take on Moscow' I've been saying. You spawny bastard!"
I cannot contain my glee.

"So what did you do then Steve? Did you strike your famous exacta plot or did you not?"
He didn't. No sympathy from me then. I collect my lovely 40-odd notes from the newly refurbished Tote booth.
"There yooze gur, sonny. Divn't spend it arl at once, now!"
"Thank you."
Steve's grinning when I return, but in a 'you thieving bastard' sort of way. It's all good natured. I think.

Steve's big moment next. The Coral Cup. If the Queen Mother Chase is poetry, this is a limerick. I struggle to make head or tale of this race at the best of times. This year's renewal has an added twist. It's been the subject of much speculation because of the defection of Rhinestone Cowboy from the Champion Hurdle. This makes the weights for others, so the likes of Monkerhostin, Mistanoora and Rosaker all line up too. It's a very strong field.

I'm gutted for Steve. Rosaker is in mid division all through the race and never really makes any impression. The jockey doesn't put him in the race and Rosaker goes out tamely. Steve never gets to shout him on and get an adrenalin rush during the race. There's not much to show for his excellent Fundamentalist bet now and he is even harsher on himself.
"Why did I do that? Why was I so blinded by Rosaker in this race and miss the obvious bet on Fundamentalist. Basic mistake. I've cocked it up."
This one hurts.

The race is won by Monkerhostin who finds more than the rest after the last fence. Court Shareef springs a shocker when rolling up in 2$^{nd}$ at 200-1. Bloody hell.

Rhinestone Cowboy really should have been closer. His jockey, owner's son JP Magnier looked to have been badly positioned as the leaders kicked for home at the top of the hill and was too far off the pace to close the gap. He finished 3$^{rd}$. Later, on the Betfair chat forum, there is a thread entitled ' JP Magnier couldn't ride Jordan'! Harsh. But fair.

I'm still searching for a repeat of the Rith Dubh moment in the marathon National Hunt Handicap Chase. No joy this year. I have a strange old bet on a horse called Atlastaboy. Strange because I have never heard of it before and to be honest I do not know why I backed it. A mystery. My main bet is on Nicholl's Mister Banjo. He runs honourably but unsuccessfully in 7th. Native Emperor, 5-1 joint favourite wins the race.

We move down a gear. The main betting activity ended with the Coral Cup and now Dave and Jane, Steve's brother and sister-in-law arrive. They've been hob-nobbing in the best end over the other side and have decided to slum it for the rest of racing in with us. They greet me like an old friend. I'm quite touched. We mix it with the rave boys in front of the big screen behind the new stand. Jane gets the beers in. Very welcome. The hip flask is getting low.

Dave is a real trends man. He's giving it large to Steve about the pedigree of French and Irish breds in various races and chances of winners coming from outside the handicap. He subscribes to Timeform, but today he is consulting a different oracle. He flaps his Wetherby's Cheltenham Guide.
"It's all in here. No winners for this race come from stables that run their nags at dibbly dobbly northern tracks. The answers are in the trends."
The winner of the Mildmay of Flete in infact comes from about three miles off the pace. Hold up specialist Timmy Murphy leaves it sooo late again on Tikram to steal the race from Iznogoud. Nothing for us.

Dave and Jane are both from Birmingham. The longer we talk to them the more Steve's usual northern, flat-vowel accent takes on a bizarre Brummy twang. The more Steve pushes Dave on his suspect trends analysis the more he slips into a deadpan, dry, nasal 'Wayne eats Wheatos' drone. He even starts raising his voice at the end of sentences, turning them into questions. You naow worrreye mean? Curious.

Further lubrication is required. The bars around us are starting to close up so I join the scrum in the Dawn Run bar on the ground floor of the new stand. We aim to meet up by the rail for the Champion bumper. Steve says he'll come and help in a minute, once he's finished his Harry Ramsdens - another welcome addition to the new grandstand. I'm getting served now, and I could really do with an extra pair of hands. My phone jumps about in my crotch pocket. It's Steve, finally.
"Davoski, mate. Where are you? I'll pick up the beers."
"Nice one. In the Dawn Run bar, bottom of the grandstand. Turn right when you get in, I'm near the door."
"Nice one."
The first two guinnesses are settling lovely. Where's Bacchy? The phone again.
"Right hand side? I can't see you. There isn't a bar on the right hand side. That's the Tote booth."
"I'm nowhere near the Tote booth. Look these beers are ready"
"Dawn Run bar, did you say? Oh, I'm in the Desert Orchid bar. That's upstairs isn't it?"
Fuck's sake.

Dave is bemoaning his luck today by the time we get back to the parched couple.
"Three fallers. Can you believe that? Three good horses hit the deck. At least I can't back a faller in this." It's the flat race next.
The field is just about ready to go. Steve makes a particularly shrewd observation.
"Look at that pace. Tsk. Another typically slowly run bumper."
I look at him to see if he's joking. He isn't.
"Steve, mate. They are just coming out onto the track!"

"Oh. So they are." He adjusts his glasses. "Well I bet it will be a messy race anyway."
This is a better quality observation. There is some horrible jostling down the back straight. After some interference, one of the horses goes down in a heap. It doesn't take long to establish that the faller is Blazing Liss. Dave's horse. Now he can genuinely bemoan his wretched luck. Backing a faller in a flat race.

Total Enjoyment wins it for the Irish. I've backed a couple in this at big odds. My best bet, the French raider Royal Paradise runs with credit, but doesn't get to land a blow.

Dave and Jane are coming back tomorrow, so we arrange to meet them in the Courage End again. We are off to see what Cheltenham town centre can offer on this glorious Paddy's Night.

After a warming pie and chips, first call is O'Neill's in Montpellier. We need to get hold of Andy Intersky and find out where he is headed. He texted Steve earlier in the day to say he'd landed Rule Supreme in the SunAlliance! Can't believe it. Where on earth did he pull that one from?

O'Neill's have got it sorted. They have taken over half the pavement for overflow seating and have a table and board at the end with the form pasted up from the Racing Post. We sit outside and try to track down Andy. But it's not really warm enough for outdoor drinking after dark. Andy is making for the legendary Queens Hotel, just down the road. So we do too.

This is where the party is! Or rather parties. First we try the side bar where we muscle our way past river-dancing revellers. I half expect to bump into Mona. We come face to face with the source of the dancing, a top notch diddly-diddly folk band. A bit too face to face. Steve only just avoids wearing a fiddle bow up his left nostril. Round the back we find some space. We have beer and we have music. We are happy. This side bar gives way to the main brasserie where we glimpse the blue-blazered, brass buttoned crowd tucking into prawn mayonnaise and jolly bolly. And that's just the ladies. Har har. Can't see JP McManus anywhere.

Still no Andy either. We shuffle round a bit further. Some old goose wriggling in time to the band turns round and clocks Steve. Without missing a beat she grabs his face in her chubby bejewelled hands, gives him a juicy smacker right in the middle of his face and lets him go. That's it. She grins and turns round again to carry on bopping. Steve looks a bit shell-shocked. The smeared lipstick round his chops doesn't help. But he doesn't utter a word. I'm falling over laughing when his phone rattles a tune. Saved by the bell.

We catch up with Andy in the main bar round the front. What a festival he's having. Intersky's third yesterday gave him a very respectable pay day. Rule Supreme and Intersky have kept him on a roll. He furnishes us with some fascinating insights to inside stable info and the way the syndicate works.

The glasses are dry again and I attempt to get refills. I'm gone ages having been carried away in a sea of grooving punters. This place is the business.

Andy has taken redundancy from his city job and is enjoying the freedom a bit of time and money can bring. He gets to the races as often as he can. He's single as well. No strings. His eyes are out on stalks in this place tonight. He's not alone either.

We leave him to focus down on some bird he is convinced has been giving him the eye all night. By the time we head off I am hammered. The only thing keeping me going now is the thought of finally taking on that Gloucester mix.

I can't wait to get my hands around this beast. The kebab is just as monumental as I remember from last year. Hardly surprising as I've dreamt about it every night since. Juicy and spicy and meaty and precarious. We totter up the road with over loaded hands and over whelmed taste buds. I've barely broken into the Jurassic layer before we are back at Mona's. No-one home though. Both out celebrating Paddy still.

To my utter disgust, the Mix beats me. I'm propped up at the table like a beached whale. I'm unable to move having eaten more than my own body weight in meat and drunk a swimming pool of guinness. I gaze on the wreckage of my kebab heaven and realise that I'm going to chuck away bits of pork chop, shish and doner. I am ashamed. I've eaten all the salad though.

Meanwhile Steve is chomping through his feast with gusto. He looks down his nose at me through chilli stained glasses. He can hardly bare to lay his contempt-filled eyes on me. I quietly dispose of my remains and sit silently in humiliation. I wish I'd resisted pie and chips at 6.30pm.

Mona arrives back from the Irish Club. She's had a great night out, despite the band.
Steve and I are both knackered. He slopes off to bed, but I'm up for another half an hour. I didn't mean to be. I make a mistake of letting Mona tell me a story. I think it started in the Irish Club, with a detour along the Blue Danube and involved most if not all of her children. But I'm not sure. I really should know better. Every story is a journey of discovery. Thank the Lord my Mother-in-Law isn't here. I would never have hit the sack.

## 30. CHELTENHAM 2004: THE ROLLERCOASTER

*"Three days was the mourning*
*My focus three days old...*
*True hunting is over*
*No herds to follow"*
Jane's Addiction *"Three Days"* 1990

Paul is gently swaying at the breakfast table by the time I get downstairs. He looks like I felt in that exact same position late last night. I've seen him look better. He's sucking on his first fag of the day like it's an oxygen mask, squinting his red eyes against the smoke. The dark sagging bags under his peepers contrast with the grey palour of his long face. He has a hangover. He splutters a confession to Mona in the kitchen,
"Never again, Ma. Never again."
He doesn't believe the words himself. Almost before they have spilled from his lips, he looks at Steve, flashes a cheesy grin and bellows a rankerous, gravelly smokers laugh.
"Harharharharhar!" The spark is back in his eye.

Paul didn't make it to the festival yesterday, but did get as far as Cheltenham. He was in the same O'Neill's as us, only about three hours earlier. He landed back home early evening absolutely wasted and crashed out in bed.

Steve doesn't look too bad, but I feel almost as rough as Paul looks. Last night was a top laugh.

Mona's tea sorts me out. As ever. I nip up to Asda to buy some flowers and a decent bottle of brandy to mark her hospitality. Not of the cheap rubbish we fobbed her off with last year. She knows her stuff alright. Only the best is good enough for Mona who has been brilliant again. It's chucking iT down out there. Not sure if this was forecast or not. Sir Rembrandt will like it.

Mona is off shopping, Paul is off back to bed and we are off to find some life affirming grease. But no! The Asda kitchen is fresh out of lard. The cooker is broken. So we give the brekkie a miss and head straight to the internet café.

It's busy again. We buy an hours-worth of air time, but after forty-five minutes or so my head is throbbing. There is a shooting pain behind my eyes and I'm seeing three or four ante-post markets drifting in and out of focus. I've only tinkered with a couple of bets, but that will have to do. I log out and tell Steve and I'll meet him here in quarter of an hour. I find paracetamol, water and bacon butties within lurching distance of the café.

Recovery comes swiftly. Steve is outside the café now and casts a covetous eye over my bap (singular!). It's not long before he's wading through one of his own on the way to the station.

We catch a train that has come from London. It's packed and I half expect to see the lads. Paul and Sharon can't make it this year and so Bryn's brother Pete and one of his mates have taken their places. Pete's a good lad. He likes his music and we share a passion for '70's and '80's heavy rock. Pete is a bit more catholic than me, though and he has been known to stray into some murky pop-laced waters. Witness his love of Deacon Blue and and Belouis Some. Not sure about that.

Still no sign of the boys. So me and Steve settle down to our now customary lunchtime guinnesses. There is a different atmosphere at the track today. Already it is busier and it's a different sort of crowd too. More raucous, more lairy.

I catch up with Bryn on the phone. They are off the train, but have decided to walk to the track - it's a fair old schlep - and have called in to a pub on the way. I envisage that Jenkins' weak bladder is at work here, dictating logistics. In the meantime, Steve has caught up with Dave and Jane who are stuck in traffic and not confident of getting here in time for the first. Steve takes their bets and slopes off to find a cash machine.

Both parties arrive at about the same time as I'm completing my placepot picks on the steps of the new stand. Barely time for introductions. Everyone's active getting bets down, placepots picked and fantasy selections logged with Steve. If there's any chance of overhauling Bryn in the comp then the opener, the Triumph Hurdle is probably our best chance.

Dave has a new system today. He's getting selections texted through to him from some premier mobile phone tipping service. He's looking at the tiny screen, weighing up the shortlist he has received. Steve is scathing.
"That's no service! It's some bloke sat by the pool in the Caribbean with a whisky sour on one knee and an RP on the other. He just sends you a couple of likely names and watches the wedge roll into his bank account. Tipping service my arse."
He's slipping into brummy again.
"No, Steve mate. You've got it all wrong. This guys' strike rate is rock solid."
"Yeah, course it is, he's tipping every horse is the field!"
Dave's laughing as he and Jane nip off to get their bets down.

Nick is lumping on Henrietta Knight's Tusk and I have to go for Jonjo's Cherub of course. It's Sandown revisited. I also have Zimbabwe from a long standing ante-post punt. We are by the the rail. But it's much busier today and so we watch the race unfold primarily on the screen. Tusk is prominent for a long way and so is Cherub, but for a moment it looks like Zimbabwe is travelling best of all and my hopes are raised. The picture changes in an instant at the top of the hill, as it frequently does in this particular race. The pace has been slow and suddenly there are about a dozen runners in with a shout.

Close to home I lose sight of Zimbabwe and Tusk. Cherub looks to be in with a sniff. But then I think I see Tusk back in the lead.

"Bloody hell, Nick. Is that Tusk? You could be in with a shout here. How come he's kept on so strongly?"

But it's another case of mistaken identity. It's Philip Hobb's horse, Made in Japan, sporting similar natty stripes to the Henrietta Knight beast. Made In Japan comes to take the race in style. Glad I'm not a race caller.

Cherub finished a decent 4th. Nothing for us fantasy festivalists either, but Pete has pulled out an absolute blinder. He's backed Made in Japan, a tenner at twenties, in honour of Deep Purple who's finest live album released in 1972 is entitled *Made in Japan*. Fantastic stuff. That sets him up for the day. This is punting my brother would revel in.

Once again the Stayers proves to be one of the finest races of the festival. It always seems to produce tight little fields and quality finishes. I've been burned by the race already this year with each of my ante-post selections, first, Hardy Eustace and then Rosaker, being re-routed elsewhere. So I don't see the point of getting very involved. I put a little on my old mate Holy Orders for a place and back Crystal D'Ainay to win without Baracouda. Steve and Nick both have Crystal D'Ainay the place. Back at the grandstand, and Bryn is on the grey as well. Jonjo O'Neill has two runners, Iris's Gift and Shboom. Dave is impersonating a bloke he overheard in the ring:

"It's go'a be Shbaam, carm on Shbaam", he sing-songs in his best East End accent.

I'm prepared to overlook Iris's Gift. It proves to be folly. I wasn't too impressed with his come back run in a Pertemps qualifier and Intersky Andy added weight to the concerns when he reported a bandaged and strapped Iris working on the gallops not long before the festival. That's the last time I listen to any inside stable talk.

Nick and Ben go up to the Desert Orchid bar and get me a beer in as well. It is madness up there today though. By the time I get the bets down I've lost them. The race is underway and I assume they have found a good home for my orphaned refreshment.

Iris is wonderful and Barry Geraghty rides an unimpeachable race. The incredible Bowes family, the driving force behind Limestone Lad, have a new recruit to take his place. Solerina goes a good clip in front. She's no Limestone though. She likes it softer and maybe a bit shorter. But like all Bowes animals she is genuine and does not like being passed.

These are perfect conditions for the patiently ridden Baracouda who is held off the pace. But surprisingly, with three to go Gerraghty pushes up to take the lead. He's really turning on the tap, stretching Baracouda. Solerina falls away. Just like last year it's Baracouda and Iris's Gift head to head up the hill. One trained by Jonjo O'Neill, the other owned by his landlord and patron. There is very little between them. Iris's is going like a dream, but I still expect to see Doumen cruise up alongside late in the day. But not today. Iris's early thrust seems to have taken the sting out of the French raider. He's closing but struggling to get to the grey. The Gift digs deep and finds more. He prevails by 1 ½ lengths in a tingling finish.

Crystal D'Ainay stays on for a good third. Everyone bar me collects place wedge. This is Nick's first winner of the day. That will make him feel better.

The Stayers has an uncanny knack of providing the prefect mood setter for the big one. Every year, it leaves the crowd fired up and champing at the bit for the Gold Cup. Everyone wants to see Best Mate win his third blue ribband and he'll be sent off odds on favourite. But there is no bookies massacre this year. Even if Best Mate lands the odds the boys on the boards will have made a killing on the other results. Not only have some long shots come in, but three of the four festival bankers have been turned over. Moscow Flyer went off 5-6f, Rooster Booster at 11-8f and Baracouda 8-11f. For those who took tiny prices on all four coming in, a Best Mate victory will be no compensation.

Vaughany has gone missing again. Haven't seen him since the first race. I'm sure he's around somewhere, being aloof and mysterious; taking in the sights and sounds. Pete has disappeared, too. Probably getting lashed on his winnings. His only previous experience of racing is Royal Ascot on Ladies Day. Not sure that the attire of the ladies here today quite meets his expectations judged by that benchmark.

Time to see if Henrietta's star can equal the feat of Arkle. Three back-to-back Gold Cups would be some achievement. I've had a couple of ante-post tokens go down and I'm left with a bet on one of my favourite, if frustrating fancies, Sir Rembrandt. I followed him during his novice season when he had looked the real deal. This year again he has threatened to show his class. I've stayed loyal, but he has thrown in a few inexplicably poor runs. I struck the bet ages ago and the horse has drifted since than on the basis of those howlers. I'm not minded to top up, though. I'll stick with this. The spectacle will be sufficient adrenalin rush. Steve also has Sir Rembrandt and a bet on Harbour Pilot to win and in an exacta with Matey. Pilot seems to be the each-way choice. Bryn and Nick are on him too.

Best Mate delivers. The result in the Racing Post is very clinical:

| | | | |
|---|---|---|---|
| 1. | | Best Mate | 8-11F |
| 2. | sh | Sir Rembrandt | 33-1 |
| 3. | 1 ¼ | Harbour Pilot | 20-1 |

Such dry analysis can never hope to capture the outpouring of emotion that is being wrung from the stands on this dull Thursday afternoon. Adulation and respect are gushing down the steps like a river in full spate.

The dam of affection has burst and it feels like all of Prestbury Park is awash with sentiment. Everyone's Best Mate.

It's not all romantic tear in the eye stuff though. The punters have been rewarded for their patience through the desert of turned-over favourites. A big ginger haired bloke dressed head to foot in denim and stinking of the stuff as well nearly knocks me over as he runs back to his mates in the stands. He's clutching the fatest wedge of folding stuff that I've seen since my trip to Hackney Dogs nearly 20 years ago.
"Ha Har. That's Barbados paid for. You screaming beauty!"
I assume he meant a holiday and not the whole island.

Best Mate is rightly lauded throughout the land as the best chaser since Arkle. A national treasure. The press coverage is healthy even a few days later. "IMMORTAL" screams the Racing Post. The paper goes overboard, quite frankly. They are desperate for a hero in the wake of allegations about Kieron Fallon throwing races and Sean Fox leaping off a horse in mid-race. So whilst Best Mate is in a league of his own and should be recognised as a great champion, I don't want to read any more in-depth, minute by minute accounts, days after the event, about how the Deputy Head Lad's grandson celebrated the big day.

Henrietta Knight has the best grip on reality. Apart from saying,
"That fucking awful song", as Jim Lewis's Villa chums chanted 'Best Mate' to the tune of a well known footie anthem, she also said,
"Arkle was a great horse, Best Mate is a very good horse."

But plenty in the crowd had also chosen to oppose Best Mate. At the risk of sounding a tad churlish and without casting any doubts about the horse's unquestioned hoofprint in history, me, Steve, Bryn and Nick are all getting animated about other incidents in the race. The respect will come later.

It is a classic. Thierry Doumen has chosen to take First Gold up front early on and sets a surprisingly good clip. He's determined to make it a stamina test on this rain-deadened ground. Half way up the back straight a group of three horses comes to join First Gold - Harbour Pilot, Beef OIr Salmon (or Pork And Salmon as some wag behind me keeps mouthing) and Sir Rembrandt. Sir Rembrandt is looking in fine form, riding well up with the pace. It's easy to tell when he's in business simply because of he way he travels. This horse has so much potential and he's never really shown it.

I could kick myself. I let myself think positive thoughts and sure enough Sir R clouts the fourth last. He's taken chunks out of the fence. There is a Scooby Doo style cut-out shape left in the birch after the horse has crashed through. I let out a scream. More of a wounded yelp really. Somehow Andrew Thornton hangs on and the horse recovers. He's probably lost four lengths or so.

Not many others around us have really noticed though. They are too busy watching a bit of a drama unfold on the outside. Harbour Pilot has Best

Mate pinned up against the rail. Jockey Jim Culloty isn't getting the run of the race and will have to deviate from the plan in order to get out. The group are definitely working together to force the jockey's hand. Harbour Pilot keeps Best Mate there as long as he can, but at the 2nd last Jim gives BM a squeeze and he challenges on the outside of First Gold.

But he can't put in the decisive break we are used to seeing. The ground doesn't help. The tactics haven't helped. Whatever, the champ can't shake off Harbour Pilot. Steve is having kittens. Can't see Bryn and Nick, but they must be too. Thrilling stuff. I'm agog. Can the BM be beaten? Suddenly I'm having kittens too. Sir Rembrandt is flying up the near rail. He's finally found his gears and is eating up the gap to the leaders. The TV footage gets it all wrong in the final few hundred yards. The director is doing a full-frame, flared-nostril close-up of Best Mate and Harbour Pilot slugging out the finish and ignoring the fast finishing Alner gelding on the other side of the track.

Either the collective gasp of the crowd or a swift kick in the balls from a colleague alerts the director to the charge of Sir Rembrandt. The camera pans back to give the last few strides of genuine knee-trembler. A fantastic finish sees Sir Rembrandt split Best Mate and Harbour Pilot. He didn't quite do enough to steal the glory from the Champ.

This race is a big deal for me. The Gold Cup should be the best race of the year. This renewal, though on paper lacking the apparent depth of other years, has delivered a nerve-shredding, ball tightening climax that has taken everyone by surprise. It has shown the battling spirit of a true champion who has had to dig very deep to prevail. It has given the nation an equine hero. It has seen the emergence of at least one young pretender in Sir Rembrandt and probably a second in Beef or Salmon who ran on for a very good 4th. And the race has also given me a huge personal sense of satisfaction. I am a mug punter because I fall victim to an illogical trait: loyalty. I saw something I liked in Sir Rembrandt last year and today I feel vindicated way beyond the place money I have collected for his runners-up spot.

Sir Rembrandt enters a very select band of horses that I will always have a soft spot for, will always want to see run well and will back more often than not. Others in this exclusive 'doesn't owe me a penny' league include Edredon Bleu, What's Up Boys, Springfield Scally, Valley Henry and One Knight.

My face is flushed and I'm still tingling as I meander my way back to the boys. I feel a bit intoxicated and I amble around by the bookies not sure what I'm doing. I don't get like this very often. Ben rounds me up and we go to the Desert Orchid bar. It's raining steadily by now and we struggle to meet up with the other boys in the melee. We find Vaughany and then see Bryn pass within a few feet of us holding his pint in front of him like a sceptre, parting the punters in front of him. Pete is in tow, but we can't attract their attention. So we follow in their footsteps and finally meet up by the door.

Nick and Bryn are both marvelling at the race too. They had a spectacular view of the Harbour Pilot/Best Mate incident on the rail. They have both collected place tokens on Harbour Pilot. The TV screens up here are full of Hen and Terry basking in their achievement. But I want to see the finish of the race again. I think.

The Foxhunter's comes and goes in a blur. An old friend Earthmover wins well and for the 2$^{nd}$ time in this race. Trainer Paul Nicholls is having a much better festival now.

I catch up with Steve by the rail for the Grand Annual. Dave and Jane are there too. Steve doesn't appear to be as misty-eyed as me about the Gold Cup. That particular 1-2-3 was the worst result for him. He would have had handsome payouts on either Sir Rembrandt winning, Harbout Pilot winning or a Best Mate-Harbour Pilot 1-2. His place wedge on Sir Rembrandt seems to provide him with little solace as he relives those final few yards up to the finish when lip licking turned to arse kicking. My touching eulogy to the exploits of Sir R cut no ice either.

Jane shows us her placepot card. She has picked the winner in every single race so far today - bar the lottery 1$^{st}$! Nightmare. If she'd only backed them all individually too! The Grand Annual is a good race. I've backed a long shot Ground Ball who is given a fine ride and I think he's going to win over the last fence, but he can't concede the weight to St Pirran. The Nicholls trained gelding completes a cosy enough win to give the Ditcheat handler back to back victories. I can't complain. Ground Ball was game enough, but could find no extra.

The boys are spread far and wide today. I seem to be meeting up with them only sporadically. I'm with Ben talking about the Cathcart. He's having no luck again. He admits that the only winner he's ever had was at Exeter last year when he backed the wrong horse by accident and it won doing handstands. That doesn't seem to matter though. His indestructible good humour is legendary.

Vaughany joins us after some more promenading around the course. We plot up a trio of bets. My mind is already made up. Richard Guest is turning out Our Armageddon again after his poor show in the Arkle on Tuesday. (Blimey, was that only Tuesday?) Guesty wouldn't be unleashing Armageddon again unless he had come out of the earlier race in A1 condition. He has a reputation for treating his animals well. Steve reckons his horse-boxes have carpets and curtains.

So I get 8-1 about him. The Cathcart is traditionally a strong race. Often the most competitive of the non-Grade 1 races. Possibly it's a weaker affair this year. Certainly a smallish field. But La Landiere, Iris Royal and

Impek have strong credentials and the Pipe-trained Don Fernando could be a danger. Cases for them all, but I'm happy with the bet.

The apprentice Larry McGrath gives Our Armageddon a fantastic ride. He is Richard Guest's work rider and knows the horse well. He later claimed that this helped him look after the horse in the Arkle. Our Armageddon leads from pillar to post. He sets a strong gallop from the off and he is simply magnificent in repelling all the sorties made against him. La Landiere is the first to drop away. Impek comes and fades, and it then looks like Iris Royal is going best of all. This is worrying. But then he finds very little off the bridle.

Our Armageddon is relentless and gives me an uplifting victory. I over-react to this one. I'm leaping about the betting ring, whooping like an American. Ben and Vaughany both look at me a little warily. Like you do when someone throws a tantrum in Tescos. Neither of them says anything, but they are thinking either that I had my mortgage on that one, or that I am a bad advert for going to the races. In reality I think I am letting off some tension from that awesome Gold Cup. Some of that raw emotion has been channelled into this win.

Six of us collect for the final rites of the Fantasy Festival. No-one has reeled Bryn in. He sits atop the pile on the strength of an outstanding Hardy Eustace punt and it will take a shock of monumental proportions in the County Hurdle to overhaul him. We all plump for outsiders, mustering whatever stakes we have left. There are no upsets. Sporazene comes late to take Copeland on the run in and then has to fend off a late rally from Hawadeth. He does and in so doing presents the top festival trainer to Nicholls and the top jock gong to Ruby Walsh.

I'm starving. Building up and then pouring out so much nervous energy in one afternoon has left me aching inside. I need emotional nourishment that only Harry Ramsden can provide. But Harry is all out of fish. And forks. So whilst I'm scalding my fingers on gravy bubbling at close to boiling point inside my steak pie, Nick and Pete scale the grandstand steps three at a time to squeeze in a pint before we make for the train. They return thirsty and disgruntled. The bars closed before the last race. What kind of cack-handed policy is that? Sure, the course needs to be cleared up. But serving beers after racing has finished would actually help take the heat out of the crush at the exit points and lessen the scrum at Cheltenham station as well.

It's with a hint of resignation that we take our places in the crush. Nick isn't too happy about this. Getting a drink at the festival today has been bloody hard work. There were more people here than on the other days and a lot were not interested in the racing at all. The plan, as we shuffle past stables, horse-boxes and buses, is to amble into town and find a pub for a couple of beers before getting the train. I'm not sure what happens, but we end up walking all the way back to the station without sampling any of the pubs en route.

The station is swarming, of course, but by good fortune a carriage door stops right in front of us and gets the biggest cheer of the day. A few beers flow on the train home and I pull out the schedule of shame for the last time. This has been the most frenetic and intense period of betting in my life. I set my stall out to make a profit at the Festival and abandoned any hope of a careful and disciplined strategy in pursuing that end. Scattergun is an inadequate description of the approach I took. The effect was closer to the pebble-dashing of a toilet bowl after a good curry. And yet. And yet, in the final analysis, crawling from the wreckage of a dozen failed doubles, myriad token bets and a sea of ante-post mayhem emerges a skinny and shame-faced £19 profit. That's warts and all. Nineteen sodding quid.

But I shouldn't be so hard on myself. It is a genuine profit. I had winners every day, including in the first three races on Queen Mother Day. I've turned up wins from all manner of bets - ante-posts, place-doubles, singles and exactas - thereby just about validating the pebble-dash approach. I really can't complain. I came with money to spend and I wanted to have a bet. Well I did that. I've lodged 54 separate bets on the 20 Festival races since October, at a total stake approaching £300. I got all that back and another £19. It's surely the hardest earned score I've ever won.

Steve does his provisional tot up and has a bleak story to tell. Despite his sensational Brave Inca win 20 races ago, he's managed to come out of the betting bonanza showing a small loss. I'm not at all sure how he managed that after such a flying start.

I'm feeling more subdued by the time we approach Paddington. Truth is I'm absolutely bloody knackered. These last three days have felt like a marathon. Steve and I have joked about the test of stamina that the Festival demands and with one eye on next year when there will be an additional day I seriously wonder what I'll do. Up until now I have always assumed that I would ultimately find the lure of four days of quality racing irresistible. But the way I feel now I wouldn't like to say that I'll be here every day next year. It's not just the stamina. Changing the format by putting on a few extra races changes the complexion of the event. I fear for the quality threshold if more handicaps and novice events are introduced to pad out the cards.

It has been a good three days. In spite of the odd quibble about touts, louts, bars and screens. Another fine Festival, with some of the best racing I've seen. And the end of an era, no less. If today was the last of the three-day Festivals then it's gone out with its reputation intact. If today was the last of the Thursday Gold Cups, then it's gone out on the highest possible note. A zenith. A peak. A pinnacle.

If there is a post script to these events, it is provided by Bryn and Nick who go to Twickenham on the Saturday following the Festival to see England v Wales in the Six Nations. Their glowing reports about the facilities and services contrast starkly with Cheltenham. 70,000 people had no problems getting served food or alcohol before during or after the game, had unrestricted views of all the action all the time, didn't have to queue for the loos and were shepherded in and out of the stadium in an efficient manner. Racing faces some stiff challenges if its showpiece events are not to be elbowed off the sporting map.

## 31. THE CHARMING DASH

*"Early morning, get ready to run,*
*Though it's hard to see clear*
*For we might disappear*
*With the prize hardly won."*
Magnum, *"The Prize"*, 1983

My horse, Dashing Charm, is belatedly making is seasonal debut. Connections (technically, I guess that should include me!) have settled on a low key Huntingdon Sunday fixture. He's running in a bumper, the second race of his career.

Finding a race for him has had more false starts than your average General Election campaign. Set backs have included a cough, a cold, weather too wet and weather too dry. Bloody hell, talk about wrapping him up in cotton wool. You'd think this horse was a full brother to Shergar. Frustrating, but the animal's welfare comes first. I accept that.

Then we had a farcically protracted campaign to find the horse a suitable race. The form book has been consulted, thumbed, pored over and multiple entries were made in Bumpers and novice hurdles at some of these fair island's most far flung locations. Dashing Charm's emergence into the limelight has been a tantalising 'will he, won't he' soap opera for the last six weeks. I even rang the club's hotline during Cheltenham week because there was a chance the beast might turn out at Sedgefield the day before the Champion Hurdle in some dodgy egg and spoon race. He didn't make the cut. Just as well.

Given this fixture and fitness epic, I feel I really should see the race. Just to see the horse turn up on the track would be a victory of sorts. The next hurdle (even though this is only a bumper) is getting an owner's ticket. After all, what is the point of horse ownership - even on this club membership basis - without an owners badge? But no joy. I do not get through the ballot. It makes me wonder how many members there are with a share in this beast. There are ten tickets up for grabs and I don't get one.

But I resolve to go anyway and be a paying punter in the cheap seats. It's not an easy decision. There are competing pressures at home. My eldest daughter has a ballet exam and my youngest is generally a demanding little creature. But this was Helen's Christmas present to me and she too wants me to get some value out of the membership.

I e-mail Mike at the club in the hope that someone pulls out and I can pick up the spare. At about 5.30pm, my luck changes. Mike calls.
"Hi Dave. Are you still planning to come racing tomorrow?"
He's got a ticket for me, I reckon. But he wants me to commit before he offers it up. Canny bugger.
"Yeah, definitely. I'm looking forward to seeing the horse.

"Good, because I've got a free owners ticket for you. One of the club members has had to drop out as the family have come down with chicken pox"

"Oh that's such a shame."

Ouch. Was it only three years ago that I irresponsibly deserted a chicken pox-infested household to go to my first three-day Festival? I'm so shallow.

"But good news for you if you want the ticket. That's the way it goes sometimes."

"Yeah, that's fantastic. I'll take the ticket."

And then the immortal words....

"Just go to the Members entrance and there will be a ticket for you there."

Right. Sort out the logistics. Huntingdon is OK to get to. Usually. Straight down to Euston, short stroll to Kings Cross taking in the modernist British Library edifice and gloriously gothic St Pancras Station en route, followed by an hourly 50-minute shuttle into rural Cambridgeshire. But the infamous West Coast Modernisation, a lumbering and painful, overblown and overbudget rail engineering project with an unspecified completion date, is causing protracted havoc with the service from this corner of Hertfordshire.

Weekend services are particularly prone to carnage. Sure enough, a quick check reveals that emergency engineering announced only yesterday will sabotage the service tomorrow. I try to assemble a straight story from the incomplete information provided by three separate calls to National Rail Enquiries. It seems that the works are due to be completed by lunchtime. Or I can get down to the next station on the line - Hemel Hempstead and pick up a regular service from there. This is taking more planning than Cheltenham.

Whilst I'm on the web, strangling screams of frustration at the rail system, I do a bit of research. Last time Dashing Charm's trainer, Chris Bealby, had a winner at Huntingdon it returned at 66-1 in a bumper. And the jockey booked for tomorrow's ride is Paul Maloney who rode a cracking double at Towcester when I was there earlier in the week. Hey hey! Good omens.

I'm reassured. After a cosy night's kip, dreaming of the winner's enclosures around the country, I awake refreshed and ready to take the first steps on the road signposted *'Ambition Fulfilment. This Way'*.

The family even has time to squeeze in a traditional Sunday morning outing to the Supastores. B&Q for some patio furniture and Curry's for a washing machine. It's this kind of time honoured, established activity that keeps the fabric of families as tight as a snare drum. But we've bonded for too long over the white-goods counter and we have to shift a little to get round to the station in time for the first train.

"See you later, girls. Good luck with the ballet, Elizabeth. Catherine, be good for Mummy. Thanks for the lift Helen. Byeeee"
"Good luck Daddy. Where are you going again?"

This is where the shit hits the fan. I've been drip-fed duff information. Stitched up like a kipper. There are no trains to London. Buses all the way. I make enquiries of one of the many luminous green-vested Silverlink attendants about the next bus. My gaze follows his jabbing finger in the direction of the last bus just turning out of the car park. Preceded by wife's car. Bollocks.

12.40 is the first train of the day. I curse again. No chance of getting to Huntingdon for the first race. The arrival time of the train starts to slip a little. And a little more. My stomach tightens. The TV display has given up the unequal struggle and resorts to blinking *'delayed'* in fat yellow letters instead of an estimated arrival time.

A care-worn, harassed Australian customer services rep snaps shut her mobile phone and swaps it for a mega phone.
"The train is delayed. I don't know when it will turn up. We've found another bus. As an alternative to the train, anyone who wants to take the bus to Euston, it will be leaving from the forecourt in about five minutes."
They've *found* a bus? I bet they don't have this carry on in Bendigo Springs. I bet she wishes she'd taken the safer option to work with her country-folk in an Earl's Court pub.

Reluctantly I leave the platform with everyone else, casting a longing look down the empty track. Cold rails to hell.

The coach shuttle is a disaster. The driver doesn't know the way and he takes a wrong turning in Watford. We do a complete circuit of the Mirror Print Works on the outskirts of town followed by a tour of myriad side-streets trying to find the railway station. After 20 minutes stuck in traffic near the by-pass there is open hostility on the coach.
"If he don't know his fuckin' way round the A41 he shouldn't be doin' the fuckin' job", is one of the more constructive remarks.

Another guy blowing his top at the inept driver is with his family trying to get to a West End matinee performance on time for a birthday treat. I shuffle uneasily in my seat.

The bus sits outside Watford Junction station waiting for new customers. The coach driver has disappeared and a couple of the more irate passengers get off to find out what's happening. It is they, rather than the driver that come back and tell us that the trains are now running from Watford and the bus will be going no further. Bastard. I knew it. I should have stayed at Hemel. Wrong decision.

I charge through the barriers and up the stairs. I never move this enthusiastically when I'm commuting. Unbelievably, a train is just departing from platform 9. It isn't even full. Surely the platform manager must have known that there was a coach full of people in the car park waiting for trains. I swear and actually kick the guard-rail running round the waiting room. It hurt.

I'm starting to lose heart now. The train info suggests tentatively that the next direct London service might be 1.55. But it appears to be running late already. It's about 1.15 and I begin to wonder whether I should just turn round and go home. There is a train on Platform 10. It goes to Brighton via Harrow, Kensington and Clapham Junction. At least it is vaguely the right direction. I leap on just as the doors are closing. This is harum scarum stuff. I'm not even in London yet.

I'm trying to catch my breath. In my mind's eye I see the last couple of minutes as something out of a Western. I'm Clint Eastwood and I'm looking at the train indicator, weighing up what to do. Maybe I'm chewing resolutely, but calmly on a piece of old gum. Maybe I'm distractedly spinning my shiny pistol around the fingers of my left hand. I take a long look at the London platform and narrow my eyes. Then a long look at the Brighton train. With a quiet nod I coolly board the Brighton train. The doors sliding shut immediately behind me ruffle my poncho but not my pose.

In reality, I'm more like Manuel out of Fawlty Towers. I'm stood in front of the train indicator dithering and dallying. First I take a few hurried steps towards the London platform before I stop and grasp my head in frustration. Then I move towards the Brighton train before halting and blaspheming.
    "Fuck, fuck, fuck, fuck"
I go back to the train indicator and search for some illumination. I have the deepest scowl burnt onto my features.
    "Meester Fawltee. Whata you wanna mee todooo now?", I should be asking, droopy moustache twitching with nervous tension.
Then at the very last moment I plunge for the Brighton train like the manic waiter from Barcelona and scramble aboard by the skin of my pinny, grin unnervingly at the other passengers and prop myself up against the opposite door, slipping as I do.

I have some quick decisions to make now. I pull out my Betfair diary and consult the tube map at the back. I need to get to King's Cross from this train which cuts out central London. Clapham Junction involves too many changes. There are no tubes from Olympia and West Brompton on a Sunday. No choice then. I get off at Harrow and Wealdstone to get the Bakerloo line which will take me right into Zone 1.

The Clapham Junction train pulls away at the moment I'm reading the tube map info. It tells me that Harrow doesn't currently enjoy a Sunday

Bakerloo line service. Trains into London start further down the line at Queens Park today. That's handy then. Boy, have I cocked this one up.

I'm still running through options in my increasingly crowded and dark brain when I notice a bit of movement on the platform. People shifting around like they are getting ready for a train. I spin round to see a Silverlink Metro service arriving. Hallelujah! My first piece of good luck. This is a tortuous stopping service all the way to Euston. I need to be on the 2.20 from KX if I have any chance at all of seeing some racing today. It will be tight. I count down every single stop, willing the doors to bleep-bleep as soon as the train comes to a stop. It's torment.

Next thing, I'm skittering down Euston Road, hurdling rough sleepers and leap-frogging concrete bollards. People jump out of my way as they hear my laboured breathing and heavy footfall approaching behind them. I'm no athlete.

But I've gained a bit of time and I clamber in to the Cambridge train with a Racing Post, a racing heart and a beetroot face. I hope there aren't rules about deportment in the Owners Enclosure.

Throughout this chaotic journey, I haven't had chance to look at the form or check what the RP says about my horse. I flick to page 73 and cast my eyes over the runners for the 5.10 Hemingford Grey Standard Open National Hunt Flat Race (Class H) Winner £1,876. Hmm. Don't think my share of the prize money is going to make me rich, then.

Dashing Charm is Number 4, resplendent in red colours with a blue stripe. He gets an RP rating of 69. This isn't good, though there are two others with an even lower rating. The spotlight analysis is crushing.
    "Left toiling in rear on run for home when tailed in off fast ground Worcester bumper last June; cannot fancy."

The journey out to Huntingdon is in marked contrast to the last few hours: calm, quick, pleasant. I jump in a taxi out to the track. It's not long before I'm directing the taxi down the track marked 'owners and trainers'. I leave him a healthy tip and he shoves off. I've got too smug. This entrance is for the trainers, grooms, head lads and the like. Pukka race folk who have a proper job and proper connections. I trudge off before I make any more howlers. I find the main entrance and more accommodating 'members, day members and owners' gate. This is me.

    "Hello. You should have a badge for me. David Atkinson, City Racing Club. Bit late. Ha ha. Train trouble. I've got a runner in the 5.10."
I wince. That last bit I couldn't deliver with any confidence. It's the sort of thing I dreamt of saying. When it came to the delivery, it sounded weak and made up. If I was a proper owner I wouldn't need to emphasise the point.
    "Oh yes, here you are Mr Atkinson. And a complementary race card. Have a lovely day."

Oh yes. I will. Oh Yes.

I fumble with the strings attached to the badge, trying to attach it to my jacket. In doing so I almost stumble into Nicky Henderson who is leaving the parade ring to watch the next race. Oh my God. I've only been here 30 seconds and I'm already mixing with the game's premier trainers. This is too much.

I'm in time to see the 3.40. The day's exertions have rattled me and I decide to have a bet and watch the race before meeting the Club members. I need to regain some composure.

I back Nicky Henderson's runner Late Claim. Rude not to after our introduction just now. We are almost mates and this is practically a tip. It's a 2 mile novice hurdle, but this doesn't stop the horse fading badly in the last half mile. There is a very close finish and I couldn't call the winner between Stolen Song and Tai Lass as they flash past the stands. Stolen Song prevails.

OK. I'm steeled. The club members are meeting in the owners' bar of the main grandstand. I swear my chest swells as I stride in. The doorman (who would not be out of place at The Ritz in my eyes) clocks my badge flapping freely in the Spring breeze and pushes open the door. I breathe deeply. Smells like any other bar in the world. Stale fag smoke, flat beer and recycled air conditioning. But this is my bar. The owners' bar.

Mike told me that he and the other club officials would be wearing red jackets. I easily spot a group of four - two blokes and two girls - who fit this description, mingling with half a dozen people who I assume are the other members. I wander over and introduce myself. Mike's on the phone and the other red-fleeced clubbers point at him and say it's him I need to speak to. Not a trace of a Geordie twang. Clearly it's just the Tote red jackets that bring out this curious trait.

I fall into conversation with Bill from the club. I say I'm late because of my train nightmare. He takes one look at me and says,
    "You look like you need a drink! The bar is over there."
He knows me for all of 30 seconds and he's worked me out! He's bloody well right. I must looked frazzled after my ordeal. The journey out from Peterborough was calm, but clearly it did not give me sufficient time to disguise the trauma of the first 3 hours of the journey.

I return with my pint and I do actually feel more relaxed. Bill is a quietly spoken, stocky bloke in his late forties at a guess. He tells me he's only working with Mike because he's at a loose end these days. He comes along on race days to help with all the bits and pieces that need sorting out. He knows Mike from their Army days years ago and hooked up with Mike again after his own engineering employment which had taken him as far afield as the Falklands had run into the ground.

Bill is so laid back. He doesn't know much about the horses or about the game. He doesn't bother about a bet. This is all about a day out, being involved and helping out a mate. He is a very engaging, thoughtful chap and contrasts markedly with Mike. Mike is finally off the phone and is scurrying around us shaking hands, nodding the odd comment and making himself busy. He's quite a short guy, clipped blond hair and looks a few years younger than Bill. After a few minutes, Mike gives a sort of schoolteacher like chat about Dashing Charm, known by everyone here as 'Tickle' and today's events.

"He's been working well at home and Chris is pleased with him. He is still only young and we are looking forward to a long career with him. Today's race is a bumper. That means there are no fences and it's just a flat race. He has taken on some hurdles at home, but he won't be trying that today."

Hmm. This is hardly a Racing Post analysis of his prospects.

"Is the plan to step him up to longer distances after today", I ask.

"Yes. We already think he will stay 2 ½ miles and touch wood, after today, he'll try that distance over hurdles."

That's about it before Mike issues some instructions about meeting up before the race and slips back into his phoning/handshaking routine. I grab a couple of words with him. He seems like a buzzed-up teenager, not able to hold his attention on anything for more than a few seconds. He's very enthusiastic which is great to see and he cares deeply for the horses. He rides out Tickle most days.

The owners who have shown up today come from right across the racing spectrum, hence Mike's very general pep-talk a few minutes ago. I'm chatting to a young couple who bought each other shares as Christmas presents. They've never been racing at all before. First time. They remind me of giggling teenagers, arm in arm, pointing and laughing at anything they have never seen before. Another couple, much older and looking well off, go racing regularly and seem to have an interest in a couple of the club's horses. Eric - big bloke, blingage, camel hair coat and booming gor-blimey voice - tells me all about his best bets and how to pick a winner at Leicester, his local track. He must be a used car salesman. He's a good laugh, at least in moderation, and I watch the next race with him and his quietly spoken, demure missus from the grandstand.

I don't get a sniff of a win in the race, but at least my blood pressure has returned to normal and I've stopped spitting barbed wire about Network Rail. I have a good look at the course. There are a couple of decent races here each year. The Peterborough Chase, synonymous with Edredon Bleu is probably the pick. The circuit is quite small and even in 2-mile events the field comes passed the stands twice. I crane my neck to see them round the tight bottom bend. Rarely, for a course these days, there is no giant screen to concentrate on when the field is down the back straight. The course is not exactly top drawer in terms of quality and quantity of facilities, but the environment is lovely here on the outskirts of town and the track has encouraged an open and accessible policy. There is plenty of room to move around and explore, fostering a relaxed atmosphere. The facilities must heave under the pressure of a Peterborough Chase crowd though.

I decide to explore the facilities in more detail and plunge nose first into a thai chicken concoction from a van near the horse walk back to the unsaddling enclosure. Wonder if it makes the horses hungry. I'm standing near the winner's enclosure when Terry Biddlecombe squeezes under the rail and passes within a foot of me. For a moment I think he's going to steal my noodles. But he simply passes an enquiring glance and heads off to the stables. No sign of Hen Knight today but the stable has a couple of runners here today. Mixing with the stars, me. I'm getting to like this owner's stuff.

I bump in to Bill just as I'm binning the mangled remnants of the Thai extravaganza. It only gets 5/10. If you read this, Terry, go for the chippy instead! I tell Bill that I'm having a great day and that I'm surprised how many top trainers there are here. He says that's good but I don't think he really knows who Terry Biddlecombe and Nicky Henderson are.

The novice chase is a reasonably good looking race and I back Bill's Echo. It's the first decent fancy I've had so far today. Bill and I settle on the rail beyond the winning post for this one. He talks lovingly about the grace of horses then surprises me when he says that his first love is really motorbikes. He also tells me about a fantastic walk he did across Northern Spain as part of an international challenge. He ended up staying on for months after the walk had been completed. We went there on holiday there last year and he knew the bit the stayed in, Cantabria, well. He loves the people and I think he left part of his heart in La Coruna.

Timmy Murphy left part of Bill's Echo at the last fence. My bet was coming to take the race, I'm convinced, under a typically late, driving finish from the in-form jockey. But he clouted the final obstacle and went down in a heap.

We join the rest of the team by the parade ring for Dashing Charm's race. Mike is still buzzing about, but there's not much to be seen yet. I meet the other two red-jacketed club officials. Kate and Lynn are the stable staff. Both teenagers who love horses and are charged with looking after Tickle. Mike is organising a collection for Kate who is the horse's groom. She's been with him up until recently and is more excited than any of us about seeing him in the ring.

Mike points out Chris Bealby, the trainer and not long after Dashing Charm, or Tickle, whichever you prefer, comes out of his box. There are too many of us to go into the ring with Mike and the trainer. Shame. I'd have enjoyed that part as well. Maybe next time.

Tickle looks very well. He's a chestnut colour, quite big and appears quite fit enough to my uneducated eye. But this is his first run since June last year, so is bound to need a sharpener. He's big enough compared to the other runners. I think I actually do say "chaser in the making" to someone in our group who nods back at me with a knowing expression. Some traditions need to be kept intact.

Jockey Paul Maloney receives the briefest of final instructions from Chris Bealby before mounting our horse, pause there, ……our horse…., and cantering onto the track. Chris joins us in the grandstand which is great because I really wanted to have a bit of a chat with him. At least he's making the effort to join the members and is an approachable sort. I ask him about long-term plans for the horse.

"Yes, we think he'll go chasing. Seems the right sort. See what happens today though. Needs a bit more experience."

He speaks in clipped tones from a giant height. I'm on the step above him in the stand and I'm still peering up at him. You can tell he's a trainer a mile off. He wears a check flat-hat pulled down low over his eyes. He's wearing a grey barbour zipped up half way with regulation brown v-neck pullover and contrasting shirt/tie combination peeping out from underneath. But the give-away must be the crazy mustard cords keeping his pins warm. Where do they sell this gear?

I don't get chance to congratulate him on his tremendous bumper record at Huntingdon or to ask whether he's expecting a repeat. He's been collared by Mike again who clearly feels he's the only one qualified to engage the trainer in proper racing talk. He's probably right.

I need to get a bet on and I bag 66-1 each way on the Atkinson beast. Ha ha. They are at the start by the time I join the gang. Bealby has his bins focused on the field. I do a double take at the size of his hands. They are like shovels. Absolutely massive. He's obviously bred from solid farming stock.

As the race gets underway, Bryn fires me a text to say he's watching the race and the Charm looks well placed in mid Division. Indeed he is. The field passes us with our boy held up sensibly in the pack.

"Go on Tickle. You show 'em." It's the stable girls next to me.

The race kicks on a gear down the back straight and Dashing Charm is quickly outpaced. He can't stay with the leaders and Maloney is barely asking him for an effort. Henrietta Knight's horse Racing Demon comes away to win the race, but all of us are still looking down the track. Dashing Charm stays on well and picks off a few stragglers to finish a well beaten but not disgraced 10$^{th}$ at 40-1.

The stable girls are bitterly disappointed and desperately trying to see the bright side.

"At least he wasn't last"

"Yeah, but this was a decent race, remember. Lots of good stables were represented here", I offer.

"Yeah, that's right", they leap on my solace. In a manner of speaking.

"And he hasn't run since last June. He's bound to be rusty." I almost believe the excuses myself.

There's time for a group photo and a bit more chat before I decide to make for home. Bill tries to buy me a pint, but given the histrionics involved in getting here, I see sense and head for the courtesy bus back to the station. This has been some day.

Think I'd better call home.

"Hello Daddy."
"Hello Elizabeth. How did your ballet test go?"
"Oh, it was OK. Wendy said I did well."
"Brilliant. Well done.
"Hello Daddy. I've been a good girl today."
"Hello Catherine. That's really good. Is Mummy there?"
"Yes, I think so"

Long pause.
Longer pause.

"Hello? Dave?"
"Hiya. It's me. What sort of day did you have?"
"Fine. I didn't know you were calling. I just walked in to the living room and the phone was off the hook!"
"Cheers Catherine!"

They've had a top day anyway. And they even saw the race.

"Which one's Charming Dash, Mummy?" had asked Elizabeth.

"That's Daddy's horse", had said Helen, pointing at the red and blue clad jockey, "Dashing Charm."

"It doesn't look like Daddy", she had replied. Helen looked a bit perplexed before she worked out what our eldest meant.

"No, no he's not riding it, honey. He's just gone to watch it with some other people."

I think she was a bit disappointed.

The club is quite pleased with Tickle's run, apparently. I checked the website for any follow up, and not only is there a picture of us all by the parade ring, but the price for shares in the horse has been put up by another £50 quid or so on the strength of this performance. There's optimism for you.

## 32. RIVAL ATTRACTION

*"The new seasons come and go*
*At the dog and pony show*
*Gonna sit and beg and fetch the names*
*And follow the dress codes."*
Green Day, *"Fashion Victim"*, 2000

Today I'm experiencing a 'morning after' effect. Yesterday, Friday, we made our debut at Royal Ascot. And it has prompted me to think about it for a moment. It's time to take stock. Draw breath. Pause a while.

We have come a long way from Fantasy Cricket, via Cheltenham and half a dozen tiny tracks to "the highlight of the flat season, a landmark event of the British Summer and a celebration of nearly 300 years of history and tradition" (it says here in the programme).

Except all the boys didn't quite make it as far as the Queen's Acres. Just Nick, Bryn, Steve and me. The hard core. Vaughany got caught at work. Never even left the office. Again. We had to flog his ticket to a tout. That's sticks in the craw. I was surprised, because I thought Royal Ascot was very much his scene. Ben didn't make it either. He got a bit closer, however. The text to Nick said,
"Made it to Ascot station. Chucked up. Decided to go home again. Have a belter."

Ben's been following Euro 2004 more closely than the rest of us. Yesterday he had his own 'morning after effect' following England's win against Switzerland the previous evening. Ben had also been to Lisbon for the England-France match. Bought a ticket at the last minute and found he couldn't get a direct flight to Lisbon. So he flew to Seville and hired a car. What game. In years to come I'm sure the scars of those two Zidane goals in added-on time will fade. Shattering.

Like this year's Cheltenham festival, Royal Ascot is approaching a bit of a watershed. Whilst the greatest Steeplechasing event moves to four days, its flat equivalent moves to Yorkshire. At least for 2005. The course is to have a £180m facelift in time for 2006 and the Knavesmire will host the event in the meantime. York finally becomes the Ascot of the North for real.

Royal Ascot was not like any race meeting I have ever been to before. From arriving at Waterloo and being slack-jawed at the stunning array of skimpy dresses and bare flesh, to the obnoxious posh nobs on the train, to the seething hordes of revellers and picnickers on Ascot's lawns, I had seen no sports event quite like that before. The day was not really about racing.

We entered into the spirit, too. Nick turned on the style as we were shunted through suburban London. He pulled out a bottle of champers to mark the occasion. Very nice too.

"Anything they can do....", grinned Nick as he glugged fizz into some quality plastic glasses for the four of us.

He was not wrong. I looked around and the majority of passengers were similarly indulgent. Champagne, Pimms, red wine, spritzers...was that a cocktail brolly sticking out of a margarita? The lot. The whole train was a surreal assemblage of toffs' treats. Cool boxes and hampers cluttered up the aisles, boxes of strawberries littered the luggage racks and hats the size of small gazebos poked me in the eye.

The sights that greeted us on the course put Waterloo station and the train journey into perspective. All four of us spent the first hour exhibiting chillingly accurate Sid The Sexist characteristics. Bulging eyes out on stalks, swivelling rubber necks and dropping jaws. There were some deep politically incorrect comments passed around about the totty on view.

Royal Ascot is perceived as unique. I'm starting to understand why. This week is no longer the preserve of the upper classes, minor royals and débutantes on the Henley/Lords/Wimbledon circuit. The Royal Enclosure may still be filled with peers of the realm, but they represented a minority of yesterday's crowd. The proles in the grandstand and the silver ring swelled the attendance to a massive 70,000. The standard maintained by the toffs for loud suits, posh frocks and flash picnics is now aped year after year on the other side of the tracks. Perhaps here there is a little less sophistication. Everywhere the blokes were looking at the birds. Strappy dresses, skimpy skirts, tight flesh, emboldened by high heels, tattoos and bleached blonde hair ensured our attention was diverted away from the racecard for plenty long enough.

Bryn made an effort to live up to the sartorial reputation of the festival. He looked particularly well-attired in a natty red sports jacket. Put the rest of us to shame. Nick, clad in a dirty old anorak should have been barred entry at the turnstiles. Shocking attitude. But Bryn might have had cause to regret his choice of jacket about half way through the afternoon:

"Here, mate, didn't I see you at Butlins last year? Haharharhar."
"Oi, red-coat. What's your best joke?"
"Here comes the entertainment to keep the toilet queue amused. Can you juggle?"
After about the eighth jibe I think his patience began to wear a bit thin.

The racing across the whole festival is absolutely impeccable. The very highest standard competition is maintained. There are six group 1 renewals amongst a total of 16 group races offering over £3m in prize money. The handicaps, too, are amongst the richest and most keenly contested of the summer. Friday, the fourth of the five day extravaganza was no exception, though it was probably not the most mouth-watering card of the feast. The highlight looked to be the Group 1 Coronation

Stakes, a mile event for 3 year old fillies. Attraction, a classic filly unbeaten in seven starts was the one they all had to beat. She had won an unprecedented English/Irish guineas double already this season and had come back from serious injury last season. And she possessed the most talked about legs in racing. Wonky, apparently. Her owner/breeder, the Earl of Roxburghe had tried to flog her at one point, but nobody was interested on account of the filly's dodgy pins! She is the apple of trainer Mark Johnston's eye and I was looking forward to seeing her run into history.

She did too. In a scintillating flag-to-post win, she simply galloped her opponents in the dust. There was a doubt about her ability to run round the bend - those legs again - but she handled it perfectly, although she appeared to change lead legs a couple of times. But what sets Attraction apart is the ability to find more at the business end of the race. The front running tactics are well known, after all she's won dual Guineas like that. A couple of horses tried to stay with her in the early part of the race, Secret Charm and Royal Tigress. They were the first to be burned out. When the challengers, Moon Dazzle and Majestic Desert, finally appeared out of the pack at the two furlong marker, Attraction simply stepped on the gas, found some blistering acceleration and cruised away. She was still extending a comfortable 2 ½ length lead when she blasted past the winning post. Jockey Kevin Darley had chance to check his pose, grin at the crowd and wag an imperious index finger. Number 1. No doubt.

The bookies had tried to get Attraction. They didn't fancy her and instead of going off odds-on as her previous performances should have warranted, the SP was an almost value-like 6-4. A good day for the favourite backers.

That was about it for the racing. We all had bets in every race and no-one won a bean until Bryn had a token bet on a 9-1 shot, Unscrupulous, in the last race of the day. He won his day's gambling wedge back and maybe even enough for a round of drinks.

If we'd had school report cards for the afternoon, every one would have been marked 'easily distracted'. Although the racing was undoubtedly of the highest order, there were simply too many other competing interests. It didn't help that we were well away from the finishing post and so we were very reliant on the big screens. I swear I didn't see a horse in the flesh at all in some races. That said, the start for the 2m listed race was a right treat because it took place directly in front of us at the 2 furlong pole. I've never been close enough to see at first hand the field mill around in front of the stalls, load up and then bolt from the traps like shots from a gun. I couldn't see Alice Plunkett giving the low down on the horses at the post for the telly, but Nick took some photos to mark the occasion anyway. Just to show that we weren't ogling the fillies on our side of the fence all day.

The distractions weren't limited to the babes in the crowd. There were the beers too. Surprisingly easily to get at, given the huge numbers at the track. It was made far easier by the appearance of vendors sporting backpacks full of chilled Fosters, dispensing refreshment via an intricate tube and trigger system. We hailed them many times during the afternoon with a hearty "Brendan! Oi Brendan Foster! Over here mate!" This was Bryn's christening call, betraying his athletics background.

Supping Brendan's Fosters, however, had its natural consequences. Nick of course succumbed first to the 20 minutes toilet syndrome, but we all followed suit. If getting ale was easy, taking a leak was not. The queues were monumental. We all went missing at various times during the afternoon, sometimes skipping races, to take a leak. This became a theme of the day. It turned out that Steve had to jump off the train home at Richmond so that he could relieve his burning bladder! It became so bad that any scrap of space was being urinated on behind the stands. One perfectly innocent privet bush had been found a new use as a trough and had scores of people gathered round it to relieve themselves in communal harmony. By the time I used it the grass was sodden and yellow. I expect the bush is dead today. An hour or so after that Bryn reported that coppers had started hauling people out to stop them using it as a toilet. Lovely job.

By the end of the day, my view of Royal Ascot had matured. I realised that I was holding a ring-side seat at a freak show. For most people this is a cracking day out and a bit of a laugh. But there are some worrying signs, like the over the top dress and behaviour, that betray this festival as a 21st century extreme corruption of some ancient fertility ritual. The bastard offspring of traditional Summer celebration.

There are a couple of dominant influences at work. Firstly there's a subtle class war thing going on. The toffs through in the Royal Enclosure have a sneer at the proles over the other side trying to muscle in on their event; and in return the hordes in the Grandstand and the Silver Ring cock a snoot at the snobs and reckon they know how to turn on the style when they fancy it too. Add to this the massive corporate hospitality freeloaders and there is already a heady cocktail of attitude and alcohol.

Then there is the cattle market effect. The blokes in their Armani suits, sharp shades and the birds in their outrageous dresses, and ostentatious hats are simply preening their plumage in a radical version of the mating game. This point was rammed home on my train home from Clapham Junction when a "buying an' selling geezer, if you get my drift", still wearing his Versace wrap-around eye wear at 10.30pm bent my ear about his day at the races.

"Carl, that's me. Get to see the Racing Post before anyone else. Sort involved, y'know."
He hunched his shoulders at this remark as if to add gravity to the revelation. Carl was a genuine gambler, if anything he said was to be believed, and punted heavily when he felt he was on to a good thing. He knew his horses too. We had a decent banter about the horses we'd seen and admired this season. But he hadn't seen a single race that day. He'd

had two bets and didn't even know whether they'd come in. He was asking me the results. He had spent his day in the Grandstand flirting, chatting up, drinking bubbly and getting up to no good. He was married with kids but said he would never take them to Royal Ascot,

"because it ain't about that is it, geez? Royal Ascot's like Christmas, yeah. It only comes round once a year. You don't need to be cluttered up wiv the family when you've got all that totty dripping out of the stands. No mate. You know what I mean, dontcha? We don't mean nuffin' by it"

Such is the impenetrable language of 'a nod is as good as a wink' after a hard day's partying. We shook hands and embraced at Watford Junction like we'd been best mates all our lives.

Royal Ascot feels like a bit of a watershed. I realised that I was there for a good time. And I got a good time. But it's less to do with the side shows and the freak shows and more to do with the racing. I was there for the racing. With this revelation comes an acknowledgement that I was in a minority yesterday! At this particular event, anyway.

Confirmation then, that I've travelled a long way since that day five years ago when we decided that a trip to the Cheltenham festival might be a bit of a blast. Horse racing is here to stay for me. I'm even sampling some of the delights of horse ownership. I may only be dipping a tiny toe into a vast ocean. But I like what I've seen so far.

Bryn's on the road too. He's extended his sporting portfolio to embrace mastery of racing as well as just about every other mainstream sport found on satellite TV and a few that aren't. The balance on his on-line Blue Square account is all the justification we need.

Even Nick offers up poignant observations and thoughtful commentary about the races. Despite his maintenance of a healthy scepticism about the skill in making any serious money at this game, he has a bottomless enthusiasm for a day's racing, based on a deep held passion:

"I don't care about the losers. I just like drinking", he uttered in a desperate moment at Royal Ascot the other day. Respect for that view, tongue in cheek though I know it is.

Steve's travelled the furthest. He continues to reel in some big winners regularly and is mining a rich seam of assured punting on the flat, more so than over the jumps. Another season like this and he'll be punting professionally. An exit strategy. That would be the best ending for this little collection of racing accounts. Maybe that's for the next volume.

CPSIA information can be obtained at www.ICGtesting.com
Printed in the USA
LVOW12s1718060814

397843LV00018B/969/P